Wendell Berry and the Agrarian Tradition

American Political Thought
edited by
Wilson Carey McWilliams and
Lance Banning

Wendell Berry and the Agrarian Tradition

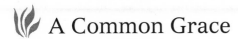 A Common Grace

Kimberly K. Smith

 UNIVERSITY PRESS OF KANSAS

Published by the University Press of Kansas (Lawrence, Kansas 66049), which was organized by the Kansas Board of Regents and is operated and funded by Emporia State University, Fort Hays State University, Kansas State University, Pittsburg State University, the University of Kansas, and Wichita State University

Library of Congress Cataloging-in-Publication Data

Smith, Kimberly K., 1966–

  Wendell Berry and the Agrarian tradition : a common grace / Kimberly K. Smith.

    p. cm. — (American political thought)

Includes bibliographical references and index (p.).

  ISBN 0-7006-1230-0 (cloth : alk. paper)

    1. Agriculture—United States.   2. Agricultural conservation—United States.   3. Sustainable agriculture—United States.   I. Title.   II. Series.

  S441 .S72 2003

  306.3′49′0973—dc21   2002013584

British Library Cataloguing in Publication Data is available.

Printed in the United States of America

10 9 8 7 6 5 4 3 2 1

The paper used in this publication meets the minimum requirements of the American National Standard for Permanence of Paper for Printed Library Materials Z39.48-1984.

FOR MY PARENTS,

for their stewardship and uncommon grace

CONTENTS

✔ PREFACE

This book concerns Wendell Berry's reformulation of democratic agrarian-ism, one of the most enduring and influential of America's political tradi-tions. In the following pages, I explore Berry's critique of American society and his case for an agrarian republic by analyzing his social, moral, and political theory. More fundamentally, however, this study is an exploration of Berry's moral vision—a vision that becomes more relevant, I believe, even as we move farther from our agrarian past.

Berry's central teaching is that the world is not, and never will be, a safe place. Humans have always faced danger and uncertainty, and human action has always had unpredictable and often deadly consequences. His under-standing of the human condition echoes in many respects that of the classi-cal philosophers, who warned that if we are more than beasts, we are also less than gods. As individuals, we will never be fully self-sufficient, and even as a community, we will never have full control over the conditions of our own existence. This lesson is crucial, according to Berry, because our misguided attempts to make the world safer and more predictable can lead only to violence, brutality, and cruelty. He suggests that instead of seeking greater control, we must learn how to achieve a fully human life—to real-ize our best possibilities—in a dangerous and unpredictable world. And that, in turn, requires us to cultivate certain virtues—moderation, prudence, pro-priety, fidelity—as well as a deep understanding of our dependence on one another and on the natural world. This book, then, is not only an attempt to introduce Wendell Berry's work to students of agriculture, social theory, moral philosophy, and political thought. It is also an exploration of the prob-lem of living a meaningful life in a world filled with both deadly perils and unimagined possibilities.

Berry sometimes describes his intellectual activities, like his farming, as group projects—the products of a community engaged in the task of cultural stewardship. I've come to look on my own writing in the same light. This book was a collective effort, and one that I hope others will continue. Those who have already contributed to the project (albeit unwittingly) include Wendell Berry himself and Jack Driscoll, who first introduced me to Wendell Berry's work. Others have provided more direct support, in the form of comments, conversation, criticism, and research assistance. They include Barbara Allen, Bob Pepperman Taylor, Eric Kos, Mika LaVaque-Manty, Ted Clayton, Connie Price, Carol Rutz, Jim Fisher, Ionia Italia, Jennifer Manion, Mary Freier, Sheri Breen, Steve Campagna-Pinto, Jon Lauck, Dave McGowan, Jim Chen, Fred Woodward, and the excellent editors and staff at the University Press of Kansas. Not all of these people would approve of the final result (some would even consider the whole project misguided). Nevertheless, they deserve much of the credit for what is valuable in the following pages. I will, as always, take the blame for the rest.

⚘ INTRODUCTION

Jane Smiley's *A Thousand Acres* begins with the return of Jess Clark, a tree-hugging, draft-dodging organic farmer, to his rural Midwest hometown. The neighbors greet him with open arms and poorly concealed suspicion. They're dismayed as much by his unorthodox farming methods as by his cosmopolitan lifestyle (he's a *vegetarian!*). Resentment simmers. "He doesn't *feel* critical," they complain, "and he wants to be our friend, but he wouldn't do things our way, and he probably wouldn't have us do things our way, truth to tell."[1]

Truth to tell, he wouldn't. But he *does* at least want to be their friend, and that's an improvement—a sea change, in fact—in the long-standing conflict between environmentalists and farmers. Smiley's Jess heralds an important, if incomplete, transformation in farm politics: the "greening" of American agrarianism. Jess is a fictional representative of the ecology-oriented "back-to-the-land" movement of the 1970s, which brought an influx of young, college-educated erstwhile suburbanites into the countryside. There they organized into groups like Rural America and Rural Coalition, aimed at joining traditional farm politics with issues such as the environment, housing, health care, education, and energy. Their activism, as historians Theo Majka and Patrick Mooney put it, "began to erode the traditional political animosity between environmentalists and agriculture as a whole."[2] Thanks in large part to their efforts, the defense of rural community and the small farm has become intimately—if problematically—linked to the defense of the earth.

Wendell Berry is a central figure in the greening of American agrarianism. Since the 1960s, he has been a leading expositor of a set of ideas designed to forge a politically effective union of small farmers and environmentalists. His success, as Smiley's story suggests, has been mixed; in addition to persistent political conflicts, class, religious, and lifestyle differences continue to trouble the tenuous partnership. But the effort promises to leave a durable legacy nonetheless. By importing an environmental sensibility into traditional agrarianism, Berry and his fellow travelers have revived and transformed a major branch of the American intellectual heritage.

Like the twentieth-century environmental movement generally, Wendell Berry's ecological agrarianism is a response to the social and environmental problems created by the transition to an advanced industrial economy. But while most American environmentalists have concentrated on the use and protection of the wilderness, Berry has focused on how industrialization has affected the countryside. Born in rural Kentucky in 1934, Berry witnessed firsthand the rise of corporate, industrial agriculture after World War II and the resulting dislocation and decline of rural communities. That transition is both the impetus and the context for most of his writing. From a political standpoint, his work can be read as a defense of small farmers and rural community, which he treats as a critical and diminishing resource in American society. From a philosophical standpoint, however, his work is an attempt to understand the meaning of the life of the traditional farmer, a way of life seemingly at odds with the values on which industrial capitalist society depends. Thus Berry's agrarianism aims to explain and defend the value and meaning of a particular conception of farm life in an industrial capitalist society.

Of course, Wendell Berry is hardly the first American to champion the yeoman farmer. The claim that small family farmers are especially valuable to the republic has been a commonplace in American politics since the founding. Agrarians have argued that farmers, by virtue of their labor and economic circumstances, are more likely than most other kinds of citizens to develop virtues that are essential to republican government, such as frugality, discipline, self-reliance, and respect for law and order. Berry's argument is similar, but instead of contending that small farmers are vital to the political or economic health of the country, he claims they are essential to its *ecological* health: it is environmental rather than political values that farmers cultivate—virtues that are (he claims) otherwise lacking in industrial capitalist regimes. This apparently minor refinement of conventional agrarianism leads to surprisingly unconventional results. To make his case, Berry has to reexamine, reinterpret, and sometimes even reject the values that have traditionally been central to American agrarian thought, including individual independence, the sanctity of property rights, and the meaning of economic freedom. In short, he reworks the basic assumptions, both moral and sociological, underlying the agrarianism he inherited from his Populist predecessors. The result is an incisive critique of industrial, corporate capitalism and the concepts of autonomy and freedom it rests upon—as well as a provocative blueprint for an alternative, ecologically sensitive agrarian society based on the value of stewardship.

This study offers a summary and critique of the social, moral, and political dimensions of Berry's ecological agrarianism. It is necessarily a very general overview. Over the past thirty years, Berry has written on topics ranging from agricultural technology to theology to literary criticism, and produced more than thirty books of essays, poetry, and fiction (as well as countless uncollected pieces). This is a daunting body of work just to synthesize, much less examine in detail. I have therefore focused on explaining how the various aspects of his thought—on ethics, sustainable agriculture, religion, politics, and technology, to mention a few—might be brought together to form a coherent agrarian philosophy. This is just a road map to his ideas; a more nuanced and detailed exploration of each subject I must leave to future commentators.

It may seem surprising that such a road map is needed—that Berry's ideas, which have been circulating for over thirty years, haven't already generated more critical commentary.[3] But such inattention is perhaps to be expected, given the status of agrarian ideology in the scholarly community generally. Richard Hofstadter's interpretation of agrarianism as reactionary nostalgia for a preindustrial, noncommercial past remains academic orthodoxy. Scholars tend to assume that agrarian ideology has little intellectual content or practical significance; indeed, they have been proclaiming its demise for over fifty years.[4] Those of us who venture into this apparently unpromising field may dispute that judgment; we may insist that agrarianism is a complex and dynamic tradition that has generated a wealth of progressive ideas.[5] Our conclusions have (so far) failed to disturb conventional wisdom. In vain do we insist, with Andrew Angyal, that Berry's agrarianism "is no mere sentimental attachment to the past, but a compelling critique of progress and of the kind of society ours has become." Or agree with Patrick Murphy that

> Berry does not seek a return to some "Golden Age" of good farming, but rather the restoration of a relationship to the land, a rooting of the individual to a specific place, one that will compel him through identity and a sense of responsibility to seek the most ecological means to maintain both sides of that identity in harmony.[6]

Despite his popularity, Berry's agrarian philosophy suffers the critical neglect usually afforded history's losers.

But if agrarianism is no more than a nostalgic longing for bygone days that has long since outlived its usefulness, then how can we account for its persistence in farm politics? The periodic resurgence of grassroots farmer protest movements—in the 1950s, the 1970s, and more recently—tells another story: all of these movements drew on agrarian language and images to win broad public support for policies that would benefit the ever-shrinking minority of American farmers. Agrarian ideology has, if anything, become more ubiquitous as farmers seek allies and policy makers try to make sense of the economic and social problems facing rural America. Its persistence suggests that there is more to this tradition than scholars have recognized: that it expresses values many Americans embrace, that it offers a useful way to understand the problems of farmers and the rural community generally, and that it may even point us toward solutions.

The alternative hypothesis, at any rate, seems to be that agrarianism persists because a significant number of Americans are merely irrational—hopelessly nostalgic, impractical, sentimental—on the subject of farming. That may sound right to their critics, but it's all too easy to assume irrationality on the part of one's political opponents. It's more reasonable to assume that many proponents of agrarian ideas are intelligent and serious-minded, and that the persistence of those ideas into the twenty-first century is due to their philosophical or political value. That is not to say that agrarianism has survived unchanged since Jefferson's day, however. On the contrary, its vitality is due to its ability to adapt to new conditions; Berry's agrarianism is not Jefferson's, nor the Populists'. That is precisely his significance: by importing environmental ideas into the framework of agrarian thought, he has revitalized agrarianism and helped to ensure its continued relevance to American social and political thought and practice.

If Berry has been neglected as a philosopher, his literary accomplishments have attracted more attention. A partial list of his honors includes a Guggenheim Fellowship (1961–62); a Rockefeller Foundation Fellowship (1965); a National Institute of Arts and Letters Award (1971); a Friends of American Writers Award for his novel *The Memory of Old Jack* (1974); the Jean Stein Award from the American Academy and Institute of Arts and Letters (1987); the T. S. Eliot Award for Creative Writing from the Ingersoll Foundation (1994); and a number of honorary doctorates.[7] As one would expect, Berry's rise to prominence in the literary community has been accompanied by the development of a considerable body of literary criticism examining his imaginative prose, his poetry, and his poetics.[8] Those familiar with this critical work will likely be disappointed that I haven't engaged it more directly in this study. Instead, I have treated Berry's novels and stories primarily as elaborations of his social and moral theories. Admittedly, that decision is problematic; disregarding the literary dimension of these obviously literary works undoubtedly limits my ability to explain them. Reading Berry's novels as exercises in moral and social philosophy, for example, leads me to downplay the subtlety of his thought as it is revealed in those novels—which are, by the nature of the genre, more open to ambiguity and complexity than the essays. As literature, Berry's fiction and poetry lead us beyond the clarity of philosophical systems into the particularity, contingency, and mystery of human experience. Thus in my search for consistency and clarity in Berry's thinking, I confess I've failed to convey the richness, the openness and ambiguity, of these literary works. My only defense is that Berry is not always a novelist or poet; often, he is a social and moral critic, attempting to realize not only literary but also philosophical and ethical values. If I don't do justice to his work as literature, I hope I may do justice to it as moral and social criticism. And it is perhaps not too much to hope that a better understanding of his philosophy will lead to more insightful critiques of his work as literature.

As for Berry's philosophy, it's fair to point out that Berry is a particularly lucid writer and probably does a better job of explaining himself than I do. My justification for this project is the sheer volume of his explanation; his body of work is so extensive that some attempt to distill, organize, contextualize—and of course critique—his ideas is called for. Nevertheless, as Berry himself points out, "Most of the time, when you have explained something, you discover leftovers. An explanation is a bucket, not a well."[9] I've discovered quite a lot of leftovers. For example, a literary career spanning more than three decades calls for a study of its development over time, which this book does not provide.[10] I have for the most part treated Berry's philosophy as a consistent whole rather than a work in progress—an approach made possible by the fact that most of the basic elements of his thought are already present in his earliest works. They have been elaborated, but not substantially altered. I have remarked on the development of his thought only where I have noticed significant change (in his views on religion, for example).

I've also failed to investigate fully Berry's relationship to conservative thought. This may seem an unconscionable oversight. His insistence on the importance of tradition, the value of community, and the dangers of liberal individualism would seem to put Berry in the same company as Edmund Burke and Michael Oakeshott—or at least those peculiarly libertarian conservatives that we find in the United States.[11] The point is well taken; nonetheless, to read Berry as a conservative, or at least *merely* as a conservative, may be misleading. I've found Berry's debt to conservative thought harder to specify and account for than his debt to agrarianism and environmentalism. He was undoubtedly exposed to conservative ideas simply by growing up in Kentucky in the 1930s and 1940s; states' rights theories would have been prevalent in his childhood and in the 1960s, when they were revived in response to the civil rights movement. But when Berry discusses his intellectual influences, he never mentions conservative theorists (with the important exception of the Vanderbilt Agrarians). His inspirations are people like Thomas Jefferson, Henry David Thoreau, Liberty Hyde Bailey, Albert Howard, Wallace Stegner, Edward Abbey, and Gary Snyder. Moreover, many of the apparently conservative elements of his thought, such as his preference for decentralized government, his critique of individualism, and his case for strong communities, may in fact be derived from the environmental tradition. Untangling these influences is too complex a project to undertake in this study. I therefore leave them tangled, and address Berry's relationship to conservatism only briefly in chapters 4 and 8.

Instead, I focus primarily on Berry's relationship to the American agrarian and environmental traditions, which I spend a good deal of time exploring—most of the first two chapters, in fact. Working through this introductory material may discourage readers eager to get to Berry's own ideas. But it's essential if we are to understand both what Berry is saying and what he is trying to do by saying it. He insists that he is not inventing anything new; in fact, he tersely dismisses the whole idea of originality: "I fail to see how an individual brain alone can have any originating power whatsoever." The hope of humanity is not originality in any case but "our ability, in time of need, to return to our cultural landmarks and reorient ourselves."[12] His goal, then, is to *revive and renew* the intellectual traditions he has inherited. That interpretation of his project derives from an important element of his social theory: the claim that the way to establish a proper relationship with the past is through a conservative but critical stance toward tradition—and that industrial society undermines our ability to adopt such a stance. Thus Berry's attempt to recover his own intellectual heritage not only exemplifies what he means by renewing and reviving tradition, it is meant to rectify what he considers to be a basic problem with industrial society: its lack of connection to the past. Clearly, in order both to understand this project and to evaluate how well he has accomplished it, we must begin where he does—with the agrarian and environmental traditions.

Beginning with those traditions will also help us to better appreciate Berry's significance to the history of American thought in general and to the modern environmental movement in particular. That significance is easy to undervalue, particularly if we make the mistake of reading contemporary environmental sensibilities and ideas into early agrarian ideology—an error all too common in histories of environmental thought. We are tempted, understandably but incorrectly, to read environmental concerns into Thomas Jefferson's economic and political arguments for small farms (Berry himself tends to misread Jefferson this way). Or to conflate Thoreau's pastoralism and celebration of the simple life with Jeffersonian agrarianism.[13] As I will argue, both interpretations are misleading, and both obscure Berry's contribution to the agrarian tradition. If Berry's ecological agrarianism doesn't look particularly innovative to us, it is because he makes the marriage of agrarian and environmental thought seem so natural that we assume agrarianism *always* implied ecological sensitivity—or that ecological sensitivity always implied support for family farming. It did not; indeed, for much of American history agrarians had little interest in environmental issues, and environmentalists for their part have had little good to say about farming. Berry's importance to the evolution of these traditions lies precisely in his ability to resolve their fundamental ideological differences.

And so does his importance to environmental and farm politics. Here also it is easy to underestimate Berry's contribution. If we focus on conventional measures of political activism—protests, lobbying, formulating policy proposals, engaging in electoral politics—Berry doesn't look like a major political figure. He has for the most part eschewed such overtly political activities in favor of developing and publicizing his ideas. But ideas do matter to politics—even farm politics.[14] Ideas and the languages in which they are articulated can have a number of consequences for political action. Berry himself insists upon this point, and explains his own motivation and purposes in explicitly political terms. I will examine that explanation, and Berry's understanding of the relationship between language and politics generally, in chapters 2 and 7. Here I will simply underscore the more obvious reasons that Berry's ideas may be relevant to environmental and agricultural politics. First, it is easier for a political actor to pursue a course of action if she has the intellectual resources to *justify* that action.[15] An advocate for farmers, for example, will be more likely to form an alliance with environmentalists if she can justify that alliance—to herself, tc her peers, and to the people she represents. An ideology that persuasively links environmental protection to the defense of farmers can therefore help to create and maintain such alliances. Second, an actor's ideology shapes her perception of what the problem is (is it poverty, environmental degradation, loss of community?) and what courses of action are possible (legislation, moral reform, community activism?). Thus the shape and direction of a political or social movement may be determined in part by the ideology the actors bring to the movement. Berry's ideas, I would argue, contribute to the contemporary environmental movement in both respects: his reformulation of agrarianism has helped to shape our understanding of the problems agriculture policy should be addressing, as well as facilitating actions, alliances, and strategies that earlier versions of agrarianism made difficult or even unthinkable.

That claim should lead us into a discussion of the meaning of the term "ideology," which one would expect to figure prominently in a study such as this. I'd like to bypass that discussion, however. In fact I seldom refer to "ideology," which carries connotations I'd like to avoid—particularly the implication that we are talking about an unchanging, coherent philosophical system that can be abstracted from and explained without reference to the way it has evolved in the context of political conflict. I rely instead on the concept of *intellectual tradition,* which I understand much the way Berry does: traditions are not unchanging systems handed down intact from one generation to the next, based on certain fundamental philosophical principles. Rather, they are an evolving collection of ideas and rhetorical strategies that tend to cluster together and to be associated with certain political goals. Traditions are not static; as they are passed down from one generation to the next, they must be reworked to apply to new conditions. People draw on their inherited intellectual resources to solve practical problems, and in doing so they leave those resources changed—enriched, one hopes, but sometimes diminished. Thus we should not expect traditions to be philosophically coherent systems (although one may develop a philosophically coherent system out of a tradition's elements). Of course, we can often find common threads that survive over the ages. But in general, political traditions are not defined by a set of fundamental philosophical principles so much as they are defined (often in retrospect) by the evolution of their principles or merely the continuity of their specific political goals. We recognize that John Locke and Martin Luther King Jr. both belong to the liberal tradition not because they adhere to the same basic principles but because we can trace King's intellectual genealogy from Locke and because, in some broad sense, we understand them to be pursuing the same goals.

So it is with the agrarian tradition. We can trace Berry's intellectual descent from Jefferson (whom he quotes frequently) through the Populists and their political successors (including Berry's father), and identify the ideas he borrowed from the twentieth-century back-to-the-land movement and the early sustainable agriculture advocates. I will argue in the following chapters that he is part of an identifiable tradition of agrarian thought aimed at protecting the interests of small farmers, as well as a tradition of environmental thought aimed at establishing a more meaningful and less damaging relationship to nature. But, as we shall see, to place him in these traditions is to say very little about the content of his agrarianism. The point of talking about traditions is not to categorize Berry's thought but to understand how he uses his inherited intellectual resources to make sense of the new and perplexing problems facing agriculture, rural communities, and American society in general.

The plan of this book is as follows. Chapters 1 and 2 offer a brief history of American agrarianism and environmental thought, respectively, with a focus on clarifying the ideological conflict between them. Ironically, this conflict centers on the one commitment that both traditions share: the moral ideal of rugged individualism. Their respective interpretations of that ideal, I argue, account for the ideological divide that separates them. As I demonstrate, however, over the course of the twentieth century, environmentalism and agrarianism gradually moved away from their concern with individualism and converged on the political goal of defending family farming. That convergence prepared the ground for the sustainable agriculture movement of the 1960s and the emergence of Wendell Berry as a major voice in the environmental movement.

Chapters 3 and 4 turn to Berry's social theory, exploring his argument that a vital rural community of small farmers is essential to maintaining a sustainable, ecologically sensitive agriculture. This section shows how Berry's emphasis on the conditions necessary to creating a culture of stewardship unites environmentalism and agrarianism on the common ground of supporting rural communities. Chapter 5 then addresses the most frequent criticism of Berry's social theory: that it is mere utopianism, born of a romantic nostalgia for a way of life that never could or did exist. I argue that this charge is based on a misunderstanding of Berry's rhetorical strategy and method of moral reasoning.

In chapters 6 and 7, I explore Berry's moral theory, reviewing his critique of individualism, his interpretation of the virtues of the small farmer, and his understanding of the meaning of a life of stewardship. I contend that Berry's moral philosophy attempts to shift agrarianism and environmentalism away from rugged individualism and toward a new moral ideal, a concept he calls "grace." In the process, he elaborates an ethical system based on ecological virtues, reinterpreting the meaning of both farming and the wilderness in light of this ethic.

Finally, chapter 8 reviews Berry's critique of contemporary politics and his argument for decentralized democracy. Berry's political theory, which echoes Thoreau's critical perspective on politics, is less developed than his moral and social theories. Nevertheless, it offers insight into the relationship between language and politics and the role of political action in a life devoted to stewardship. Moreover, his analysis of the conditions necessary for meaningful political action offers a starting point for revitalizing national politics and humanizing government. I conclude by considering Berry's contribution to American agrarianism as an intellectual tradition and his significance to contemporary environmental and farm politics.

Chapter One

Agrarian Visions

When asked why he has devoted his life to the defense of small farmers, Wendell Berry recounts a story his father used to tell him:

> The first time he [Berry's father] remembered waking up late in the night was when he was about seven years old. His daddy sent the crop . . . to Louisville. Then the night before it was going to sell, they sat up talking about what they were going to do when they got the money, and it was kind of a happy, optimistic evening. Then my father heard his daddy get up, at probably two o'clock in the morning, to get on his horse to go to the train and go to Louisville, to see his crop sold. And he got back without a dime. They took it all. The crop . . . about paid the warehouse commission.
>
> My father saw men leave the warehouse crying and he said, when he was a little boy, "If ever I can do anything about this, I'm going to."[1]

Inspired by that memory, John Berry spent his life pursuing what his son calls an "agrarian vision": "to have an economy here that could support small farmers and keep them on the land."[2] That vision, Berry tells us, informs his own life and work as well. In short, he describes himself as the inheritor of his father's quest for agrarian justice.

But to say that Berry is just following in his father's footsteps is to oversimplify the complex process of inheriting a tradition. John Berry was a farmer and lawyer in Henry County, Kentucky, where his family had lived since before the Civil War. Henry County is characterized by small, self-supporting farms and a highly diversified agriculture. But, as in much of Kentucky, tobacco is the primary cash crop, and John Berry's involvement in farm politics centered on tobacco. In 1924 he became involved in the effort to found a cooperative association of burley tobacco growers, which

11

brought him into contact with Democratic congressman Virgil Chapman. He worked for Chapman in Washington D.C. for three years; when he returned, he helped to found the Burley Tobacco Growers Cooperative Association, serving as its vice president and then president for many years. Through this legal and political activism he tried to protect the economic interests of the local farming community, to ensure that they would realize an equitable return on their labor. His younger son John would take up the same cause as a lawyer and politician, representing small farmers in the state senate and serving as president and general counsel of the Burley Co-op.[3] For Wendell, however, pursuing his father's vision would mean traveling a less conventional path.

The farming community Wendell Berry grew up in was, in some respects, very much like the one his father knew. The transition to industrial agriculture was slow in Kentucky; hard hit by the Depression, in the 1940s it still lagged behind the rest of the country in urbanization and economic development. Berry learned to farm with mules and horses as his father had, and to value the community of small, independently owned farms that still survive in Kentucky. Between 1954 and 1987, the number of farms in Kentucky declined by only 9 percent; 75 percent of Kentucky's farms are still under 180 acres. The majority of these farms remain in the hands of individuals or families, and in 1980 over half the population of the state lived in rural areas (compared with less than 25 percent in the United States generally).

But Kentucky was not unaffected by the forces that were transforming the agricultural economy throughout the country. During the second half of the twentieth century, the relative importance of agriculture in the state's economy declined dramatically. In 1940, more than one-third of the labor force worked on farms; by 1990 that figure had declined to less than 4 percent. Significantly, few farmers now derive their principal income from farming, and, as of 1990, agriculture constituted the largest source of income in only five counties. Meanwhile, the number of factories in Kentucky increased by 42 percent between 1939 and 1947, and the number of manufacturing workers increased by 69 percent.[4] This transition to an urban, industrial economy forms the general context for Berry's thinking about agriculture, community, and the environment. "I began my life," he says, "as the old times and the last of the old-time people were dying out." Thus in his "acceptance of twentieth-century realities there has had to be a certain deliberateness." His thinking, he says, has been critically shaped by the fact that he was "born with an aptitude for a way of life that was doomed."[5]

Actually, Berry's early career suggested an aptitude for a very different way of life. He received a bachelor of arts in English from the University of Kentucky in 1956, then continued on to receive a master's degree, apparently intent on pursuing an academic and literary vocation. His first job was teaching English at the small Baptist Georgetown College near Lexington. After marrying Tanya Amyx, daughter of a University of Kentucky art professor, in 1957, he took a fellowship to study creative writing at Stanford with Wallace Stegner. His first novel, *Nathan Coulter,* was published in 1960. In 1962, he took a position in the English department at New York University, after traveling in Europe for a year on a Guggenheim Fellowship.[6] In short, he was following a typical career path for an aspiring writer, moving from his rural roots to an upwardly mobile, cosmopolitan lifestyle. Reflecting on this period, he mused,

> Hadn't I achieved what had become one of the almost traditional goals of American writers? I had reached the greatest city in the nation; I had a good job; I was meeting other writers and talking to them and learning from them; I had reason to hope that I might take a still larger part in the literary life of that place.[7]

Instead, however—to the surprise and consternation of his friends—after a year Berry gave up his position at New York University to join the faculty of the University of Kentucky. He had decided to move back to Kentucky and become a farmer.

That decision cost him "considerable difficulty and doubt and hard thought." Well-intentioned colleagues urged him to reconsider, insisting "you can't go home again" and warning him of "the Village Virus."[8] "It was feared," he reports, "that I would grow paunchy and join the Farm Bureau."[9] But those who see in Berry a nostalgia for an imagined utopian past should take note of his response to these warnings:

> I knew as well as Wolfe that there is a certain *metaphorical* sense in which you can't go home again—that is, the past is lost to the extent that it cannot be lived in again. I knew perfectly well that I could not return home and be a child, or recover the secure pleasures of childhood.[10]

Nevertheless, "home—the place, the countryside—was still there, pretty much as I left it, and there was no reason I could not go back to it if I wanted." On a deeper level, he concluded that "Kentucky was my fate—not an altogether pleasant fate . . . but one that I could not leave behind simply by going to another place." The world, he believed, "would always be most fully and clearly present to me in the place I was fated by birth to know better than any other."[11]

Berry's return to Kentucky baffled his friends, but in retrospect we can see it as an early manifestation of the broader social trend in the 1960s toward "dropping out" and pursuing alternative lifestyles. Berry was hardly a hippie, of course, but neither was he a typical farmer. Rather than following the advice of experts and modernizers to "get big" and make use of the latest agricultural technology, he bought a small "marginal" farm and set out to reclaim it, using traditional methods of farming. His aim was not to be successful by conventional standards—to pursue wealth and status—but to find a level of satisfaction and independence in a life not overly dependent on government, corporations, or markets.

Inevitably, Wendell Berry's lifestyle invites comparison to the traditional Jeffersonian yeoman farmer, for whom the chief goals of farming are independence and virtue. Indeed, Berry himself claims the Jeffersonian legacy, insisting that his goal is to revive and renew the American agrarian tradition.[12] But that claim raises more questions than it answers about Berry's aims and reasons. The agrarian tradition he invokes is a complex phenomenon; it has been used to support economic liberalization and economic protectionism, political equality and social hierarchy, agricultural modernization and a return to "the simple life." Berry may be attempting to realize an "agrarian vision"—but what exactly is that vision? Which agrarian tradition is he trying to revive?

The agrarian tradition has ancient roots in Western thought, but exploring those roots would take us farther afield than we need to go.[13] I want to focus instead on American democratic agrarianism: a specific set of ideas, claims, and political programs that have been set forth over the past two hundred years by a varied assortment of Americans, most tracing their inspiration back to Thomas Jefferson.

Defining traditions is a tricky matter, both because they are always on the move—merging, mutating, bifurcating, spawning offspring—and because their meanings are typically the subject of political conflict. "Agrarianism" covers a lot of territory. For Carl Taylor, for example, agrarian politics revolves rather tediously around agricultural prices, markets, and the availability of credit. James Montmarquet, on the other hand, considers as central the belief that "farmers are, on the whole and as a result of their distinctive experiences, more virtuous than those engaged in urban, commercial activities." Others emphasize the proposition of the eighteenth-century Physiocrats that agriculture is the true source of national wealth. The term has also carried the implication of coercive equalization of the ownership of cultivated land, and "agrarian" is sometimes used to refer to any movement defending the interests of farmers, or to movements expressing resistance to industrialization generally.[14]

My definition may only perpetuate the confusion, but it's probably too much to ask that such an ideologically charged term confine itself to one meaning. Indeed, as I argued in the introduction, agrarianism should be viewed less as a static philosophical system than as an evolving collection of ideas and rhetorical strategies. Thus we should not expect to identify a set of philosophical principles shared by all agrarians. We can, however, identify a specific political tradition of American democratic agrarianism, characterized by a claim that all its proponents have made in some form: that the family farm is the chief repository of the virtues necessary to the republic. That claim links Thomas Jefferson with John Taylor of Caroline, Booker T. Washington, the Populists, and modern agrarians like Wendell Berry. Its rhetorical value to its proponents is that it allows each to present himself as an inheritor of the Jeffersonian tradition. Its analytic value is that it allows us to distinguish democratic agrarianism from related or similar intellectual traditions.

Consider, for example, George Washington's Cincinnatus-like retreat from the cares and concerns of public affairs into private rural domesticity.[15] Washington's embrace of the simple life represents less a celebration of agriculture itself than a conviction that the ordinary life of the common man (typically, of course, a farmer) offers greater incentives to virtue than the life of great political leaders. This claim, a familiar support for agrarian views, stems from an ethical tradition rooted in a distrust of glory seeking and aimed at encouraging political leaders to retire gracefully from public life rather than causing personal and public chaos by clinging to power.[16]

Similarly, we should distinguish the literary tradition of pastoralism. This set of images, themes, and tropes is usually traced back to Virgil's *Georgics,* which, as Victor Davis Hanson put it, "romanticized the harmony and community of the countryside, in implicit contrast to the bustle and impersonality of urban life."[17] Hanson contrasts Virgilian pastoralism with a tradition of complaint stemming from Hesiod, whose *Works and Days* was "a more melancholy, more angry account of the necessary pain and sacrifice needed to survive on the land."[18] Both traditions have been influential in American letters; although Virgilian pastoralism may be the dominant mode, America is not without her Hesiods. They include Hamlin Garland's bleak stories of the middle border, O. E. Rölvaag's *Giants in the Earth* (recounting the misfortunes and hardships of Norwegian homesteaders in Dakota), and Steinbeck's *Grapes of Wrath*. Hanson points out that this bleaker literary tradition focuses on the character of the farmer: independent, often unpleasant, not always virtuous, but a vivid and powerful alternative to the values of urban society.[19]

Histories of agrarian thought typically conflate the political tradition of agrarianism with its literary counterparts. There is some justification for doing so; pastoral themes often lend rhetorical support to agrarian politics, while agrarian ideology can offer philosophical support for pastoral tropes. Nevertheless, for our purposes it's useful to distinguish the literary tradition of pastoralism from the political tradition of agrarianism. Agrarians do not always draw on pastoralism; on the contrary, they often explicitly reject romanticized visions of rural life in favor of hardheaded economic and political analysis. Similarly, pastoral themes and images may be associated with political programs other than agrarianism (preserving the wilderness, for example)—or with no political program at all. So treating agrarianism as conterminous with pastoralism can be misleading. Thoreau, for example, is undoubtedly a major figure in the pastoral tradition. Perhaps for that reason he is often cited as representative of a nature-loving kind of agrarianism that celebrates farming primarily for its spiritual value. There is a strain of romanticism, including the New England transcendentalists, that maintains that contact with nature and the cycle of birth and decay can bring one closer to God, or some sort of spiritual reality. But this tradition has been at least as hostile to farming as it has been to industrialization. As I will discuss in the next chapter, Thoreau himself exemplifies an ambivalence toward farming deeply ingrained in American thought.

That ambivalence, in fact, makes it unwise to insist too hard on the distinctions among these traditions that I have identified. Americans' attitudes toward farming have actually been quite complex, often mingling varieties of agrarianism with related or opposing traditions. Crèvecoeur's *Letters from an American Farmer,* for example, draws on many of the above traditions—a desire to live closer to nature, a complaint about the hard lot of simple farmers, and a conviction that virtue lies in avoiding involvement in high politics—to justify his (or his protagonist's) plan to abandon war-torn New England and go live with the Indians.[20]

This ecumenical approach to agrarianism probably helps to maintain its richness and vitality. More problematic is the common confusion of democratic agrarianism with its aristocratic cousin, an elitist ideology that evolved in the South before the Civil War. The confusion stems in part from the fact that both traditions claim descent from Thomas Jefferson, whose endorsement of the agrarian life is familiar to the point of triteness:

> Those who labor in the earth are the chosen people of God, if ever He had a chosen people, whose breasts He has made His peculiar deposit for substantial and genuine virtue. . . . Corruption of the morals in the mass of cultivators is a phenomenon of which no age nor nation has furnished an example. It is the mark set on those, who, not looking up to heaven, to their own soil and industry, as does the husbandman, for their subsistence, depend for it on casualties and caprice of customers. Dependence begets subservience and venality, suffocates the germ of virtue, and prepares fit tools for the designs of ambition. . . . While we have land to labor then, let us never wish to see our citizens occupied at a workbench, or twirling a distaff.[21]

Such language accounts for Jefferson's reputation as friend and defender of the yeoman farmer. But it doesn't explain his association with aristocratic agrarianism. Although he accepted the notion of a natural aristocracy, he insisted that the natural elite may arise in all walks of life. Hence his plan for public education and a vital local government, both devices to sift the wheat from the intellectual and political chaff.[22] His democratic sympathies seem beyond question.

Nevertheless, it's significant that many of his policy proposals, including his "ward" system of local government, aimed at identifying talented individuals and sending them to college, where they would be educated in the liberal arts in preparation for careers as statesmen. Farming may be adequate training for republican citizenship, but political leaders apparently need a different sort of education. This is not to suggest that Jefferson expected statesmen to abandon the farm altogether; he himself remained actively involved in operations on his plantation, and insisted his children do so as well. But the sort of work he thought appropriate for a gentleman farmer was not the backbreaking drudgery that constitutes the bulk of agricultural labor. Rather, he pursued scientific studies and other intellectually stimulating pursuits—the kind of "work" usually considered appropriate to *leisured* gentlemen.[23]

Is Jefferson's agrarianism then inherently elitist, assuming a stratified society with a leisure class perched comfortably on the top? There's little doubt that he considered leisure as well as labor important to cultivating republican virtues. His praise of the yeoman farmer is based in part on the dubious claim that they have plenty of leisure—and education as well: "Ours are the only farmers who can read Homer," he boasted.[24] Thus the farmer he celebrated appeared to be a fairly prosperous one, with plenty of hired hands, if not slaves. Certainly he didn't have in mind the subsistence farmers scraping out a living on the frontier.[25]

On the other hand, like most eighteenth-century Americans, Jefferson worried about the corrupting effects of wealth and apparently believed that small-scale commercial agriculture would not allow the ordinary farmer to get rich.[26] So his vision of American agriculture turns out to be a mélange of elitist and democratic ideals: small family farmers relying principally on their own labor but not working too hard, producing enough for themselves but also for the market, actively engaged in commerce but not pursuing excessive wealth, and spending their spare time reading Homer and keeping informed about (but not too involved in) national politics. There may be a few American farmers who have achieved this ideal. It describes Wendell Berry pretty well, in fact. But most of Jefferson's intellectual heirs have simplified his vision considerably, emphasizing either the elitist or the democratic elements. Hence his reputation as both champion of the small farmer and apologist for the planter aristocracy.

Jefferson's fellow southerners didn't hesitate to exploit that ambiguity. His conviction that leisure and mental cultivation were critical to developing civic virtue, along with his distaste for manufacturing and industry, paved the way for the variety of agrarianism that emerged in the South during the antebellum years, an aristocratic ideology designed to defend slavery. John Taylor of Caroline, a contemporary of Jefferson, planted the seeds of this school of thought with his defense of the peculiar institution. Although he declared slavery "a misfortune to agriculture," he disagreed with Jefferson's contention that it was morally corrupting. On the contrary, he argued that masters would love liberty all the more for their practical experience with slavery.[27] Defenders of slavery such as George Fitzhugh later developed this idea. Fitzhugh maintained that slavery was necessary to the maintenance of republican government and higher civilization; democracy, he worried, leads to a general retrograde in "the departments of genius, taste

and art." "The [modern] world," he complained, "seems to regard nothing as
desirable except what will make money and what costs money." The march
of democracy will therefore create a desperate situation in which "there is
not a poet, an orator, a sculptor, or painter in the world."[28] Fortunately, the
South, because it has slaves, may be spared this decline into bad taste:

> Our citizens, like those of Rome and Athens, are a privileged class. We
> should train and educate them to deserve the privileges and perform the
> duties which society confers on them. Instead of, by a low demagogu-
> ism, depressing their self-respect by discourses on the equality of man,
> we had better excite their pride by reminding them that they do not
> fulfill the menial offices which white men do in other countries.[29]

According to Fitzhugh, civilization depends on aristocratic pride and a sense
of noblesse oblige, which the institution of slavery promotes.

Fitzhugh's elitist ideology was hardly representative of mainstream
southern agrarianism, which remained predominantly democratic. In fact,
some commentators, pointing to Fitzhugh's negative view of agricultural
labor, have suggested that he wasn't an agrarian at all. But his defense of
slavery appealed to more than a few defenders of southern agriculture, including the influential journalist Edward Ruffin.[30] Industrial production can
rely on slavery as well, of course. But agriculture, according to many antebellum southerners, was a more appropriate pastime for a gentleman, and
more conducive to cultivating the intellect and sensibilities than the crass,
noisy, busy pursuits of industry.[31] It would be self-defeating to preserve slavery in order to cultivate the arts and then abandon agriculture for soul-killing
industrialization. Thus Fitzhugh's defense of slavery did not depend on but
was intimately associated with an endorsement of agriculture as more civi-
lizing and humane than industry.

Emphasizing the superiority of agriculture to industry allowed aristocratic agrarians to rely heavily on Jeffersonian language. But aristocratic
agrarianism differs from the democratic variety in stressing *leisure* as the
defining characteristic of rural life. Aristocratic agrarians drew an important distinction between the dull, routine, *laborious* part of farming and the
ennobling, intellectually stimulating "scientific" part—managing a farm and
workforce, cultivating new varieties of crops, pursuing theoretical knowledge relevant to agriculture. The scientific part (the part Jefferson, for example, was actually involved in) was appropriate to a gentleman. The dull
routine part was simply degrading.[32] Aristocratic agrarianism therefore as-
sumed a division of labor that would give the planter a good deal of leisure

time for democratic politics and other civilized pursuits. Yeomen farmers, while virtuous in their own crude, uncultured way, would hardly have the time or education for politics. Obviously, they would need a leisure class to provide leadership.[33] This recognition of the importance of leisure to politics and the arts is thus central to aristocratic agrarianism, providing crucial support for their hierarchical vision of society.

Its concern with leisure and the role of the liberal arts in maintaining civilization has earned aristocratic agrarianism adherents even in the twentieth century; as we will see, it remains an important source of inspiration for Berry as well. But it is democratic agrarianism that most powerfully informs Berry's work. Unlike their aristocratic counterparts, democratic agrarians want to lodge political power and the preservation of civilization in the hands of ordinary, hardworking farmers. They therefore emphasize labor, rather than leisure, as the primary source of agrarian virtue. For democratic agrarians, the virtues of yeomen farmers arise directly out of their constant, physical, and laborious relationship to the land, rather than their leisure to engage in intellectual, political, and artistic pursuits. This conviction has helped democratic agrarianism retain its vitality into the twentieth century—although not without undergoing significant transformations.

On one basic tenet, democratic agrarians from Jefferson to Berry would agree: The farmer's labor not only creates material wealth,[34] but cultivates virtues necessary to the nation's welfare. This concern with civic virtue derives from the tradition of civic republicanism, in which ownership of land figures as a central requirement of citizenship, providing both economic (and therefore political) independence and a concrete interest in defending the freedom and laws of the republic.[35] The republican and agrarian traditions are so closely connected in Anglo-American thought that it's probably pointless to try to disentangle them. But it's important to note that republicanism and agrarianism can fit together in different ways. For example, republican theorists influenced by the seventeenth-century British theorist James Harrington value land because it provides the wealth and leisure to participate in politics and perform one's military duties—arguments that were adopted by southern aristocratic agrarians.[36] America's democratic agrarians, in contrast, value not simply owning land but also *farming* it. Democratic agrarians share the conviction that actually working the earth is necessary to cultivate republican virtues. Where they disagree is over which virtues the farmer's labor cultivates.

Jefferson's list of virtues reflects typical eighteenth-century concerns. He argued that farming instilled such desirable traits as industry, frugality, humility (in the sense of lack of unseemly ambition), and a reliable interest in law, order, and individual rights.[37] Most important, however, farming cultivated independence—specifically, independence from the ties of patronage and the economic influence of employers that threatened to corrupt the political process. "Dependence," Jefferson warned, "begets subservience and venality." Independence is a theme common to American democratic agrarians, but Jefferson wasn't worried about the dependence of commercial farmers on agricultural markets (which has proved to be among the most problematic of small farmers' dependencies). Rather, he was concerned about the dependence of workers on employers, which gave employers too much influence over workers' political opinions and activities. And equally troubling to his republican sensibilities was manufacturers' dependence on "the casualties and caprices of customers"—that is, on consumers' whims and fashions. Jeffersonians argued that markets for the "luxury" goods produced by manufacturers—like buckles, lace, or plated candlesticks—could collapse overnight when fashions changed, throwing people out of work. Markets for basic agricultural commodities, they claimed, were more reliable ("as long as eating is the custom of Europe," as Tom Paine put it).[38]

Jefferson, then, was concerned primarily with protecting farmers from economic dependence on the rich and on unstable markets. John Taylor went further, arguing that farmers must be assured of economic prosperity—not just independence—because political power follows wealth and farmers constitute the majority. If they are left impoverished, they will lack political power to check interested minorities and, instead of a healthy republic, we will be left with an aristocracy of the "idle classes" (bankers, speculators, and people living off government sinecures).[39] Thus Taylor gave considerable attention to what one might expect to be a major theme of agrarianism: how to be a good farmer. Because successful farming was important to his vision of an agrarian America, his ideal farmer had to have certain stewardship and intellectual virtues, as well as rugged independence. In fact, Taylor wrote extensively on soil fertility—not because he was concerned about environmental integrity for its own sake, but because it affected the prosperity and therefore political status of farmers.

This focus on political status was Taylor's legacy to democratic agrarians.

His argument that political status was linked to good husbandry, however, was never a prominent element of the democratic tradition. In fact, it was aristocratic agrarianism, which defended agriculture as a way to develop intellectual virtues, that held the most promise of developing into an environmentally sensitive agricultural ideology. By the time the science of ecology came of age in the late nineteenth century, however, aristocratic agrarianism was in decline—and those who sought to revive it in the 1930s had little interest in agricultural science or ecology. Research on soil fertility and erosion did continue throughout the nineteenth century, of course. Eventually (as we will see) such research contributed to the twentieth-century permanent agriculture movement. But in general, the science of agriculture evolved independently of both aristocratic and democratic agrarians. The former was more concerned with rescuing some remnant of antebellum southern society, while the latter (much to the frustration of the experts) remained more interested in economics and politics than in techniques for preventing soil erosion.[40]

Thus Jefferson's legacy evolved as it fell into the hands of actual yeomen farmers, beginning with the Jacksonian democrats and culminating in the Populist uprising of the late nineteenth century.[41] Instead of following up Jefferson's and Taylor's interest in a more scientific approach to farming, democratic agrarians revived their calls for political and economic independence. Drawing on what we have come recognize as basic democratic agrarian principles—the moral and economic value of labor, the demand for economic and political equality, and the value of individual independence—the Populists launched a general attack on the emerging industrial order, particularly its concentration of wealth and erosion of competitive capitalism. Their struggles for reform and regulation of the money, land, and transportation systems demonstrate the radical potential of agrarian thought.[42] Rather than examining their specific policy proposals, however, I want to focus on their reinterpretation of the Jeffersonian virtuous farmer.

The Populists' list of agrarian virtues resembled Jefferson's in some respects. Industry and frugality, certainly; Populists loved to compare themselves favorably to city folk who neither worked nor saved. Farmers' wealth, what little there was of it, came through labor, "business tact and thrift," while the city was filled with speculators: "The Ghouls of Wall Street," in Jonathan Periam's overheated rhetoric, are "intensely selfish, guilty of the meanest subterfuges, often lacking education, successful by dint of cunning, and unscrupulous to the last degree." They "rope in" the unwary clerk, steal his pitiful savings and reduce him to poverty and disgrace.[43] Such corruption is only to be expected from people who make a living without breaking a sweat; Populists remained faithful to the long-standing agrarian conviction that labor is man's proper function and the true source of the nation's wealth.[44]

For the Populists, however, it wasn't only agricultural labor that produced civic virtue. In an attempt to forge an alliance with workers, Populists developed a "producerist" ideology that held the labor of the industrial worker and the farmer equally valuable to the republic. For Jefferson, the superiority of agricultural labor had been premised in large part on the variety and intellectual stimulation such work provided. In contrast, Populists had little to say about how labor cultivated intellectual virtues. Labor, for the Populists, invariably meant manual labor; they valued such moral virtues as discipline and ruggedness, which were clearly shared by many industrial workers. Thus, although they never lost sight of the special claims and concerns of farmers, Populists did not rely on invidious comparisons between agriculture and industry; rather, they compared farmers and workers both to the "idle" (upper) classes.

Similarly, like Jefferson the Populists valued political independence, but they reinterpreted independence as freedom from partisan influence (rather than freedom from wealthy patrons). Since partisanship interfered with their efforts to build a third party, freedom from unthinking party loyalty became an important item on the Populist agenda. But they qualified their endorsement of political independence with the recognition that effective political action requires organization, and organization involves some limits on individual autonomy. Populist rhetoric is thus littered with oddly dissonant calls for unity: "The independent manhood of the country is rising up," proclaimed James Davis—but those independent men are immediately lost in an organic unity: "An army of oppressed producers are organizing for victory. . . . Upon their banner they have inscribed 'Liberty, Justice and Equality.' A million hearts are beating in response to these sentiments."[45] If farmers fail to assert their rights, warned Periam, "they will cease to be free agents." But their best hope is in precisely that, in "their Societies, their Clubs, their Granges." "In *union* there is strength."[46]

Nor was the conflict between organization and individual independence the only inconsistency in Populist rhetoric. They also lauded the farmers' traditional interest in law and order (based on the fact that farmers own property and therefore want protection for property rights)—but they undermined this lawfulness by insisting that the current government was hopelessly corrupt and lawyers and politicians were useless parasites. Respect for law, they pointed out, sometimes requires resistance to unjust legislation and police abuse. ("The tree of liberty," as Jefferson wrote, "must be refreshed from time to time, with the blood of patriots and tyrants.")[47] On the other hand, Populists expressed an almost touching faith in the power of legislation to cure the inequities of industrial society—a position that brought them into conflict with Jefferson's famous endorsement of limited government. Even the cleverest Populists had a hard time finding Jeffersonian arguments to support their calls for national regulation of railroads, telegraphs, and other corporations.[48]

The theme of humility also eroded under the pressures of the Populists' political activism. Populist rabble-rousers, trying to stir up resistance, talked self-respect and empowerment, not humble acceptance of one's lot. James Baird Weaver's stirring 1892 "Call to Action" called on farmers to show their "enlightened self-respect," and offered them the kind of fame usually reserved for the political elite:

> It is glorious to live in this age, and to be permitted to take part in this heroic combat is the greatest honor that can be conferred upon mortals. It is an opportunity for every man, however humble, to strike a blow that will permanently benefit his race and make the world better for his having lived.[49]

Obviously this call for farmers to abandon their traditional humility was driven by a desire to mobilize mass political action. But downplaying humility wasn't just a matter of political expediency for the Populists; it also reflects the ideological distance between the early and later agrarians. Where Jefferson, the Virginia gentleman, saw a collection of small landholders minding their own economic business and uninterested in challenging the social hierarchy, Populists saw a downtrodden mass suffering from the depredations of the aristocracy of wealth and badly needing a dose of self-esteem. Humility was a problematic value for them, as it is for anyone involved in the politics of class and status.

Consider Booker T. Washington's dilemma. Given the influence of Populism in the South, it made sense for him to use agrarian rhetoric to defend the interests of blacks, who were mostly southern farmers. But the problem of humility brought him up short: His advice to blacks to stay on the farm and cultivate agrarian virtues, while calculated to advance the economic status and therefore political power of the race, sounded to many like a cowardly refusal to challenge oppressive social conventions. In contrast, W. E. B. DuBois, who was sympathetic to the agrarian critique of industrial capitalism, drew more heavily on the aristocratic tradition. For DuBois, the virtue of the agrarian South was that it supported a class concerned with humane values—a class (he contended) that should recognize its fellow natural aristocrats, no matter what color their skin. His somewhat elitist agrarianism sounds less humble, and has therefore seemed to later generations a better vehicle for status politics.[50] Humility, in short, is at the center of conflict over social status. If we interpret humility as the virtue of "knowing one's place," we must ask what one's place is and whether it can be defined without reference to existing social hierarchies—a question that Berry takes up as one of his central themes.[51]

The basic concern of Populist politics, however, was not simply status but economic autonomy—interpreted, however, as the ability to make a fair profit on the market rather than merely the ability to subsist on the products of one's own labor. Echoing John Taylor, Populists claimed that individual political rights are meaningless to the poor; political freedom requires an equitable distribution of wealth. The concentration of wealth in the hands of corporations, they insisted, turned yeomen farmers into "serfs" or "slaves."[52] James Weaver, for example, interpreted Anglo-American political history as a continual struggle against the concentration of wealth ("One of the main charges against Charles the First, was that he had fostered and created monopolies. His head went to the block.") The current economic system, he maintained, was no better than "corporate feudalism."[53] The power of money is the power to oppress; the struggle for a more equitable distribution of wealth is therefore a struggle for political liberty.

This concern for economic autonomy led to a broad attack on corporations, monopolies, and the institutions controlling credit—the centerpiece of the Populist agenda, and their most enduring legacy to twentieth-century agrarians such as Berry. Corporations, Populists complained, "are the forces against which we are to contend." The corporation was a monstrous creature, an "artificial person." Once brought to life, "this individual . . . soon began to bend to its uses the forms and powers of the law." By its "gigantic combinations, its control of the money of the nation, by its gradual building up of a system of indebtedness of colossal magnitude," it has made the "toiling millions" into "the tools of a few plutocrats."[54] Corporations use their economic power to corrupt legislatures, which are then induced to grant them special privileges, resulting in monopolies destructive of economic competition and begetting the "un-republican vices of fawning, subservience, and venality."[55]

The problem with corporations, however, is not merely their economic power and ability to corrupt legislatures. Rather, it is the very nature of these amoral creatures: "These corporations . . . are moved only by an exhaustless greed for lucre, without one human sympathy." They are "soulless." Sounding a theme that would echo into the twenty-first century, Populists complained that corporations *at best* act on self-interest; too often the "capriciousness of officials" governs their decisions; the welfare of the local communities that depend on them are "a secondary and trivial consideration."[56] Moreover, because they act only through agents, "the natural persons who own and move their power, look to them only for an increase of gains, and feel no personal concern for the moral quality of the acts which produce money." Thus "the individual is merged in the money-machine of which he is an integral part, and the morality of its action is the morality of the company, not his."[57] Corporations, in sum, concentrate wealth, destroy competition, corrupt legislatures, disrupt local communities, disempower the citizens, and demoralize their own officers.

Populists therefore called for large-scale government regulation of corporations and limits on the acquisition of wealth—all in the name of protecting civic virtue and individual (economic and moral) autonomy. I don't want to oversimplify their views, however. There is also plenty of Populist rhetoric extolling the virtues of organization, the unfairness of asking individuals to take care of themselves, and generally raising questions about the political and moral value of independence. We have to rise above "survival of the strongest," insisted Lorenzo Dow Lewelling. "It is the duty of the government to protect the weak."[58] Jacob Coxey frankly admitted that his ragged army had come to ask for help; the struggle for existence was just too hard.[59] Many Populists sounded as if the age of individualism were over: If "the corporation has absorbed the community," then "the community must absorb the corporation. . . . A stage must be reached in which each will be for all and all for each."[60] Nelson Dunning insisted that organization "is now the motive power that rules and guides the world"—and that's a good thing. The people should simply learn how to use the advantages of organization to combat tyranny. Collectivization, according to Ignatius Donnelly, is the answer to corporate power.[61]

This inconsistency illustrates not mere carelessness or a lack of sincerity but a problem that will continue to infect agrarian politics up to Berry's day: the difficulty of basing a political movement aimed at strengthening community control on the value of independent, individual action. That the Populists regularly asked people to accept all sorts of legal restrictions in the name of protecting individual liberty and economic independence apparently didn't trouble them much. Berry's point, as I interpret him, is that it should have. The problem of reconciling individualism with the needs and demands of farmers should have led to a more thoroughgoing critique of a basic agrarian tenet: that the virtue most necessary for free, popular government is self-reliance. Instead, this celebration of individual autonomy remained central to the democratic agrarianism that Berry inherited, forming an important ethical basis for farmers' attacks on big business and industrial interests.[62]

Conspicuously missing from those attacks on industrialism, on the other hand, is any hint of ecological sensibility. The Populists' perspective on the environment is summed up in Ignatius Donnelly's 1891 prophecy: "The time may come when the slow processes of agriculture will be largely discarded, and the food of man be created out of the chemical elements of which it is composed, transfused by electricity and magnetism. . . . Our mountain ranges may, in after ages, be leveled down and turned into bread."[63] Donnelly actually *looked forward* to a world without mountains or endless waves of grain. Like most Populists, he favored technological progress and showed little concern either for sustainability or for preserving the pristine beauty of the American wilderness. In this respect, too, Berry's agrarian vision would differ substantially from that of earlier democratic agrarians.

As the new century opened, however, the agrarian tradition was about to undergo another transformation. During the early decades of the twentieth century, a new, broader discourse about American agriculture took shape in the academic and policy community. While the Populists and their successors continued to pursue economic reform almost exclusively, a small but influential back-to-the-land movement brought attention to rural communities and to the social, spiritual, and aesthetic rewards of farming.

The twentieth century witnessed an increased interest among policy makers and social reformers in the condition of rural America. Ironically, this interest coincided with one of the most prosperous periods in American agriculture. Farm prices rose regularly every year between 1897 and 1910, and farmers actually began to sound optimistic about their economic prospects and the future of agriculture.[64] From another perspective, however, agriculture was in decline. Although the number of people on farms continued to increase until World War I, the percentage of the population involved in agriculture was decreasing, from 50 percent in 1870 to 30.7 percent in 1910 to less than 25 percent in the 1920s. The decline was due in part to the very success of agricultural development; the increased use of machines and other intensive practices allowed for more production with less labor. But it also reflected agriculture's inability to compete with other sectors of the economy for labor. Farmers, despite their increasing prosperity, continued to make less money than workers in many other occupations. In addition, the quality of rural life left much to be desired; rural folk complained of bad schools, bad roads, isolation, and the lack of urban amenities.[65] So views on farming in the early twentieth century were mixed: While the more successful farmers would look back on this period as the golden age of American agriculture, others viewed it as the beginning of a major crisis in rural America.

Those who saw a crisis brewing were an eclectic group of intellectuals, including literati, professors, government officials, and urban reformers, who worried that the loss of farmers signaled the end of the Jeffersonian vision of America. As the country became urban and industrial, they feared, agrarian virtues—virtues critical to maintaining a republic—would disappear. Thus to halt or at least slow down this urban migration, they called for improvements in the quality of rural life and the rewards of agriculture. Americans, they insisted, must be induced to go "back to the land." Although never as strong as its European counterpart,[66] the American back-to-the-land movement did boast some eloquent spokespersons: John Crowe Ransom, Allen Tate, Ralph Borsodi, and Scott and Helen Nearing were among those who embraced farming as a way to cultivate independence, security, health, and leisure. Their efforts to halt the forces of industrialization were entirely unsuccessful, of course; although some of these writers were widely read, the movement as a whole never enjoyed mass support. Nevertheless, these advocates for rural revitalization made a significant contribution to agrarian thought, developing themes that the Populist tradition had largely ignored.

Such themes are illustrated in *I'll Take My Stand,* a classic statement of postbellum southern agrarianism and an important precursor to Wendell Berry's work.[67] *I'll Take My Stand* is the manifesto of the Vanderbilt Agrarians, a philosophical and literary group that took shape in the 1920s around the leadership of John Crowe Ransom, Donald Davidson, Allen Tate, and Robert Penn Warren.[68] The immediate impetus for the book was the 1925 Scopes trial, which prompted many caustic attacks by eastern journalists on southern rural "backwardness." Annoyed, the group (calling themselves "Twelve Southerners") published this collection of essays to defend southern agrarian society as superior to northern industrialism.[69] The result is a critique of American industrial civilization that, to many scholars, sounds quite contemporary.[70] But the Twelve Southerners' agrarianism is actually rooted in the past. In *I'll Take My Stand,* the aristocratic version of the Jeffersonian vision is revived, along with its endorsement of social hierarchy and its concern with leisure, aesthetics, and the intellectual and spiritual virtues of the good farmer.[71]

The Twelve Southerners hardly spoke with one voice, but they all agreed that industrialization destabilizes community, threatens the humanist tradition, and destroys any possibility of achieving a good, truly human life—conceptualized as "a kind of imaginatively balanced life lived out in a definite social tradition."[72] Their major themes are the moral effects of industrialization, the case for social hierarchy, and an analysis of the social conditions necessary to preserve the intellectual tradition of civic humanism. These are, rather unconvincingly, marshaled in defense of the South against northern industrial imperialism. The result closely tracks the aristocratic agrarianism of nineteenth-century theorists such as George Fitzhugh. For example, John Crowe Ransom's "Reconstructed But Unregenerate" begins with a defense of the antebellum South, which was, he claims, "unique on this continent for having founded and defended a culture which was according to the European principles of culture."[73] In other words, it was feudal, hierarchical, and traditional. These features allowed it to cherish a set of values antithetical to those of industrial society. Southern society, uninterested in material "progress," was characterized by leisure and, therefore, culture. Southern agriculture involved little physical labor, he insists. Rather, its goal was "to put the surplus of energy into the free life of the mind."[74] This was its chief virtue; a lifestyle devoted to leisure allowed for the cultivation of the arts and an appreciative, humble stance toward nature. In contrast, northern "urbanized, anti-provincial, progressive and mobile American life" is "in a condition of eternal flux."[75] This condition of constant change prevents people from developing attachments and therefore impoverishes their emotional life. Moreover, devotion to material progress forces them into a combative relationship with nature and enslaves them to constant toil. The desire to dominate nature eventually "brutalizes" their lives.[76]

Ransom's debt to antebellum southern agrarians is clear in his one-sided picture of planter culture as leisurely and civilized. But in case his aristocratic tendencies need further evidence, he goes on to criticize social mobility as destabilizing to community.[77] Although he suggests that slavery was merely an inessential local custom, he insists that the South's virtue lay in its stable social hierarchy: "The good life depends on leisure, but leisure depends on an establishment, and the establishment depends on a prevailing magnanimity which scorns personal advancement at the expense of the free activity of the mind."[78] In other words, unquestioning acceptance of one's lot in life frees one from all that pointless striving for material goods.

This elitism, which infects most of the essays in the book, mars what would otherwise be a persuasive, if not particularly original, critique of industrialism. The claim that industrialization destabilizes community, undermines tradition, and cultivates a hostile, combative stance toward nature has been echoed by more egalitarian and progressive theorists, including Berry.[79] But the Twelve Southerners' critique of industrial society is tied inextricably to their case for social hierarchy. Agrarian society, under their reasoning, can escape the defects of industrial society only if it maintains a leisure *class*. Unfortunately for their argument, farming is a leisurely way of life only for the gentleman farmer who relies on slaves, hired workers, tenants—or machines—to work the land. Thus if the Southerners' agrarian society is more hospitable to noninstrumental values, it's not because that society has more farmers, but because it has more *aristocrats*. The heart of the Agrarians' argument is that only a leisure class commanding traditional authority can maintain the cultural cohesion necessary to sustain a humane civilization. Their goal is not to improve the political or economic status of farmers, but to create an aristocracy that would pose a counterbalance to the values of industrial capitalism—a class concerned with tradition, leisure, and the art of living.

The Vanderbilt Agrarians represent only one vision of a reformed rural America, of course. Not all back-to-the-land advocates were so enamored of rigid social hierarchy. But those who shared the Twelve Southerners' concern about cultural decay resulting from industrialization often shared their elitist attitudes. For example, Ralph Borsodi, a prominent spokesman for the back-to-the-land movement in the 1930s, revealed his ideological orientation by quoting Nietzsche approvingly and complaining of the way industrial society favors inferior, "quantity-minded" men over superior "quality-minded" men—men who appreciate beauty and the finer things. Individuals, he insisted, are not equal, so "we cannot say that all men are equally entitled to a voice in the counsels of the state."[80] What mankind needs "is an aristocracy of truly superior persons." Only when the masses understand and accept that fact will we achieve cultural renaissance.[81]

On the other hand, Helen and Scott Nearing, among the most well-known advocates of the simple life, were socialists whose goals were eminently democratic. In *The Good Life*, Helen Nearing explains why she and her husband left the city in 1932 to live on a small farm in Vermont: "We were against the accumulation of profit and unearned income by non-producers." They wanted to dissociate themselves from such exploitation and cultivate a true sense of community: "individuals, householders, villagers and townsmen living together and cooperating day in, day out."[82] Although the Nearings shared the aristocratic agrarians' concern with leisure, aesthetic values, and intellectual cultivation, their case for the simple life sounds more like Thoreau than George Fitzhugh. They merely sought "a simple, satisfying life on the land, to be devoted to mutual aid and harmlessness, with an ample margin of leisure in which to do personally constructive and creative work."[83]

Whether they drew on aristocratic agrarianism or Thoreauvian simplicity, however, most back-to-the-land advocates focused on the aesthetic and spiritual rewards of farming. Although economic independence was a chief goal, particularly for those writing during the Depression, they had little interest in the Populists' plans for reforming the market economy to make commercial agriculture more rewarding. Instead, resurrecting Jefferson's notion of economic autonomy, they advocated subsistence agriculture as a way to reduce dependence on international markets and on industrial production, as well as fostering a more spiritual and less instrumental relationship to nature. It's important to note, however, that this call for a more spiritual relationship to nature was not typically accompanied by a keen ecological sensibility. Borsodi and the Vanderbilt Agrarians showed no awareness of ecology at all. And even the more progressive Nearings, who sought "at-one-ness," were informed about soil conservation, and cared deeply about animal rights, did not develop sustained ecological arguments for adopting the simple life. The back-to-the-land advocates were less interested in ecological integrity than in social and moral reform.

That interest in reforming American society through moral regeneration distinguishes the back-to-the-land movement from Populist-style agrarianism. Unlike Populism, the movement did not, in general, speak from or to the concerns and values of ordinary farmers; as many commentators have noted, the movement was largely the province of dissatisfied urban intellectuals seeking to escape from the pressures of city life. Thus we might not expect this variety of agrarianism to have a significant influence on a rural Kentucky farmer like Wendell Berry. On the contrary, however, the simple life did have a few advocates in rural America—even in Kentucky. The most important of these advocates, for Berry, was the writer and painter Harlan Hubbard.

Harlan Hubbard was an inspiration and role model for Wendell Berry. Born in 1900 in Bellevue, Kentucky, Hubbard moved to New York at age fifteen, studying art at the National Academy of Design and then at the Cincinnati Art Academy. But he returned to northern Kentucky in 1919 and settled in Fort Thomas, working as a day laborer and caring for his mother. When she died in 1943, Hubbard and his wife, Anna, built a boat and set off on what Berry calls their "great adventure."[84] For forty-two years, they lived on a riverboat floating up and down the Mississippi and its tributaries and on a small homestead at Payne Hollow, on the Kentucky shore of the Ohio River. Their lifestyle was inspired largely by Thoreau, but as Harlan Hubbard explained, "I had no theories to prove. I merely wanted to try living by my own hands, independent as far as possible from a system of division of labor in which the participant loses most of the pleasure of making and growing things for himself."[85] Thus they "departed from the life of the twentieth century as their families and friends were living it and as they had been expected to live it themselves."[86]

The Hubbards were still living in Payne Hollow in 1964, when Wendell Berry visited their homestead. Although the couple was "already more or less legendary by then," he hadn't yet heard of them, and the visit seems to have been serendipitous. Nevertheless, he tells us he wasn't surprised by their lifestyle; he was in fact "somewhat prepared" for them.[87] He recognized that their way of life, although unconventional, was "an exemplary way of living in America." Like other "American settlers," they wanted "a kind of freedom and a kind of integrity that they could not have in any other place." According to Berry, Harlan and Anna Hubbard were self-consciously seeking to realize the Jeffersonian ideal, to revive (in Harlan's words) "a strain of Americanism almost lost."[88] It was a project Berry not only understood but sympathized with; in Hubbard he found another link to the Jeffersonian tradition that would justify his own decision to return to Kentucky.

It is significant, however, that Berry's account of the Hubbards' life, like Harlan Hubbard's own account, mentions Thoreau much more often than Jefferson. The Hubbards may represent one sort of twentieth-century agrarianism, but their "simple life" philosophy also has roots in a competing, and sometimes opposed, tradition—a tradition that claims Thoreau rather than Jefferson as its chief inspiration. We will explore that tradition and its relation to agrarian thought in the next chapter. First, however, we must consider the fate of the Populist legacy in the twentieth century and its influence on Wendell Berry.

While advocates for the simple life were exploring the social and cultural potential of rural living, the Populist tradition continued to focus on the economic prosperity of the American farmer. Although the Populist party dis-integrated after the 1896 election, the political tradition was inherited by a series of successors, such as the Non-Partisan League, the American Society of Equity, the Farmers' National Holiday Association, and the Farmers' Union. These organizations addressed a number of farm-related issues, but their primary interests were marketing and price control. Farmer coopera-tives in particular were the centerpiece of much early twentieth-century Pop-ulist agitation, particularly in Kentucky.

Populism had always had a strong presence in the tobacco-growing regions of Kentucky, which boasted 226 chapters of Farmers' Union in 1908.[89] The most famous—or infamous—result of this influence was the vio-lence that erupted in the Black Patch region of western Kentucky between 1906 and 1910. Vigilantes who came to be known as the Night Riders at-tempted to coerce farmers to join the Planters' Protective Association, a coop-erative organized to oppose the international tobacco cartel.[90] The Planters' Protective Association failed, but the Populist spirit survived, if in less radi-cal form. A wave of cooperatives were organized in Kentucky in the 1920s and continued into the 1930s—including the Burley Tobacco Growers Co-operative Association, with which John Berry was intimately involved.

Of course, by the 1940s, most of the Populists' policy proposals—in par-ticular price supports and other forms of protection from unstable markets—were accepted, even entrenched, elements of agricultural policy. When John Berry appeared before the Senate Committee on Agriculture and Forestry in 1948, he sounded much like the staid Farm Bureau representatives, advo-cating price supports that would guarantee farmers "parity"—that is, roughly the same return on labor as other sectors of the economy receive. (In prac-tice, parity meant a price that would give farm products the same buying power they had between 1909 and 1914, the golden age of American agri-culture.) "The parity concept," he declared, "is the happiest and most for-tunate thought that has visited the minds of statesmen of this country in generations. It accords with our way of life and gives real and tangible meaning to the philosophy of equal opportunity."[91] The connection between price supports and equal opportunity was a legacy from the Populist tradi-tion, but John Berry's optimistic, even cheerful, tone poses a stark contrast to the angry protests of the earlier era.[92] His testimony is wholly free of the declamations against evil corporations or impassioned pleas for justice that characterized Populist rhetoric. This variety of Populism was a domesticated version, seeking accommodation rather than revolution.

Neither the anger nor the more radical style of protest disappeared from

Kentucky politics, however; in the early 1960s they erupted violently in the coal-mining regions of eastern Kentucky. For decades, eastern Kentucky had suffered under conditions of poverty and corporate exploitation similar to that of the Black Patch region during the Night Rider era. The situation became particularly desperate in the 1950s, when the "coal barons," protected by their hegemonic control of politics in the region, adopted the environmentally devastating practice of strip mining. During the 1960s, however, federal poverty relief and community organizing programs disrupted the coal barons' political control, giving rise to organizations such as the Appalachian Volunteers and the Appalachian Group to Save the Land and People. These groups drew on the native history of popular resistance in the region to create opposition to the coal companies in general and strip mining in particular.

Among the leaders of the resistance was Harry Caudill, a Whitesburg attorney and author of *Night Comes to the Cumberland,* an eloquent and influential indictment of corporate abuse and exploitation in the Appalachians.[93] Caudill's rhetoric, echoing the rich, effusive style of nineteenth-century Populists, contrasts strikingly with John Berry's restrained testimony before the Senate. Coal, Caudill declared,

> has always cursed the land in which it lies. When men begin to wrest it from the earth it leaves a legacy of foul streams, hideous slag heaps and polluted air. It peoples this transformed land with blind and crippled men and with widows and orphans. It is an extractive industry which takes all away and restores nothing.[94]

By the 1950s, "the greater part of the region's mineral wealth had lain in the iron clutch of absentee corporations." Clinging to their archaic legal privileges, abetted by legal decisions "medieval in outlook and philosophy," these soulless corporations turned to strip mining—and then "the shades of darkness moved close indeed to the Cumberlands."[95] Sounding familiar Populist themes, he blamed morally bankrupt corporations and a corrupt political establishment for the disruption and demoralization of the agrarian communities of eastern Kentucky.

Wendell Berry first encountered Harry Caudill in 1965, at a meeting of the Appalachian Group to Save the Land and People. He had read *Night Comes to the Cumberland* two years earlier; its author, he remembered, spoke that night "with the eloquence of a resolute intelligence and with the moral passion of a lawyer who understood and venerated the traditions of justice."[96] Caudill's speech indicted the corporations and the political system, the "gleeful yahoos who are destroying the world, and the mindless oafs who abet them."[97] To the conservative (not to say paranoid) Kentucky political establishment, this sort of talk sounded like communist agitation. But to Berry, Caudill's complaints were perfectly in tune with American political traditions: Like Harlan Hubbard, Caudill was "recalling us to what, after all, we claim as 'our' principles."[98]

Caudill, however, was not calling for a return to "the simple life." On the contrary, he favored federal policies promoting economic development of the Cumberland, on the model of the Tennessee Valley Authority (TVA). "The transformation of the Tennessee Valley," he claimed, "demonstrates that enlightened government intervention under the auspices of careful planners can accomplish far-reaching economic and social improvements."[99] Rather than withdrawing into private domesticity, he wanted to encourage industrial development and political action at the national level. Superficially, at least, his vision for a reformed rural America had little in common with Harlan Hubbard's, or Jefferson's—although Ignatius Donnelly might have approved.

The striking differences between Harry Caudill and Harlan Hubbard—both native Kentuckians, both major influences on Wendell Berry, and both arguably inheritors of Jefferson's mantle—underscore the complexity of the agrarian tradition that Berry is trying to revive. His project is as much a synthesis as a recovery, a critical examination and careful selection from the variety of agrarianisms he has inherited. We will find in his writings echoes of Harry Caudill and the Populist tradition, celebrating the working man and teaching distrust of the establishment and corporate America. Similarly, we will discover a critical engagement with the Twelve Southerners' highly literate defense of southern agrarianism against northern industrialism. And of course we can detect the inspiration of advocates of the simple life, such as Harlan and Anna Hubbard.

None of these influences, however, entirely account for Berry's interest in environmentalism and sustainable agriculture. Protection of the environment was not a major concern for either the Populists or the advocates of the simple life. If it became a theme in both traditions, it did so late in the day—not until the 1960s, in fact, when Berry himself was already beginning his career. Berry may be an inheritor of the agrarian tradition, but he is also a reformer of that tradition, bringing to it an ecological sensibility lacking in earlier agrarians. The next chapter examines the intellectual sources of that sensibility.

Chapter Two

The Greening of Agrarianism

In 1989, Terry Tempest Williams accompanied Wendell Berry into the desert to attend a memorial service for Edward Abbey. As Williams remembers, Berry found the desert beautiful but strange. Although he had traveled to Europe, Ireland, and South America, here near Moab, Utah, he felt "as far away from Kentucky as I have ever been."[1] Apparently, the journey helped Berry to better understand Edward Abbey, a man he had known for many years but never met in person.[2]

There was much about Abbey that someone like Berry might find difficult to understand. Abbey was by his own admission a desert rat, often crude and belligerent, a vigorous defender of wild nature and rugged individualism. Berry, in contrast, is notoriously polite, an eloquent spokesman for civility, domesticity, and the social virtues. He was never entirely comfortable in Abbey's world; when Williams invited him to take a trip down the Colorado River, Berry responded graciously but cautiously: "It sounds like a wonderful adventure, but I'll have to check my schedule for next year. It seems to me I may have a dentist appointment around then."[3] Despite their differences, though, Berry embraces and is embraced by many of Abbey's allies in the wilderness preservation movement. Much of his work is aimed at building conceptual bridges between wilderness advocates, who champion nature raw and dangerously pristine, and agrarians, for whom nature must be transformed and given value by human labor. His distant friendship with Edward Abbey is a measure of both the difficulty and the success of that project.

To contemporary readers the difficulty may seem puzzling. After all, the connection between the protection of small farms and protection of the environment, to modern environmentalists, often looks natural and obvious. But it was slow to emerge in the United States; farmers and environmentalists have been at odds with one another in this country for most of the last two centuries. This political animosity contrasts strikingly with the much warmer relations between greens and agrarians in Europe, where small farmers have long defended their interests using the language of environmentalism. Anna Bramwell accounts for the difference by arguing that in Europe, nineteenth-century environmentalism developed in close conjunction with efforts to preserve rural life and rural landscapes. In Germany, for example, concern for the environment was linked to a search for national identity that emphasized the rural roots of German culture and celebrated the organic, authentic, earth-bound peasantry. Many English environmentalists were similarly concerned with defending farmers against industrial encroachment—not only to protect the physical environment but to save the remnants of a disappearing folk heritage.[4] Thus early European environmental politics often connected the defense of the earth to the defense of rural community.

Bramwell notes with some bemusement that American environmentalists seem to be oblivious to this rich European tradition. She undoubtedly overstates the case,[5] but it does appear that the communitarian and organicist elements of nineteenth-century European agrarianism made few significant inroads on America's liberal consensus. Environmental thought developed differently in the United States, where the most influential environmentalists focused not on preserving rural life and landscapes but on protecting or managing the wilderness: Conservationists such as Gifford Pinchot concentrated on rational use of natural resources for the public good, while preservationists inspired by John Muir fought for protection of natural areas in their pristine condition.[6] Although often at odds with each other, they shared a common challenge in the flood of homesteaders making constant demands for more farmland.

The convergence of environmentalism and agrarianism did not take shape until the sustainable agriculture movement of the 1960s—and it was hardly a natural or inevitable development. True, most wilderness advocates shared the Populists' interest in preserving individual independence in a society being rapidly engulfed by collectivization. The two groups even used the same language, extolling the rugged individualism produced by man's interaction with nature. But the similarities between agrarians and environmentalists are deceptive. In fact, their respective pursuits of individual autonomy have masked, and sometimes aggravated, the profound conflicts between them. Although farmers and environmentalists would eventually unite in resistance to the industrialization of agriculture, their ideological differences would persist until Wendell Berry and his colleagues in the sustainable agriculture movement began to bring a greener, and less individualistic, perspective to traditional agrarianism.

American environmental thought, particularly the preservationist tradition, has had a complex relationship to agrarianism. While agrarians claim a somewhat erratic descent from Jefferson, preservationists claim a similarly uncertain legacy from Thoreau, that cranky and brilliant worshipper of the American landscape. Berry shares this legacy as well; indeed, his agrarianism is in large part a critical engagement with *Walden*—which itself can be read as a critical engagement with Jeffersonian agrarianism. But what Thoreau may be saying about agrarianism, or nature generally, is far from clear.

According to the conventional reading, *Walden* is a romantic celebration of nature, a call for a pure, unmediated relationship to the physical environment as a source of spiritual enlightenment. This is the Thoreau who called a young man's encounter with the forest an introduction to "the most original part of himself," and condemned him "who would carry the landscape, who would carry his God, to market, if he could get any thing for him." It is the Thoreau who left off eating animals in order to live by higher principles, and held that spiritual benefits are the "highest reality"—the ascetic who sought to transmute "what in form is the grossest sensuality into purity and devotion."[7] We might call this an Emersonian reading. It sees behind Thoreau's love of nature the whole transcendental paraphernalia: physical nature as emblematic, corresponding to a higher, spiritual reality attainable through heroic feats of imaginative or intuitive transcendence. For Emerson the value of nature depended almost entirely on its link to spiritual truth—a view that elevated nature worship to the status of religion, and justified Emerson's rejection of conventional organized faiths.[8] Thus an Emersonian reading would see Thoreau as a contemporary incarnation of the ancient hermits and prophets seeking spiritual insight (and autonomy): heading into the wilderness only to transcend it.

The world-denying Thoreau, however, doesn't square with the sensuous materialist who was refreshed by the sounds and smells of commerce, of

the stores which go dispensing their odors all the way from Long Wharf to Lake Champlain, reminding me of foreign parts, of coral reefs, and Indian oceans, and tropical climes, and the extent of the globe. . . . Here goes lumber from the Maine woods, which did not go out to sea in the last freshet, risen four dollars on the thousand because of what did go out or was split up; pine, spruce, cedar, —first, second, third and fourth qualities, so lately all of one quality, to wave over the bear, and moose, and caribou. Next rolls Thomaston lime, a prime lot, which will get far among the hills before it gets slacked. . . . This closed car smells of salt fish, the strong New England and commercial scent, reminding me of Grand Banks and the fisheries.[9]

Here Thoreau sounds more like an advocate of globalization than a pure spirit devoted to the simple life. He delights in thinking himself a "citizen of the world" and glories in the majesty and power of the locomotive—if only it were made for more noble ends![10] His ambition is centered in *this* world, the world of sights and sounds and smells all deliciously available to his devouring senses. This reading of Thoreau (call it Whitmanesque) sees his nature worship as part of an all-encompassing sensual materialism, a love for the world in all its rich particularity.

Then there is Thoreau the agrarian—the halfhearted agrarian, we should say—who wondered about the meaning of "this small Herculean labor" of "half-cultivating" his beans. "The labor of the hands, even when pursued to drudgery," he mischievously suggests, "is perhaps never the worst form of idleness." Such pursuits are "a rare amusement," but "continued too long, might have become a dissipation."[11] Perhaps farming need not be degrading, he muses, but this once-sacred art "is pursued with irreverent haste and heedlessness by us, our object being to have large farms and large crops merely. We have no festival, nor procession, nor ceremony." He complains that "by avarice and selfishness, and a grovelling habit . . . of regarding the soil as property, . . . the landscape is deformed, husbandry is degraded with us, and the farmer leads the meanest of lives."[12] So much for the virtues of farming and manual labor. To the extent that it is a mere commercial activity, it loses what value it might have in bringing us into contact with the natural world. "The true husbandman will cease from anxiety" in a most uneconomical way, "and finish his labor with every day, relinquishing all claim to the produce of his fields, and sacrificing in his mind not only his first but his last fruits also."[13]

Ironically, this critique of farming is based on the value of individual independence—the very virtue celebrated by agrarians. *Walden* is in some respects a critique of agrarianism, claiming that agrarians fail to realize the ideals they embrace: "I see young men . . . whose misfortune it is to have inherited farms, houses, barns, cattle, and farming tools; for these are more easily acquired than got rid of. Better if they had been born in the open pasture and suckled by a wolf." He wonders, "Who made them serfs of the soil? . . . Why should they begin digging their graves as soon as they are born?"[14] The price of the farmer's alleged economic and political independence, according to Thoreau, is a life of social conformity and unthinking habit, as well as the intellectual and spiritual degradation resulting from grueling manual labor. The freedom to vote is meaningless if you haven't the leisure, intellectual independence, and freedom from social pressures to be unconventional, to express your essential self through political action. Thus Thoreau too might be seen as a descendant of Jefferson—a wayward offspring seeking to reform agrarianism through a radical reinterpretation of its central value.

More commonly, of course, we see Thoreau as a lover of nature, not farming. But even as a nature lover he can be frustratingly ambivalent. Roderick Nash, for example, sees in Thoreau a reformulation of the pastoral ideal. He points to Thoreau's insistence that an ideal life would combine the best of both wilderness and civilization—not in the way that conventional pastoral visions did, by taming the wilderness, but by preserving both in their pure state.[15] Thus in his 1862 essay "Walking," Thoreau calls for "absolute freedom and wildness" as contrasted with "a freedom and culture merely civil." But his experience with wilderness, as Nash points out, sometimes left him dispirited and morose: He found it "grim and wild, "savage and dreary," "a place for heathenism and superstitious rites—to be inhabited by men nearer of kin to the rocks and wild animals than we."[16] One can lose oneself, one's sense of self, in the woods. So Thoreau longed for wilderness, but from the safety of the semitamed borderlands. As Nash put it, "Thoreau . . . arrived at the middle by straddling. He rejoiced in extremes and, by keeping a foot in each, believed he could extract the best of both worlds."[17]

Even this ingenious reading, however, may work too hard to find a consistent philosophy in Thoreau's writing. Thoreau wanted no disciples; if he preached anything it was a quirky, spirited independence. And even his brief for independence offers no neat answers. His experiences at Walden instead bring into focus the array of dependencies available to us, and the trade-offs we make as we decide on whom (or what) to depend. Shall we forswear dependence on commerce and society? Then we are dependent on our bean field and our own (often tedious) labor. Shall we build our own houses ("for there is some of the same fitness in a man's building his own house that there is in a bird's building its own nest")? Then we must borrow an axe (because "perhaps it is the most generous course thus to permit your fellow-men to have an interest in your enterprise").[18] This refusal to offer a consistent, ready-made ideology may itself be seen as an endorsement of intellectual autonomy. "I would not have any one adopt *my* mode of living on any account," he insists. "I would have each one be very careful to find out and pursue *his own* way, and not his father's or his mother's or his neighbor's instead."[19] But to encourage intellectual autonomy is not to tell us what our proper relationship to the natural world ought to be. Even his call for the preservation of both civilization and wilderness seems designed to keep our options open, rather than to counsel a particular stance in relation to either. Thoreau thus turns out to be at least as problematic a founder as Jefferson is.

These Thoreauvian tensions between dependence and autonomy will resurface in Berry's struggle with the conflict between individualism and community. Thoreau's more immediate descendants, however, have been less sensitive to the complexities inherent in the concept of autonomy. Calls for self-reliance appear constantly in the tradition of nature writing that inspires American preservationism, but they are typically much less nuanced than Thoreau's. John Muir, for example, was deeply concerned with how reliance on nature could facilitate independence from society, but his version of individual independence is innocent of Thoreau's qualifications and hesitations. His conception of self-reliance makes extraordinary demands on the nature lover: He dangles precariously from the top of a pine tree arching over a sheer cliff in the middle of a thunderstorm; he heads up into the mountains in the midst of blizzards, burying himself in the snow until the thaw; he walks a thousand miles alone through trackless wilderness, "joyful and free."[20] Such feats offer an almost superhuman ideal of physical freedom and self-sufficiency. He even reduces his diet to bread and water to secure "full independence of any particular kind of nourishment" ("as if one couldn't take a few days' saunter in the Godful woods without maintaining a base on a wheatfield and grist mill").[21]

Nor is physical independence sufficient. Muir's nature worship can also be interpreted as a bid for spiritual autonomy—in this case, freedom from the rigid Calvinism of his youth. Muir found in nature a different gospel, teaching God's benevolence: While his father taught him that sinners would burn like the branches they were casting on a brush fire, "those terrible fire lessons quickly faded in the blithe wilderness air; for no fire can be hotter than the heavenly fire of faith and hope that burns in every healthy boy's heart."[22] Just "let children walk with Nature," he advised, "let them see the beautiful blendings and communions of death and life, their joyous inseparable unity, . . . and they will learn that death is stingless indeed, and as beautiful as life. . . . All is divine harmony."[23] Muir's natural religion is Christian to the core, infused with "divine uplifting, transfiguring charity,"[24] but it undermines the authority of religious institutions as effectively as Emerson's transcendentalism. Nature not only instructs the attentive student in spiritual truths, She also teaches sympathy, the divine love for creation that transfigures the soul. Who needs man-made churches when God's forest cathedrals are available?

Muir's individualism, particularly his concern for individual self-development, also informs his view of farming. Like Thoreau, Muir criticizes the life of the farmer as too laborious and constraining, leaving little time for intellectual pursuits or aesthetic appreciation of nature. He does recognize that farm life can teach one about the natural world; he and his brothers, he recalls, developed a strong sympathy for the animals they worked with on his father's farm (although they never had as much time to play with the animals as they would have liked). Nevertheless, Muir's distaste for the crass pursuit of wealth, combined with his growing unhappiness with his fellow citizens, defeated any real appreciation for frontier society. *My First Summer in the Sierra,* his most popular work, is suffused with a dislike of society verging on misanthropy: He would be happy, he insists, alone in the mountains forever, "nor would I be lonely; loved friends and neighbors, as love for everything increases, would seem all the nearer however many the miles and mountains between us."[25] And the more mountains between him and his traveling companions, the better. He has nothing but contempt for the sheep ranchers he's stuck with: "The California sheep-owner is in haste to get rich. . . . This quickly acquired wealth usually creates desire for more. Then indeed the wool is drawn close down over the poor fellow's eyes, dimming or shutting out almost everything worth seeing." The shepherds are no better: "Though he is stimulated at times by hopes of one day owning a flock and getting rich like his boss, he at the same time is likely to be degraded by the life he leads. He is solitary most of the year, and solitude," Muir marvels, "to most people seems hard to bear." The shepherd too is blinded, or deafened, by the sheep: "Even the howls and ki-yis of coyotes might be blessings if well heard, but he hears them only through a blur of mutton and wool, and they do him no good."[26]

This contempt for society, coupled with his almost superhuman ideal of physical self-reliance, explains why Muir's philosophy, despite its spirituality and emotionalism, continues to inspire a macho kind of individualism among many preservationists—a theme that Berry will find particularly problematic.[27] Consider Edward Abbey's *Desert Solitaire,* which contains

one of the most memorable definitions of rugged individualism in the canon
of American literature:

> Cutting the bloody cord, that's what we feel, the delirious exhilaration
> of independence, a rebirth backward in time and into primeval liberty,
> into freedom in the most simple, literal, primitive meaning of the word,
> the only meaning that really counts. The freedom, for example, to com-
> mit murder and get away with it scot-free.[28]

Lest we think he's exaggerating, he goes on to explain in vivid detail just
how sickening society is:

> *My God!* I'm thinking, what incredible shit we put up with most of our
> lives—the *domestic* routine (same old wife *every* night), the stupid and
> useless and degrading *jobs,* the *insufferable* arrogance of elected
> officials, the crafty cheating and the *slimy* advertising of the business-
> men, the tedious wars in which we kill our buddies instead of our real
> enemies back home in the capital, the foul, diseased and *hideous* cities
> and towns we live in, the constant petty tyranny of automatic washers
> and automobiles and TV machines and telephones.[29]

Marriage, politics, unjust wars, ugly cities; in a stunning rejection of conventional values, he holds them all equally repulsive. Abbey desires no reform
of society, no alternative version of the degrading jobs, the domestic routine. He just wants the opportunity to escape—"a temporary legal separation," as he puts it. He even takes spiritual autonomy to its logical extreme:
"God? . . . who the hell is *He?* There is nothing here but me and the desert."[30]
And that, apparently, is the way he likes it.

Abbey's rant against society is hardly idiosyncratic; its seeds were planted
in Thoreau's half-cultivated bean field. Like Thoreau, preservationists have
based their critique of American society—of industrialization, the pursuit of
wealth, the concern for social status, and other standard forms of corruption—
in large part on the value of individual freedom and independence. The virtue
of pristine nature is that it offers an escape from the constraints, demands, and
corruptions of society. It may of course have other values, even intrinsic
value—but that, I would contend, is not the primary ethical insight driving
this tradition.[31] Rather, preservationists have relied most heavily on the anxiety voiced so eloquently by Thoreau, Muir, and Abbey: the fear of individuality being submerged in a tide of social conformity.

Importantly, American preservationists did not exempt rural society
from their critique. Farmers are just as bad, maybe worse, than the rest of

us, busy despoiling God's garden in pursuit of useless material goods. Where agrarians see in farming a path to economic and political independence, preservationists see just another kind of slavery—to social conventions, domestic responsibilities, the drudgery of agricultural production. Farming is at best morally dangerous and at worst degrading; Muir's immigrant farmers and sheep ranchers are as blind to nature's beauty as any slum dweller. If we're looking for an intellectual foundation for an environmentalist/agrarian alliance, then, preservationism doesn't seem to be it.

The other major branch of environmentalism, however, looks more promising. The roots of conservationism are distinct from those of preservationism. Indebted more to Jeremy Bentham and Charles Darwin than to Thoreau, it is largely free of the romantic dispositions of the preservation movement—including the concern for individual self-development that drives preservationists' critique of agriculture. As an intellectual movement based on nineteenth-century developments in biology, geology, and ecology, conservationism aimed at putting natural resource policy on a scientific basis.[32] Its grounding in natural sciences gave the movement the potential to bring a truly ecological perspective to public policy, including agricultural policy. Unlike preservationists, conservationists were not openly hostile to agriculture; on the contrary, they embraced agricultural productivity as a central concern of natural resource policy. Nonetheless, ideological conflicts between farmers and conservationists proved as intractable as the conflicts between farmers and wilderness lovers.

Conservationists did share some ideological ground with farmers—particularly a common hostility to the big corporations that wanted public lands to remain open to unrestricted private development, a policy that troubled small farmers as much as scientists. Gifford Pinchot, the movement's chief spokesman, portrayed himself as a friend of the farmer and occasionally supported their demands (for irrigation projects, for example). Sounding a Populist note, he complained that "great areas of the public domain have passed into the hands, not of the home-maker, but of large individual or corporate owners whose object is always the making of profit and seldom the making of homes." He warned that "unless the American homestead system of small free-holders is to be . . . replaced by a foreign system of tenantry, there are few things of more importance to the West than to see to it that the public lands pass directly into the hands of the actual settler."[33] His policies, however, did little to further that goal. On the contrary, conservationism aimed at public ownership and elite professional management of natural resources, and often resulted in reserving lands from homesteading to create forest and wilderness preserves.[34]

Nor did conservationism share the central value of agrarian ideology. Its chief values were efficiency and public spiritedness, not individual independence or freedom. Pinchot, despite his occasional paeans to the self-sufficient farmer, typically coupled talk of rights with an insistence on duties, to the nation and to future generations. "In dealing with our natural resources," he declared, "we have come to a place at last where every consideration of patriotism, every consideration of love of country, of gratitude for the things that the land and the institutions of this Nation have given us, call upon us for a return."[35] We have a duty to see "that those who are coming after us shall have the same opportunity for happiness we have had ourselves."[36] Democratic agrarians had argued that farming instilled patriotism; Pinchot was less willing to take agrarian virtues on faith. To him, the problem was *how* to encourage farmers to subordinate their individual interests to the good of the nation.

Theodore Roosevelt apparently saw no contradiction between his vigorous support for conservationism and his eloquent endorsements of rugged individualism, but the contradiction was there and often erupted into open conflict. But even if conservationists had succeeded in winning over farmers, they wouldn't necessarily have created an environmentally sensitive agriculture. Conservationists, as historian Donald Worster points out, actually weren't very good environmentalists.[37] While Pinchot's philosophy encouraged a long-term perspective—a critical element of ecological sensitivity—it didn't demand a holistic one. Pinchot's land use policies were aimed at resource development and exploitation, not ecosystem preservation.[38]

On the other hand, the conservationists' commitment to science did eventually bring them into contact with the emerging discipline of ecology, a new, holistic approach to the life sciences. The rise of ecology had dramatic consequences for conservationists' thinking about agriculture. During the early years of the twentieth century, ecological thinking would be brought to bear on agriculture policy, resulting in a powerful new analytic framework for agriculture policy—a framework developed most fully in the Country Life movement.

Actually, "movement" may be too grand a name for an idea that never earned a significant following even among the intellectual elite; it remained largely the pet project of Theodore Roosevelt and Liberty Hyde Bailey, its chief spokesman. Nevertheless, it marks a significant development in agri-cultural thought, bringing an ecological perspective to rural reform that would inspire later agrarians—Berry in particular. Although Country Life sounds much like the other back-to-the-land philosophies of this era, Bai-ley strictly disavowed kinship with enthusiasts of the simple life. His phi-losophy, he claimed, was a natural extension of conservationism. What he had in mind was not an individual quest for the good life but a new approach to rural development based on holistic—in fact ecological—premises.

Granted, these premises aren't immediately apparent in his brief for rural revitalization, *The Country-Life Movement in the United States*. There he trumpets the value of rugged individualism, claiming the countryside as its natural domain: "If we have very highly developed persons in the city, we have very rugged persons in the country." Urbanization put that rugged-ness at risk: "What future lies before the American farmer? Will he hold something like a position of independence and individualism, or will he become submerged in the social order?"[39] This apparent concern for indi-vidualism, however, didn't prevent Bailey from advocating measures to strengthen rural social organizations and government programs to improve living conditions in the country. The Report of Roosevelt's 1909 Country Life Commission (chaired by Bailey) pointed to the need for better schools, better highways, regulation of monopolies, and more farm credit to improve the fortunes of American farmers. The commission's stated goal was emi-nently holistic: to create a "farm civilization" through "domestic settlement." Accordingly, its program embraced social, economic, ecological, and even aesthetic values. If the commission's plan of action looks considerably less ambitious than its goal—proposed government action was limited to survey research, improving highways, and increasing federal involvement in pub-lic health—its framework for analyzing the problems of American agricul-ture was radically innovative.[40]

Bailey's concern with cultural revitalization and the social and politi-cal consequences of urbanization underlies his broader inquiry into man's relation to nature. That inquiry, however, ranges well beyond the sociolog-ical and agricultural issues dealt with by the Country Life Commission, and well beyond the individualistic premises of *The Country-Life Movement*. In *The Holy Earth* Bailey offers a well-developed ecological ethic. Humans are not separate from nature, according to Bailey, but are "living parts in the vast creation." This relation imposes on us a duty to respect the divinity of the earth. Reinterpreting the "dominion" mandate from Genesis, he insists that dominion be interpreted as stewardship of God's creation: It is not a right but "a duty imposed upon us . . . to exercise ourselves even against our own interests. We may not waste what is not ours."[41] The chief environmental virtues are the virtues of the good housekeeper, care and thrift—not independence or freedom. In fact, Bailey is deeply suspicious of individual property rights; the earth is common property ("dominion does not carry personal ownership"). Not only do property owners owe duties to other humans, they owe duties to other living creatures. We are to enjoy our "fellowship" with nature; "the things that grow out of the earth are . . . holy. They do not belong to man to do with them as he will."[42]

Despite this ecological piety, however, Bailey affirms and even celebrates our instrumental relation to nature: If dominion implies duties, it also implies mastery. "We may make the surface of the earth much what we will." Enlightened agriculture will "secure supplies by controlling the conditions under which they grow, wasting little, harming not." This physical mastery must be accompanied by spiritual mastery—the farmer must be able to achieve a kinship with the natural world, to "take [it] into himself" and "make [it] to be of his spirit."[43] What exactly Bailey means by this is rather opaque, but he apparently anticipated the gradual development of a rural culture that would imbue the landscape with (appropriate) moral meaning, so that rural folk would grow naturally into an ethical relationship with the land. Nevertheless, their relationship to nature is clearly that of master to servant; farmers are to be "natural" aristocrats—but in a much broader and richer sense than Jefferson ever imagined. "We can claim no gross superiority and no isolated self-importance. The creation, and not man, is the norm."[44]

Bailey's attempt to reformulate agricultural theory to embrace a range of ecological and social values provides a template for an environmental agrarianism. His conception of farming as a public profession governed by duties to society that require careful attention to ecosystem maintenance continues to appeal to contemporary environmentalists, and many of Berry's ideas echo Bailey's. In particular, Berry will rely on the notion of domestic settlement, of farming as stewardship, and the endorsement of thrift, orderliness, and care—the virtues of the good housekeeper—as central to environmental sensitivity.[45] On the other hand, the very concept of professionalism implies an ideal of mastery, a desire for control that later environmentalists (Berry included) will find deeply problematic.

That concern aside, the Country Life philosophy, by virtue of its holistic perspective on rural life and its progressive political values, had the potential to create an ideological bridge between environmental and agrarian politics. Unfortunately, it didn't fulfill that potential. It wasn't that the Country Life advocates were out of touch with actual farmers; on the contrary, they pioneered the use of survey research to identify problems that farmers themselves complained of. But Bailey never attempted to join forces with politically active farmers' organizations, and his ideas largely failed to penetrate farm politics. He placed his hopes in educational policies such as extension programs and curriculum reform, rather than grassroots organization and lobbying. Moreover, Country Life advocates never effectively addressed the political or economic concerns of farmers. They therefore missed an opportunity to link their concerns about the state of the social and natural environment to the large-scale political and economic forces also affecting the farmer.

The Country Life movement did have important offspring, however. Bailey's ecological perspective was embraced by an influential group of policy experts in the 1930s attempting to explain the environmental causes of the Dust Bowl. The Dust Bowl crisis revived fears about soil erosion, a persistent concern of American agriculturalists since the eighteenth century.[46] The New Deal response to these fears was the "permanent agriculture" school, whose apostles included ecologist Paul Sears, Hugh Bennett (head of the Soil Conservation Service under Roosevelt), and Rexford Tugwell (head of the Resettlement Administration), as well as writers Edward Faulkner and Louis Bromfield. Soil conservation was the main item on their agenda, but permanent agriculture was more broadly concerned with the cultural and ecological impacts of agricultural practices.[47]

The goal of the permanent agriculture school was to reform agricultural practice and policy in order to put it on an ecological basis. Like Bailey, permanent agriculture advocates often sounded agrarian themes, celebrating rural life as the source of Jeffersonian virtues that could revitalize American civilization. But their political agenda was far from Jeffersonian. Most of their proposals called for national planning and even collectivization. "All our experience has demonstrated that erosion can be controlled in a practical way," insisted Hugh Bennett. "The need is for forthright, determined, nation-wide action"—specifically, a "national program of soil and water conservation."[48] Rexford Tugwell called for greater government regulation of land use, as well as national planning of agricultural production as a whole, guided by scientific experts.[49] Of course, the impulse to help farmers by expanding government power wasn't new; the Populists also wanted to use government to achieve Jeffersonian ends. But the Populists at least favored institutions that kept power relatively decentralized.[50] The permanent agriculturalists, like most New Dealers, were optimistic about the potential of centralized, bureaucratic control of production.

Similarly, the permanent agriculture advocates departed from the Jeffersonian/Populist tradition by adopting the critical perspective on American farmers typical of environmentalists. The farmer emerges as the chief villain in Hugh Bennett's account of the forces causing soil erosion. Farmers have violated "many fundamental principles of sound land use," he complained. They "waded in with plow and axe, stripped nature's protective cover from the ground, and indiscriminately, without regard for the future, laid bare the rich soil to the erosive forces of wind and water."[51] Because they bought into our "false philosophy of plenty, a myth of inexhaustibility," farmers never learned to love the land and to regard it as an enduring resource.[52] Paul Sears also suggested that farmers' philosophy of quick and easy profits created the conditions that led to the Dust Bowl: "To a degree even the best citizens conducted themselves like the shell-game man at the county fair, on the basis of quick action. . . . Land was land, to be mined until it could be sold for a profit."[53]

Granted, the permanent agriculturalists were willing to concede that farmers themselves were not entirely to blame; some, like Edward Faulkner, suggested they had been duped into adopting bad practices by the "experts" in the land-grant universities.[54] But their criticism of the agricultural establishment was quite mild compared with the Populists' suspicion of the intellectual elite. Generally, the permanent agriculture movement belongs more to the environmental rather than the agrarian tradition; it echoes Thoreau and Pinchot in its hostility to the agrarian concept of farming as an activity aimed at exploiting nature to serve private interests. Advocates of permanent agriculture wanted farmers to be more concerned for the public good, if not awed and humbled by the mysterious forces of nature. Nevertheless, Bennett and his cohort were sensitive to the political and economic problems of farmers; they were after all firmly grounded in progressive politics, which had absorbed many of the lessons of Populism. So Paul Sears, for example, occasionally sounds Populist themes in his classic work, *Deserts on the March.* Taking on a favorite Populist target—credit institutions—he complains that the "pattern of farm finance which developed in the grain belt was thoroughly vicious and against the public interest." More generally he blames "the monotonous story of exploitation [of the land]" on "a system which tolerates private privilege in utter disregard of public policy."[55] Such comments point toward some important connections between economic and ecological systems, but they stop well short of a theoretical account of those connections.

That lacuna is all the more striking in that such an account was in fact available. European agrarians had been developing economic arguments for

small farms since the nineteenth century, and had produced a number of studies to show the superior productivity of small holdings to the large estates of
the landed aristocracy. These studies, explicitly aimed at land reform, were
based on the proposition that small farms benefited *ecologically* from the
intimate care and attention of the farmer. Such care, they argued, ensures soil
fertility and therefore productivity.[56] Similar claims had been made in American farm journals during the nineteenth century, and Sears himself was
familiar with the ideas of Russian anarchist Peter Kropotkin, one of the chief
advocates for land reform.[57] This is undoubtedly the reasoning that lay behind
Sears's assertion that "in every great culture that has ever existed the concentration of wealth has resulted in a degradation of the man who worked
the land and the eventual ruin of the land itself."[58] That the permanent agriculture advocates did not depend more heavily on this argument must be
attributed to their political goals, which during the Dust Bowl era focused
less on supporting small farms against competition from large farms than on
reforming the practices of farmers generally.[59]

In fact, some permanent agriculturalists rejected the link between farm
size and soil fertility altogether. Rexford Tugwell's 1929 article calling for
a permanent agriculture advocated a transition to more *large* farms, which
he argued could be operated more efficiently.[60] Tugwell had thoroughly
grasped John Taylor's principle that the prosperity of farmers depended on
soil fertility. But the conclusion he drew from that principle was that much
of the crop farming on land east of the Mississippi (where smaller, more
diversified farming was common) should be abandoned, and the farmers
either resettled or encouraged to find a new line of work. His intention to
reform or eliminate inefficient farms was embodied in New Deal policies
that sought to remove farmers from "marginal" land, as well as the Eisen-
hower administration's policy of encouraging bigger farms and fewer farmers. Both policies have received bitter criticism from defenders of small
farmers, including Wendell Berry. Tugwell was a dedicated ecologist, but in
1929—or 1939 for that matter—support for ecology did not automatically
go hand in hand with support for small farms. On the contrary, the permanent agriculturalists' preference for national planning and collectivization
often seemed to work against the interests of ordinary family farmers, as the
farmers themselves understood those interests.[61]

As the New Deal era ended, however, radical farm leaders and permanent agriculture advocates increasingly found their policy goals converg-
ing—particularly on the question of family farming. In fact, after 1940 the
permanent agriculture school started to sound remarkably like the Farmers'

Union: James Patton, who became president of the Farmers' Union in 1940, claimed that "upon the family farms grow independent, strong, alert citizens. The family farm is the final stronghold against oppression, whether economic or political, and no tyranny or 'ism' will ever thrive in a country that grounds its agriculture on that base."[62] Louis Bromfield, from the permanent agriculture camp, agreed: "Thomas Jefferson wrote . . . that the future of this country was a great future indeed, because there was so much that every man could have his own land, every man could be an independent citizen."[63] Importantly, though, this policy agreement was not the result of ideological consensus; each camp ultimately offered different reasons for supporting family farming.

The permanent agriculturalists, concerned with preserving family farming primarily for cultural and ecological reasons, relied on the argument that small farms were more careful of soil fertility. Bromfield, for example, cited the history of Rome, linking the dispossession of small farmers in favor of slave labor to "the decline in the fertility of her agricultural land through erosion and the depletion of her soil."[64] In contrast, the Farmers' Union formulated its chief defense of small farms in the traditional Populist terms of social and economic justice. Rejecting a free-market approach to agriculture policy, James Patton argued that "the market in which farmers buy the things they need and the market channels through which their commodities are processed are no longer free." They are highly integrated and concentrated, which puts smaller farmers at a disadvantage. Farmers, "the only nonintegrated basic producers," face monopolistic pricing by both their suppliers and the food processing industry.[65] The issue, for Patton, was not whether we would have a permanent agriculture but whether farmers would "retain a fair share in what they work so hard to produce"—"whether we have democracy in the agricultural economy."[66] In fact, in his vision small farmers would not pursue a more organic approach to farming; they would be as mechanized and "modern" as the large corporate farms—and perhaps even as large. "Family farming is not synonymous with either small-scale or backward farming practices. . . . It involves the use of modern farm machinery and production techniques."[67]

By the 1950s, then, two distinct arguments for small farms were in play: one from ecology (favored by environmentalists) and the other from social justice (favored by farmer advocates). Although both may be called "agrarian" broadly speaking, in fact only the second argument derives from the democratic agrarian tradition. Bromfield and his fellow travelers were more direct descendants of John Muir and Liberty Hyde Bailey than of Jefferson.

It was not ideology that was bringing the two camps closer together, but a common goal—and a common enemy: corporate, industrial agriculture.

In 1945, Ralph Borsodi summed up the problems with American agriculture in his attack on farming as a big business. Industrial agriculture, he claimed, was responsible for "the rape of the earth and the destruction of our priceless heritage of land," as well as "impoverishing our rural communities, wiping out our rural schools, closing our rural churches, destroying our rural culture, and depopulating the countryside upon which all these depend."[68] His critique was part of a general anxiety about factory farming, a term coined by Carey McWilliams in 1939 to describe a new kind of agriculture emerging in California. Factory farms, McWilliams explained, are "operated by processes which are essentially industrial in character." They rely on "an agricultural proletariat indistinguishable from our industrial proletariat": Farm labor "punches a time clock, works at piece or hourly wage rates, and lives in a shack or company barracks." Unlike the traditional farmhand, these workers have little or no contact with the real owners of the farm, who are typically shareholders of the corporation that operates it.[69] Factory farms weren't widespread in 1939, but McWilliams worried that they represented the future of American agriculture.[70]

McWilliams was right that American agriculture was about to undergo dramatic changes. The proportion of Americans engaged in agriculture continued to decline after World War II, in part because of the large-scale social and economic forces encouraging urbanization and in part because of specific federal policies aimed at taking "marginal" lands out of production. The number of farms in operation in the United States decreased from 6.5 million in 1900 to 2.2 million in 1982; the largest decline was in farms between fifty and five-hundred acres (58 percent).[71] Thus there were increasingly fewer farmers and larger farms, resulting in a steady depopulation of the countryside. Equally striking was the transformation of agricultural technology: Between 1920 and 1965, the number of tractors used on farms increased from 246,000 to 4.8 million.[72] Similarly, the 1940s witnessed a flood of new techniques to increase agricultural productivity, including high-yield plant varieties, pesticides and herbicides, and chemical fertilizers. As historian Willard Cochrane puts it, in the period between 1940 and 1970 there were three technological revolutions going on concurrently in American agriculture:

There was a mechanical revolution that led to the mechanization of almost every production process in farming. There was a biological revolution that led to drought-resistant and disease-resistant varieties, and greatly increased crop yields. There was a chemical revolution that did many wondrous things: controlled plant and animal diseases, as well as pests and weeds, and provided soil fertilization.[73]

These technological changes were accompanied, necessarily, by changes in farm finance and the agricultural economy. In 1870, human labor provided 65 percent of the total inputs in farming and capital about 17 percent. By 1976, labor inputs had declined to 16 percent and capital inputs increased to 62 percent. The substitution of capital for labor meant that farmers had to purchase a larger proportion of their productive resources, which in turn made them more dependent on credit and off-farm financing. It also made them dependent on the firms producing these resources: the petroleum, tractor and farm machinery, fertilizer, pesticide, and livestock feed industries.[74] These industries, along with those that purchase and process agricultural products, constitute the complex that by the 1950s was being referred to as "agribusiness." Although some of these firms are farmer-owned cooperatives, more common (especially in the processing sector) are large corporate organizations, often highly integrated—combining processing and distribution and even production itself.[75] To many observers in the 1940s and 1950s, it appeared that the independent family farm would soon be absorbed into a vast corporate food production and distribution complex.

Few were sanguine about that prospect. By the 1950s, criticism of industrial, corporate agriculture was coming from all quarters. These criticisms, even more than the affirmative case for small farms, were central to the eventual union of agrarianism and environmentalism. In clarifying the social and environmental costs of agribusiness, critics developed the major themes that would inform the sustainable agriculture movement of the 1960s and provide the foundation for Wendell Berry's ecological agrarianism.

The pioneering work on corporate agriculture's social costs was McWilliams's *Factories in the Field,* which focused on factory farms' exploitation of workers. Writing from a socialist perspective, McWilliams identified private ownership as the major problem with these industrial-style farms: "concentration of ownership," along with the availability of a large and easily exploited pool of agricultural labor, accounted for the adoption of industrial processes in agriculture.[76] His solution, however, was not to eliminate those industrial processes but to change labor relations on the farms by collectivizing ownership.[77] In fact, McWilliams's criticism of factory farms was confined to their treatment of workers; he actually praised California agriculture as "a magnificent achievement" in "its scope, efficiency, organization and amazing abundance."[78] Nevertheless, the exposé was significant in that it challenged the prevailing faith that the problems of rural communities could be solved simply by improving the efficiency of agricultural production.

More challenges to that faith were forthcoming. In 1946, Walter Goldschmidt, a sociologist with the federal Bureau of Agricultural Economics, published a groundbreaking study on the effects of corporate agriculture on rural communities.[79] He compared two California towns, Arvin and Dinuba, that had experienced the industrialization of agriculture to different degrees. Although the two towns were originally quite similar economically and culturally, by the 1940s Arvin's agriculture was dominated by factory farms: very large farms cultivated intensively, usually in a single crop; heavily dependent on mechanization, seasonal labor, and capital investment; and owned by nonlocal corporations. Dinuba's agriculture shared most of these characteristics, but the farms were much smaller and the ratio of independent farm owners to dependent laborers was much higher.[80] Goldschmidt discovered that Dinuba was more prosperous, less stratified, and had more vital civic institutions than Arvin, a finding that he attributed to the higher proportion of farm owners in Dinuba. "The large labor population [in Arvin] means inevitably large groups with poor economic circumstances. . . . This in turn means poor housing, [a] low level of living . . . and little money for community improvement. It means that a large portion of the population has little vested interest—economic or social—in the community itself."[81]

Goldschmidt's influential study, which was issued as a committee print by the Senate Small Business Committee in 1946 and twice reprinted in their records, supported more traditional complaints, by the Farmers' Union and others, about monopolistic practices by agricultural corporations.[82] Importantly, however, it helped to redirect those complaints from the problem of preserving individualism to the problem of preserving *community*. According to Goldschmidt, corporate agriculture harmed rural communities by increasing social stratification and undermining the sense of belonging that would lead to active community stewardship. These themes of absentee and irresponsible ownership and its impact on community stewardship would become central to the defense of family farms in the 1970s, and integral to Berry's analysis of the decline of American agriculture.

Meanwhile, environmentalists were making their own case against agribusiness, arguing that absentee ownership was as bad for the soil as it was for communities. The logic behind the claim—and behind many of Goldschmidt's conclusions as well—was neatly summed up by P. Alston Waring and Walter Teller in their 1943 work, *Roots in the Earth:*

> Not long ago James Smith, a neighbor of ours, said to a group of people who had come to look at the conservation work on his place: "This farm is going to be here after I'm gone, and I guess I have a responsibility to those who farm it then to keep the soil from washing down the creek while I am in charge." . . . Somehow we gathered that James really felt that he was a custodian of that tract of 160 acres, that it would go on from generation to generation, and that while he had it he had no right to destroy it or waste it.[83]

Absentee ownership, they concluded, does not foster this sense of continuity that leads to careful stewardship.[84]

Aldo Leopold further developed the environmental case for traditional farming in his criticism of the industrial ideal of "clean farming"—"a food chain aimed solely at economic profit and purged of all non-conforming links." Farming, he insisted, should instead cultivate diversity and aim at "harmoniz[ing] the wild and the tame in the joint interest of stability, productivity, and beauty."[85] Moreover, farming could cultivate ecological sensitivity by establishing a practical relationship with nature. "There are two great spiritual dangers in not owning a farm," he maintained. "One is the danger of supposing that breakfast comes from the grocery, and the other that heat comes from the furnace."[86] Leopold suggested that farming makes the farmer aware of his dependence and impact on natural processes—but clearly it is small, traditional farms that promised to do so, not the huge industrial farms run by impersonal corporations. Leopold's depiction of traditional farming as cultivating a sense of stewardship poses a striking contrast to the more critical views offered by ecologists only a decade earlier. The farmer's instrumental relationship to nature is for Leopold (as it will be for Berry) an inducement rather than an obstacle to greater ecological awareness.

If Leopold saw small farmers as potential stewards of an environmentally sensitive agriculture, Rachel Carson's *Silent Spring,* and the response to it, went further in casting corporate power as the instigator of environmentally destructive agricultural practices. Carson's major contribution to the debate over industrial agriculture was her identification of the specific environmental harms caused by the pesticides and herbicides relied upon by modern farmers. Carson took aim in particular at the large, single-crop farms characteristic of industrial agriculture: "Single-crop farming does not take advantage of the principles by which nature works; it is agriculture as an engineer might conceive it to be."[87] The earth's vegetation, she instructs, "is part of a web of life" that we should disturb only "thoughtfully" and with "humility." Not only does industrial agriculture pose health risks to humans, according to Carson it destroys natural beauty and inflicts needless suffering on innocent animals.[88]

Carson's complaints reflect the aesthetic, cultural, and ecological values of environmentalists; in contrast, she shows none of Goldschmidt's Jeffersonian anxiety about the loss of yeomen farmers. But neither is the yeoman farmer her primary target. Rather, she reserves her harshest criticisms for chemical companies—a major part of the agribusiness complex.[89] Their reaction to *Silent Spring* confirmed the Populists' worst fears about corporate power: First they made clumsy efforts to suppress Carson's work; failing that, they ridiculed and dismissed her findings.[90] The episode helped to earn agribusiness a reputation as irresponsible, corrupt, and the chief obstacle to achieving a sustainable agriculture.

In sum, by the 1960s, agribusiness and industrial agriculture, rather than the independent family farmer, had become the favorite target of virtually all critics of American agriculture. Nevertheless, they still tended to speak different languages: while Goldschmidt and Patton used traditional Populist rhetoric to bemoan the loss of the independent yeoman farmer, Carson and Leopold used ecological concepts like "harmony" and "balance" in their analyses of industrial agriculture's impact on the environment. Ideology continued to divide them; according to environmentalists, farming practices themselves needed fundamental reform—an idea that found little support in the Populist tradition. For Populists, it was the economic system that needed reform—a project to which environmentalists had little to contribute. Limited by their conceptual frameworks, both sides failed to explore the connections between the economic and environmental problems of American agriculture. Until such an exploration took place, an effective political alliance between small farmers and environmentalists remained unlikely.

Nevertheless, the basis for an ideological convergence was beginning to take shape. The permanent agriculture school had moved beyond the rugged individualism of nineteenth-century preservationism to a more holistic concern with the cultural and sociological conditions that lead to good stewardship. The Populists' successors were also beginning to look beyond the effect of corporate power on individual economic autonomy and consider its effect on the community as a whole. The sustainable agriculture movement of the

1960s pursued these ideas. Led by such figures as J. I. Rodale, founder of Rodale Press; John and Nancy Todd and William McLarney, founders of the New Alchemy Institute; agriculturalist Robert Steffen; and food policy expert Lester Brown,[91] the movement created an intellectually vibrant community in which new—and old—ideas about ecology and agriculture proliferated.

Wendell Berry was a leading voice in this community, a "John the Baptist" of sustainable agriculture whose works were "the primers for the movement."[92] To appreciate how and why he came to occupy this prominent role, however, we have to begin with the problem he was trying to unravel: not the causes of environmental degradation or the declining fortunes of the small farmer, but the relationship between the two.

Berry's role in the sustainable agriculture movement grew directly out of his first major political cause, strip mining in eastern Kentucky. The strip-mining controversy was politically and theoretically significant in that, unlike more traditional Populist or environmental causes (price supports, monopolies, dam building, nuclear power), it explicitly linked corporate exploitation of rural communities to the destruction of the environment. Strip mining was the subject of intense political controversy in Kentucky in the 1960s, and in 1966, the Kentucky legislature (prompted in part by Harry Caudill's exposé) enacted a set of laws to better regulate coal companies' mining activities. The debates over the legislation prompted an essay, "The Landscaping of Hell," that ended up in Berry's first collection of nonfiction, *The Long-Legged House*. In this book, Berry begins to explore the interconnections between the status of small farmers and the care of the earth—the problem that would form the core of his ecological agrarianism.

In "The Landscaping of Hell," Wendell Berry describes a house in east Kentucky's coal-mining region. "As mountain houses go," he tells us, "this is an exceptionally good one." It has a neat yard with a garden and hedge fence. "One can see . . . that a man has taken a proud stand there, has put into the place the long and dear investment of his attention and love and work and hope." But overhanging the house on three sides is the "spoil bank" of the mine, which will, in rainy weather, begin to slide down toward the house. Even if it stops short of the house, "the acid water from the opened coal seam will get into the well and make it unfit for use."[93]

The miners were able to commit such damage, Berry argues, because the small farmers and home owners of eastern Kentucky were helpless against the power wielded by the coal companies. In an argument closely tracking Caudill's,[94] he points out that coal companies had bought the mineral rights in the Kentucky mountains decades ago, long before strip mining was imaginable, for "as little as a dollar an acre." Kentucky courts consistently held that the deeds to the mineral rights allowed the companies to strip-mine a farm without further payment.[95] "The mining companies . . . have made it abundantly clear that they will destroy anything, they will stop at nothing, so long as the result can be inked in black on their accounting sheet." Their political power is evidenced by their "notoriously low" property tax rates and by the overall economic depression of a region that has generated "billions of dollars" of wealth for the corporations.[96] Corporate power shields the companies from taking responsibility for the environmental damage that is disrupting local communities. For Caudill, this situation was simply another example of the economic and social injustices perpetrated by large corporations. But for Berry it is more than that: It is a vivid illustration that the health of the environment and the economic and political status of the small farmer are intimately linked. Corporations can engage in such practices precisely because small farmers—the people with the most incentive to care for the land—are powerless to stop them.

Strip-mining wasn't Berry's only political cause. He spoke out against the Vietnam War, protested the construction of a nuclear power plant near his home, and was involved in the ultimately successful effort to prevent the damming of the Red River in Powell County, Kentucky—a standard résumé for a New Left activist in the 1960s and 1970s.[97] But the strip-mining controversy served for him as the paradigmatic case of environmental damage. "So far as I know," he observed in 1972, "there are only two philosophies of land use. One holds that the earth is the Lord's, or it holds that the earth belongs to those yet to be born as well as to those now living. . . . The other philosophy is that of exploitation, which holds that the interest of the present owner is the only interest to be considered." The strip miners are the "most fanatical" believers in the second philosophy. Good farmers represent the first: "The model of good land use is to be found in a good farm."[98] That claim would have startled many preservationists, although it echoes Aldo Leopold's view of farming as stewardship. But it's more plausible when such traditional farming is compared with the "strange sort of farming" pursued by strip miners.[99] Strip mining is in fact a pervasive metaphor in Berry's work: an image of irresponsible land use and a constant reminder that the fate of the earth is inextricably linked to the distribution of political and economic power.

Berry's understanding of the relationship between society and the environment, then, is rooted in Kentucky's political and economic experiences with the coal companies. Kentucky's conservative political culture, in contrast, made it difficult for him to articulate that understanding. Although he could draw inspiration from dissenting voices such as Caudill and Hubbard, theirs were minority views—and dangerous ones. People espousing Caudill's cause were regularly harassed by the authorities; some were even brought before Kentucky's Un-American Activities Committee (established in 1968) to answer charges of sedition and communist agitation.[100] Little wonder that Berry had trouble expressing his opinions. "Though I have had many of these ideas consciously in mind for several years," he commented, "I have found them extraordinarily difficult to write about." But it was not just the risk of official persecution that troubled him; the problem went deeper: "There has not been much recent talk about them. Their language has been neglected, allowed to grow old-fashioned, so that in talking about them now one is always on the verge of sounding merely wishful or nostalgic or absurd."[101]

This point is critical for understanding what Berry is trying to do, and why his project was important to the sustainable agriculture movement: For Berry, the political problems of small farmers were in large part *linguistic*. Language, he insists, matters. "We will understand the world, and preserve ourselves and our values in it, only insofar as we have a language that is alert and responsive to it, and careful of it."[102] The rhetoric used to defend industrial capitalism—the dominant political language in Kentucky in the 1960s—was emphatically *not* such a language. Berry repeatedly draws attention to common word usages that obfuscate the moral dimensions of land use, such as the tendency to define "practical" as "whatever will most predictably and most quickly make a profit."[103] Because public debate on land use is carried out almost entirely in terms of the short-term profitability of policies, it's hard to argue or even recognize that mountains may have other uses than to make money for coal companies.[104]

The political causes and consequences of the failure of language are a central theme in Berry's work. Language, according to Berry, should serve to connect us to the world and to each other, to bring us into contact with reality and to express our designs for the future.[105] When the available languages are inadequate to these tasks—when we cannot express our pain or describe our desired future—we cannot take responsibility for our actions. "The realization that we ourselves, in our daily economic life, are causing the problems we are trying to solve," he suggests, "ought to show us the inadequacy of the language we are using to talk about our connection to the world."[106]

What Berry was searching for in 1969 was a language in which he could describe "a coherent vision of how things ought to be." In a review of a book of poems protesting the Vietnam War, he complains that the poets "are locked in this horror [of the present] partly because their inheritance has not equipped them to imagine anything in the other direction."[107] The same could be said of the policy makers, corporate decision makers, and farmers who have led America's agricultural revolution. The inherited language of industrial capitalism, the language of individual interest and corporate profit, left them ill equipped to imagine a future in which family farms and rural communities are valued and preserved. Thus to defend the family farm, Berry had to invent a new way to *talk,* to express the grievances of farmers and rural communities. His writings may be read as efforts to speak about those things—the value of farming and rural communities, the suffering created by industrial development and dislocation—previously suffered in silence by his community. They are attempts to formulate a new political language, a new set of terms and arguments for defending the family farm.

To do so, Berry has had to jettison much of the traditional vocabulary of Jefferson and the Populists. Traditional democratic agrarianism was based on the premise that the majority of Americans were farmers, so that improving the status of farmers would lead to greater democracy. But by the 1960s, farmers had become a tiny minority; their attempts to gain protection from market forces are hard to justify on the grounds of equality. John Berry's call for "parity" probably sounds to most contemporary Americans like a plea for special treatment—and the dominant ideology of industrial capitalism cuts against special protection for small farmers: Businesses must be allowed to fail, workers must be willing and able to move around the country freely as the labor market dictates, no one should be rooted to a job or community. It's inefficient. So why should the government bail out a failing farm?[108]

Some Populist-inspired advocates—notably Jim Hightower—continue to rely on the argument that monopolistic practices by the food processing and agriculture supply industries put small farmers at an unfair disadvantage.[109] Government, they contend, has a duty to level the economic playing field. Economists dispute the claim that the playing field is seriously distorted by monopolistic practices,[110] but even if it's true, it's a problematic basis for a defense of family farming. Given the economic, social, and technological forces driving the industrialization of agriculture, saving the family farm would require a great deal more public effort than simply preventing unfair trade practices. Surely a stronger argument than a dubious charge of economic injustice is necessary to justify such an effort.

Other agrarians argue that farmers should be exempted from the rigors of the market economy because farming is special. Farming is a way of life, not just a business; it's valuable either simply because it's different (and therefore contributes to cultural diversity) or because farmers have characteristics (honesty, frugality, discipline) that democracy requires.[111] Such arguments draw on Americans' powerful connection to the Jeffersonian ideal, but without further elaboration they are easy to dismiss. Legions of political scientists and economists insist that we don't actually need Jeffersonian virtues like frugality and discipline to run a prosperous, stable industrial democracy. As for cultural diversity, the argument still sounds like special pleading. After all, writing poetry or running an auto repair shop can also be considered a special, character-forming way of life, but we allow the market to thrust people out of those professions without a qualm.

Berry's defense of the family farm differs from these approaches by replacing the traditional agrarian arguments about economic and social justice, based on a desire to foster individualism, with more contemporary concerns about environmental protection and maintaining strong communities. Drawing on the permanent agriculturalists and the arguments elaborated by Goldschmidt, Leopold, and Carson, he integrates their concern for stewardship and environmental integrity into his case for family farming. Berry contends that an agrarian society, by linking individual economic and emotional welfare to the health of the land and the community, is best suited to produce the sort of people who can and will care for the environment. Like Jefferson, then, Berry insists that the family farm is the chief repository of virtues critical to the republic—but according to Berry, those virtues are ecological rather than political. His ecological agrarianism, in short, is aimed at protecting not the special interests of farmers but the public's general interest in preserving the food supply, the ecosystem, and the human community itself. The following chapters explore his argument.

Chapter Three

The Fragile Planet

Farmers, according to Thomas Jefferson, "are tied to their country, and wedded to its liberty and interests, by the most lasting bonds." Berry likes to portray himself as an intellectual descendant of Jefferson, endorsing the vision of a society of small yeomen farmers governed more by custom and tradition than government, disciplined by a liberal education, and well trained in the arts of agriculture.[1] But his reliance on Jefferson can be misleading. True, they both argue that land ownership gives farmers a permanent interest in the country's welfare. But by "welfare" Jefferson meant the *political* health of the nation; farmers, because they couldn't move their assets to another country, had an interest in maintaining a wise, free, and virtuous government in this one.[2] For Berry, the country's welfare means the *physical condition* of the land itself.

The distinction is central to Berry's reformulation of the agrarian tradition. His ecological agrarianism downplays the political role of farmers, emphasizing instead the concept of land stewardship: "Every person exercising the right to hold private property," he contends, "has an obligation to secure to the rest of us the right to live from that property. He or she has an obligation to use it in such a way as to not impair or diminish our rightful interest in it."[3] This concern for preserving the land's productive capacity, previously a submerged theme in American democratic agrarianism, becomes for Berry its chief link with environmentalism. But the connection comes at a price; it transforms the ethical core of agrarianism, subordinating its traditional focus on liberty and social justice to what Berry insists is a more pressing problem, protection of the ecosystem.

Not that Berry abandons the quest for agrarian justice altogether. He contends that the obligation to care for the land (which derives in good liberal fashion from a natural "right to life") carries with it a corresponding duty on the part of society to make the landowner able to afford to use the land and care for it properly. Clearly this duty has implications for our socioeconomic arrangements, such as restrictions on corporations, regulation of markets, and price supports for agriculture, all familiar Populist demands. Berry even gives a classic liberal justification for these protections, that they constitute a form of payment for the farmers' stewardship.[4] But the agrarian social contract differs from the liberal version in that its purpose is not to secure rights but to preserve the ecosystem. This shift from social justice to ecological integrity is the best starting point for understanding Berry's agrarianism. Here I explore its implications, both ethical and political.

Berry's case for family farming begins with the claim that family farmers are in the best position to protect the fertility and integrity of the natural environment—and protection of the environment is an ultimate, absolute value. It trumps economic growth, efficiency, even social justice, because if we don't protect the environment, it will cease to support human life. In other words, ecological values are absolute constraints on public policy. "The land," he maintains, "should not be destroyed for any reason, not even for any apparently good reason"—including feeding the starving millions, liberty, justice, democracy, or universal brotherhood.[5]

That statement would seem to leave little room for interpretation; social justice, according to Berry, is less vital than protection of the environment. But before proceeding we must acknowledge some important qualifications of his position. Berry is not interested in nature only for its own sake, or even for the sake of the mere survival of humans as biological organisms. His concern for the land is aimed at preserving not the planet itself but the possibility of *human life* on the planet. And Berry has a richly developed understanding of what constitutes human life, and what is necessary—in terms of both our environmental practices and our social institutions—to preserve its possibility. Subsequent chapters will explore that understanding; here it is enough to note that, for Berry, preserving the productive capacity of the land is a necessary but not sufficient condition for preserving ourselves as humans.

Nevertheless, he does insist that preserving the integrity of the ecosystem we depend on is our most serious challenge, and the one demanding our most immediate attention. Behind this stewardship imperative is an assumption fundamental to modern environmentalism: that the earth is fragile—so fragile it might, simply through everyday human activity, become uninhabitable for humans. Berry is particularly concerned about the environmental pressures created by industrial agriculture: intensive monoculture heavily dependent on machine power and chemical fertilizers and pesticides. This system, while allowing dramatic increases in productivity per man-hour and correspondingly cheap and abundant food, leads to soil compaction, topsoil erosion, loss of genetic diversity, pollution, and ultimately the loss of fertility (decreased productivity per acre). Moreover, because the system is much less labor-intensive than traditional agriculture, it eliminates jobs and leads to the depopulation of the countryside. Industrial agriculture thus extracts maximum short-term profits from the soil, destroying both the soil itself and the community of farmers that once depended on it.[6] The cost of our present abundance is therefore a long-term loss of fertility and productive capacity. We are, he claims, destroying the earth by farming it to death.

Such anxiety over the earth's fragility appears to be a distinctively twentieth-century phenomenon. It is fueled in part by the environmental devastation caused by rapid industrial development after 1940 (recall that Berry's earliest environmental causes were opposition to the rampant strip mining and dam building of the forties) but also, of course, by the development of the atom bomb. The specter of nuclear energy lurks behind Berry's complaint: "It is already certain that our planet alone—not to mention potential sources in space—can provide us with more energy and material than we can use safely or well. What might we bring into danger by the abuse of 'infinite' sources?" More explicitly, "the invention of atomic holocaust and other man-made dooms . . . only restores for us the immediacy of the worldly circumstance as the religions have always defined it: we know 'neither the day nor the hour.' "[7] It would be plausible and nicely elegant to assert that our sense of earth's fragility sprang full-blown out of Hiroshima.

Plausible, perhaps, but wrong; this sort of environmental anxiety actually has much older roots. But it does contrast with the kind of pessimism we encounter before the nineteenth-century industrial revolution. For example, Thomas Malthus as early as 1798 was challenging the assumption that the earth would uncomplainingly meet the demands of an ever-larger human society. His essay on population growth is often considered an important precursor to modern limits-to-growth arguments—claims that the earth's capacity to support human life is limited—and therefore a forerunner of environmentalism. But Malthus's reasoning differs from that of modern environmentalists in critical respects. While acknowledging the possibility that the earth's productive capacity may be limited, he doesn't base his argument on that claim.[8] Instead, he simply points out that the population typically increases at a much faster rate than agricultural production. Therefore, even if the earth's productive capacity is inexhaustible, there will still be a lag between population growth and production. This lag will lead to periodic crises of overpopulation and a host of miseries such as plague, famine, and war.[9]

Malthus's reasoning led him to the conservative position that utopian schemes for social improvement are misguided, at least in the absence of effective population control. But one might just as easily conclude that we must pursue scientific and technological advancement more vigorously in order to increase our productive capacity. In that sense, Malthus helped to provide the rationale for industrialization, particularly in agriculture. Mechanization, monoculture, the widespread use of chemical pesticides and fertilizers—the practices Berry insists are "destroying the land"—have all been justified by Malthusian arguments: We must use these means, whatever the cost, to feed the starving millions.

Malthus, then, should be considered less a forerunner of environmentalism than an apologist for industrialization. In contrast, the modern "neo-Malthusians" emphasize not technological lag but, first, that there may be absolute limits to the earth's productive capacity and, second, that our productive activities disturb the ecosystem so as to decrease its fertility.[10] While the first worry was familiar even to eighteenth-century economists,[11] it is the second that constitutes the heart of the "fragile planet" thesis. And most historians trace this idea, not to Hiroshima and Nagasaki, but to George Perkins Marsh's classic 1864 study, *Man and Nature*.

Marsh credits himself with being the first to explore not how nature affects man but how man affects nature. The book is a disheartening catalog of all the ways human activities—clearing forests, building dams, draining swamps, and so on—"subvert the original balance" of nature, threatening to turn the planet into a desolate wasteland.[12] It thus challenged what had been the dominant theme in Americans' approach to their natural environment: the belief that the task of the pioneer is to reduce the sublime but terrifying and chaotic wilderness to an ordered, pastoral garden.[13] Marsh argues that our efforts to bring order to the wilderness are usually misguided. In his eminently quotable style, he asserts that "man is everywhere a disturbing agent. Wherever he plants his foot, the harmonies of nature are turned to discords. The proportions and accommodations which insured the stability of existing arrangements are overthrown."[14] Man is not "of nature," he goes on, "but of more exalted parentage." Unfortunately, this "exalted" status seems to render man unfit to inhabit creation without ruining it.

Marsh's sense of the wilderness as a place of order and beauty reflects a Romantic sensibility that was becoming increasingly influential in the mid-1800s, but also significant advances in natural science stemming from the Enlightenment. In fact, his case for leaving the wilderness alone rested not on a Romantic appreciation for the beauty and spiritual value of nature but on his understanding of the role of forests, floods, and other natural annoyances in creating and preserving soil fertility. Very much a product of the Enlightenment, he had faith in human reason and even in technology, admiring for example the efforts of the Dutch to reclaim land for agricultural production with dikes. Inspired by their example, he argued that man might, through foresight and clever engineering, reclaim those lands he had laid waste through carelessness. We must, he insisted, be "coworker[s] with nature in the reconstruction of the damaged fabric."[15]

Marsh thus not only embraced the fragile planet thesis but also explicitly united it with the concept of stewardship. This connection makes Marsh an important forerunner of conservationism, despite the somewhat misanthropic perspective that permeates *Man and Nature*. Although preservationists could find support for their views in his contention that "man is everywhere a disturbing agent," his followers, including Gifford Pinchot and many other early conservationists,[16] focused more on the possibility of beneficial human action than on the threat of ecological destruction. But, their optimism notwithstanding, that threat of environmental damage is integral to the progressive conception of stewardship. We are called to be caretakers of the planet precisely because it is our actions that threaten it. To the extent Marsh popularized this idea, he may be considered the source of the fragile planet thesis.

But even Marsh had important (and largely unrecognized) precursors: The earth's fragility was already a prominent theme in American agriculture by the 1860s. The fear that poor farming methods were destroying soil fertility and thus productive capacity dates back at least to the eighteenth century. In one sense, agricultural scientists were the first conservationists, although they lacked Marsh's holistic, ecological sensibility. As pointed out in chapter 1, much of John Taylor's *Arator* focuses on improving the quality of American farming to protect soil fertility—not because he was worried about the "damaged fabric" of nature as a whole but because he considered the soil to be a vital national resource. Nor was he alone; Edward Ruffin, through his influential journal *The Farmer's Register,* preached the gospel of soil conservation and reclamation before the Civil War. Ruffin followed the lead of Jefferson, Taylor, and Thomas Paine in linking soil fertility to patriotism, advising his fellow southerners that their way of life depended on husbanding their soil with such techniques as crop rotation, contour plowing, and the use of fertilizers.[17] Thus soil fertility was a major topic of debate in American agriculture journals throughout the nineteenth century, long before the official beginning of the conservation movement.

Marsh's book is in some ways merely an extension of these debates; although he clearly favors sylviculture to agriculture (at times it seems he's never seen an environmental problem that couldn't be fixed by planting trees), his conception of environmental harm reflects a distinctly agricultural perspective: Harm is anything that renders the land unsuitable for cultivation—a standard of ecological integrity that continues to inform many modern forms of environmentalism, Berry's included. Marsh was interested in maintaining the "balance of nature" not for nature's sake, nor for the sake of its aesthetic or moral value, but for the sake of producing food.[18] In this sense he is simply a follower of the scientific agriculturalists, for whom the earth's fragility was no theoretical proposition but a continuous and vexing reality, evidenced in the reduced yields of "worn-out" fields and the ruts and gullies caused by soil erosion.[19]

Still, it's fair to say that the idea of the earth's fragility was not a dominant theme in the public consciousness, much less policy debate, until the twentieth century.[20] Early Americans had different concerns; they confronted an untamed and inhospitable but ultimately tractable wilderness. Modern Americans, in contrast, confront a planet of baffling complexity—like an alien machine of unknown and perhaps unlimited power but also incredible sophistication and delicacy. We worry not just about its capacity to produce but about our capacity to understand how it works—and our ability to destroy it through simple carelessness.[21] It is this anxiety, rather than an overconfident sense of mastery and technological competence, that drives Berry's imperative. It is *because* we lack perfect knowledge and control of nature that, when we do act, we must make the life and health of the world our first priority.[22]

Unfortunately, the urgency behind this imperative also threatens to put Berry in the same camp as "survivalists" like William Ophuls, Garret Hardin, Robert Heilbroner, and Dave Foreman. Survivalists have been widely accused of illiberal tendencies for their alleged willingness to tolerate draconian restrictions on human rights in the name of protecting the environment.[23] Such willingness is a possible consequence of subordinating social justice to environmental protection—and potentially a key point of conflict between Berry and earlier agrarians. True, Berry insists that private ownership of property is essential to good stewardship[24] and, like earlier agrarians, contends that such widespread distribution of land constitutes a barrier to tyranny. His reasoning here is rather opaque, however. Although equal distribution of wealth may contribute to the equal distribution of political power, the widespread distribution of land hardly ensures the equal distribution of wealth—land values vary widely, and there are many other kinds of wealth. But on this point Berry simply repeats the mistaken reasoning of many earlier agrarians. Where he differs from them is in his insistence that ownership carries ecological duties, and that an ecologically rational society may put severe restrictions on land use. This is precisely what some liberal theorists fear. If the survival of the human race is really at stake, it's much easier to justify restrictions that could seriously infringe personal freedom. It's hard to argue with Garret Hardin's dictum, "Injustice is preferable to total ruin."[25]

But the implications of the fragile planet thesis aren't so straightforward. Both Hardin and Ophuls, for example, do argue that a strong state might be necessary to protect the environment. But a strong state isn't inconsistent with liberalism or democracy. Ophuls criticizes liberal political institutions for their inability to adopt and implement effective environmental policies, but he insists that what he wants is a constitutional and limited, but effective, government—albeit in the hands of a "natural aristocracy."[26] And the inegalitarian implications of his solution are mitigated by his call for a transformation in the public's consciousness. His strong, effective government would have to be accepted voluntarily by a public who embraced his ecological ethic.[27] As other theorists have pointed out, democratic elections and their accompanying policy debates are good devices for winning such voluntary support.[28] Similarly, Hardin's formula for solving the overpopulation problem—"mutual coercion mutually agreed upon"—may sound ominously totalitarian, but it isn't. It's simply a restatement of the social contract of liberal political theory, through which we consent (mutually agree) to the authority of the state (mutual coercion).[29]

I don't mean to suggest that Berry would endorse Hardin's or Ophuls's vision of a strong, centralized liberal state. The need for mutual agreement on mutual coercion begs the question of where and how to achieve that agreement. As I will discuss in chapter 8, Berry (like many greens) would argue for decentralized political institutions that concentrate decision making at the local level. As I will contend in that chapter, however, vital local institutions must be complemented by a vital national government in order to achieve effective environmental management. The point here is merely that liberalism and democracy are not inconsistent with that goal.

Of course, liberalism does demand that certain basic rights be protected, and preventing ecological damage might require more severe restrictions on property and reproductive rights than Americans currently enjoy. But the definition of rights has always taken practical concerns into account. Just as freedom of speech has never meant that you can shout "Fire!" in a crowded theater, reproductive freedom need not mean that the state can take no measures to reduce population growth, and economic freedom need not mean the state cannot prevent destructive uses of property. In fact, liberal regimes have a long history of limiting property rights and regulating markets in the name of the public good—despite the emphasis in liberal economic theory on restricting government intrusion on the economic sphere.[30] We may conclude either that liberal political theory is not as protective of individual rights as some critics have claimed, or that liberal governments take liberal theory with a grain of salt. In either case, the gulf between liberalism and the survivalists isn't as deep as it seems.

Nevertheless, there is some tension between liberalism and an ethic that posits protection of the environment as an absolute constraint on policy. The problem is not that the liberal tradition is too individualistic or too protective of property rights, however, but that it teaches us to be suspicious of claims of necessity. Liberals will tolerate restrictions on rights that are necessary to preserve the state; most would agree that the security of the political community is necessary to achieving such goals as individual liberty and justice. But they are also acutely aware that the logic of this "necessary condition" argument can lead to unhappy results. Consider Hobbes's *Leviathan,* where the problem of maintaining a stable, strong state is so difficult that it overwhelms the ideal of justice (to say nothing of liberty). Justice, for Hobbes, becomes whatever the sovereign says is just, because the sovereign, to remain strong enough to preserve the state, can tolerate no dissent.

Wary of such outcomes, liberals typically treat any attempt to subordinate liberty and justice to necessity with great suspicion. An important element of the liberal tradition is the conviction that the legitimate use of government authority requires that the state's policies be submitted to rational-critical debate by an informed public.[31] Thus liberals instinctively question claims that necessity demands restrictions on rights. On examination, such claims often overstate the risks, and the policies in question prove to be poorly designed to guard against them. To liberals, then, the necessary condition argument looks less like an invulnerable foundation for a political ideology than a tempting target for critical scrutiny. Hence the friction between liberals and survivalists. Berry's claim that protecting the environment must take priority over other policy goals is a necessary condition argument: We can't have democracy, rights, and universal brotherhood if we destroy the planet. It's patently true, but, like arguments from national security, arguments from environmental integrity may be overbroad and exaggerate the risks, resulting in policies that are neither sufficiently protective of rights nor sufficiently protective of the environment. Ecological imperatives could become another set of rationalizations that any enterprising oppressor could call on to justify tyranny.

Berry, however, doesn't use the argument that way. As I suggested earlier, he is interested not merely in preserving the ecosystem, but in preserving ourselves as humans—a project that, for Berry, is wholly inconsistent with severe restrictions of freedom. As subsequent chapters will discuss, his politics lean toward libertarianism, and—like most green theorists—he argues that social and political equality are essential to achieving our environmental goals. Thus his claim that "the land should not be destroyed for any reason, not even for any apparently good reason" is not aimed at pointing out a *real* tension between social justice and environmentalism. Rather, it's aimed at demolishing the flimsy rationalizations that the government (in the person of Earl Butz, former secretary of agriculture) used to promote industrialization of agriculture and the displacement of millions of small farmers. Butz had argued that American agriculture should be made more productive so that America could extend its political influence (read: fight communism) via food exports to poor nations. "Food," he asserted, "is a weapon."[32] Berry was simply pointing out the danger of allowing such laudable goals as promoting liberty and justice to justify practices that could destroy the environment. In other words, he was just playing the old liberal game of unmasking badly justified exercises of government power.

That's not all he's up to, though. Far from encouraging an illiberal political climate, Berry contends that the fragile planet thesis can invigorate our politics by rescuing it from the mire of moral relativism. Disturbed by what he sees as a lack of conviction and seriousness in American politics, he insists that we have "exploited 'relativism' until, as a people, we have no deeply believed reasons for doing anything."[33] It's a familiar complaint: a clever relativist can dismiss any moral argument, however well reasoned, by pointing out that values are determined by contingent factors like social context and upbringing. So fundamental value conflict is inevitable; reason can't be counted on to resolve moral differences. Berry is not the only one to worry about what moral relativism implies for democratic politics: ineradicable conflict and a pervasive sense of futility, both resulting from the decline of reasoned public debate.[34] The fear is that if moral relativists are right, then no amount of rational deliberation can be counted on to bring us all to a consensus. People will cling to different sets of fundamental values, and we can't legitimately criticize them for doing so.

But we can, Berry points out, if their values support a way of life that ends up destroying the planet. This is part of the attraction of the necessary condition argument: The health of the ecosystem can serve as an absolute value for everyone because maintaining a habitable planet is a necessary condition for any community (leaving aside Jonestown-like cults for the moment) to pursue any moral ideal. As a practical matter, we just can't have a good reason to destroy the planet. Thus, Berry reasons, "we must now ask ourselves if there is not, after all, an absolute good by which we must measure ourselves and for which we must work." That absolute good, he concludes, "is health—not in the merely hygienic sense of personal health, but the health, the wholeness, finally the holiness, of Creation."[35]

It's a clever move, and one that many environmentalists rely on to provide a common ground for policy debate.[36] It is not, however, unproblematic, either philosophically or politically. First, Berry's answer to moral relativism only works if addressed to a community that is attempting to survive its current members. It's not unthinkable, for example, that an *individual* might rationally, even justifiably, pursue ends that lead to ecological destruction. (Much, of course, depends on what counts as rational—pursuing material abundance may be a rational individual strategy under some conceptions of rationality, even if it doesn't satisfy the demands of Kant's categorical imperative.) Similarly, Berry wouldn't have much to say to members of a Jonestown-like cult, people who believe Armageddon is just around the corner. If the world is ending, there's no reason to worry about the ozone layer.

So Berry's response to moral relativism isn't irrefutable. But he doesn't seem to be seeking philosophical rigor. He's approaching moral relativism as a *practical* problem, a troublesome element in our political culture that infects our lives with a sense of arbitrariness and our politics with irresolvable conflict. The cure, he suggests, is to find a value that most people do, intuitively and deeply, endorse. People who truly believe the world is ending soon can be dismissed as, if not irrational, at least irrelevant. (In fact, Berry points out that at least one group that believes Armageddon is imminent—the Shakers—already practice good stewardship. As they see it, they have no reason *not* to protect the environment.)[37] In any case, if Berry's goal is to find a value that the majority of the American public feels compelled to honor, preservation of the planet is a pretty good candidate.

Of course, consensus may disintegrate, and moral relativism reappear, once we start debating how to preserve it and who should bear the costs. Indeed, as I will discuss in chapter 5, to the extent Berry is concerned not only with protecting the environment but with preserving the possibility of a particular conception of human life, he cannot avoid grappling with the problem of moral relativism. But he seems to hope that securing agreement on the basic value of environmental integrity will at least begin the conversation the right way: as an attempt to solve a common problem rather than win an ideological war. So for practical if not philosophical reasons, the fragile planet thesis looks like a promising starting point for his argument.

Even if he can secure widespread agreement that the health of the planet is an absolute value, however, he faces another objection—and this one comes from environmentalists themselves: Defining the health of the ecosystem in terms of its ability to support human life is arbitrary. What, after all, is so special about humans? Why not define health in terms of the ecosystem's ability to support a diverse array of life, rather than simply one species? Unfortunately for Berry, this isn't merely a philosophical quibble; many environmentalists embrace an ecocentric perspective that seeks to displace our human-centered value system, including our assumption that the flourishing of the human community should be our first concern. Tracing our environmental problems to what they consider to be a fundamentally misguided worldview—a worldview based on the hubristic belief that it is human destiny to master nature—they argue that preservation of the planet requires a basic change in consciousness: We must abandon the anthropocentric mindset that values the world in terms of its utility to humans and attempt to understand our proper place in the interconnected web of life. Some take this ethic so far as to value preservation of the planet as a living organism over the preservation of individual species—including humans.[38]

Ecocentrism poses a serious ideological obstacle to an ecological agrarianism; the debates surrounding it are in fact the modern guise of the long-standing conflict between farmers and preservationists—between an instrumental and noninstrumental stance toward nature. Moreover, on a sociological and political level, ecocentric rhetoric tends to alienate American farmers; it has a New Age sound reminiscent of hippies, communes, and cosmopolitanism that is deeply at odds with the pragmatic and culturally conservative outlook that characterizes farmers as a social group.[39] Nor is ecocentrism well designed to serve the interests of farmers. By questioning the legitimacy of activities that demand an instrumental stance toward nature, ecocentrism undermines a key feature of agrarianism: the conviction that labor—actual physical interaction with the land—is the source of important civic (and ecological) virtues. From an ecocentric perspective, farming is morally risky rather than ennobling, rife with temptations to dominate, manipulate, and exploit the natural world. So it's hard to formulate a defense of farmers' interests in ecocentric language.

Not surprisingly, then, Berry is unsympathetic to ecocentrism. Unfortunately, his refusal to endorse it threatens to undermine any alliance between environmentalists and farmers. The language of ecocentrism is too integral to modern environmentalism to dismiss. Many of the movement's leaders and guiding inspirations in the United States espouse the ethic, and ecocentric language shows up on Green party platforms around the world.[40] So Berry can't escape the question: Why should we make preserving humans our first priority, especially since they've done more than any other species to harm the planet? Doesn't focusing on human survival just reinforce the mind-set that has fueled the environmental destruction we're trying to end?

He might respond by pointing out that ecocentric activists often rely on the fragile planet thesis themselves, coupling their calls for a change in consciousness with dire predictions that our way of life is leading to our extinction. Such warnings seem to assume and reinforce an anthropocentric worldview, an inconsistency that has led to much political and theoretical confusion. Andrew Dobson, for example, argues that this anthropocentric language among radical environmentalists is a hypocritical attempt to win support for policies that they favor for other, ecocentric, reasons.[41] But this line of criticism, I think, is misguided. When ecocentric activists argue that anthropocentrism will lead to extinction of the human species, they're actually offering an anthropocentric critique of anthropocentrism. That is, if anthropocentrism isn't in the best interests of humans, we should (according to anthropocentric principles) abandon it in favor of a less human-centered philosophy. Such rhetorical maneuvers call into question the logic of anthropocentrism, not the sincerity of ecocentrics.

A better approach would focus on the tenuousness of the link between anthropocentrism and environmental destruction. Whatever its value as a strategy for spiritual transformation or the basis for a more rational ethics, ecocentrism is plagued by muddy social theory. Perhaps because ecocentrism has been the particular focus of ethicists rather than social theorists (ecofeminists being an exception), ecocentric theorists seldom attempt to clarify the nature of the connection between ideology and practice. Warwick Fox's stunningly naïve assertion is typical:

> If one has a wide, expansive, or field-like sense of self [i.e., an ecocentric perspective] then (assuming that one is not self-destructive) one will naturally (i.e. spontaneously) protect the natural (spontaneous) unfolding of this expansive self (the ecosphere, the cosmos) in all its aspects.[42]

Even a casual acquaintance with the perversity of human nature should warn us against counting on our sense of self-preservation *alone* to prevent us from doing self-destructive things—like smoking, failing to wear seat belts, maintaining poor diets, and all the other things we do out of habit, stupidity, inattention, laziness, despair, and rebelliousness. (As we shall see, although Berry would like to see moral improvement on the individual level, he recognizes the need for some sort of external constraints on individual behavior as well.)

This faith in the power of individual moral transformation allows ecocentric theorists to sidestep the hard questions about cause and effect that a more sophisticated theory of social change must answer: Is it that anthropocentrism is the *historical cause* of ecologically destructive social practices, that it is a *continuing cause* of such practices, that it is *evidence* that our relationship to nature is fundamentally misguided—or is it simply that rejecting anthropocentrism is a necessary (or sufficient?) *condition* for changing that behavior?[43] Certainly the claim that anthropocentrism caused (or causes) ecological destruction is too simplistic. Like any big social problem, our poor ecological practices are driven by multiple partially independent forces. A more subtle analysis would recognize that our economic system and political institutions, along with accidents of history and the path-dependent direction of technological development, have all interacted with ideology to cause our ecological dilemmas. Nor will ideological change be sufficient to fix the problem. Even if we adopted a better attitude toward the environment, we would still have to deal with habit, tradition, entrenched institutions, global economic pressures, and a host of other obstacles to changing patterns of production and consumption.

Of course, ecocentric theorists might assert that anthropocentric ideology, while perhaps a product of certain historical practices, has taken on a life of its own, and now poses an independent obstacle to generating political support to change those practices—or at least a continuing incitement to irresponsible behavior. Under this reasoning, ideological change is a critical part of environmental politics, just as fighting racist ideology is an important part of racial politics (even though ending racism would not in itself end racial inequality). But is the analogy persuasive? True, a mass change in consciousness might make it easier to generate political support for the institutional and policy changes needed to preserve the ecosystem. It might also help prevent us from slipping back into bad practices. But here the analogy breaks down: Most social prejudices (like racism) don't threaten the survival of the human community. If, as most ecocentric theorists insist, the planet really is in danger of becoming uninhabitable, surely simple anthropocentric self-interest would be sufficient to generate support for dramatic social change. After all, if the public were rational enough to abandon anthropocentrism for a more enlightened ecocentrism, wouldn't it be rational enough to preserve the planet out of a less-enlightened self-interest?

These are, I think, significant problems with ecocentrism—but not, perhaps, insurmountable ones. Berry's objections are more fundamental and probably irremovable, rooted as they are in two basic elements of his social theory: the importance of tradition and the rejection of heroic ethics.

Berry's respect for tradition is illustrated in his first line of attack on ecocentrism: He questions the causal logic of the ecocentric argument by denying that Western ideology *is* uniformly or even predominantly anthropocentric. Here he touches on an area of vulnerability for any critique of "Western ideology." Western thought, after all, comprehends a vast array of ideas, faiths, and symbolic systems. Other critics have pointed out that the ideological culprit of ecocentrism has proven difficult to pin down—is it patriarchy, Christianity, Platonic philosophy, Renaissance humanism, or the Enlightenment?[44] And even if there were consensus on where Western civilization went wrong, the ecocentric theorist would have to explain away the continuing persistence of nonanthropocentric ideas. Some ecocentric theorists do acknowledge the presence of a Western nonanthropocentric "minority tradition"—including St. Francis, Spinoza, and other environmental good guys. But what makes this tradition the "minority"? Nonanthropocentric and cautionary themes are integral to *dominant* Western traditions. Western arrogance toward and exploitation of nature have had to contend with classical warnings against hubris and celebrations of the simple life, the Christian teaching that man is subordinate to God, and the Enlightenment notion that man like everything else is subject to the laws of physics and biology.[45] Western ways of thinking are in fact considerably more complex than the ecocentric critique typically assumes. How else could we explain the fact that ecological ideas arose out of the same Enlightenment that generated the modern technology they criticize?

This is not to say that the ecocentric critique isn't an insightful, if sometimes distorting, perspective on Western thought. Berry in fact agrees with much of it, although he usually focuses more narrowly on what he sees as typically American values: our consumerism and celebration of technology, our restlessness and individualism, our resistance to the concept of limits or self-restraint, our glorification of violence. These aspects of American ideology he considers destructive—if not the root cause at least an obstacle to a more rational relationship with nature.[46] But he warns against wholesale attacks on Western culture that might cut us off from our intellectual heritage altogether:

> If we want to use the world with care, we cannot exempt ourselves from our cultural inheritance, our tradition. . . . Most of us are in the Western tradition somewhat as we are in the world: we are in it because we were born in it. We can't get out of it because it made us what we are; we are, to some extent, what it is.[47]

Extricating ourselves from Western philosophical traditions would simply deprive us of the intellectual resources to rectify our conceptual errors and make sense of our place in the world. Inherited forms may be constraining, but they're also enabling; rebellion against such forms, while sometimes necessary, is always dangerous.[48] Instead of liberation, we may just end up with a less rich and complex conceptual framework for ordering our social world.

Such reasoning seems to reflect Berry's own professional socialization; rejecting the Western intellectual tradition would mean rejecting much of the literary canon that Berry, the writer and teacher of literature, loves. But it also reflects the importance of tradition in Berry's social theory—particularly tradition as a means of social control—which involves it in the complexities surrounding that problem. I will explore those complexities in the next chapter. Here I want to focus on Berry's second objection to ecocentrism: that calls for radical moral change are themselves morally suspect.

He explains his chief complaint with ecocentrism in *Home Economics:*

> I don't know how the human species can avoid some version of self-centeredness; I don't know how any species can. . . . We are . . . *obliged* to think and act out of a proper self-interest and a genuine self-respect as human beings. An earthworm, I think, is living in an earthworm-centered world; the thrush who eats the earthworm is living in a thrush-centered world; the hawk who eats the thrush is living in a hawk-centered world.[49]

Some defenders of ecocentrism meet this criticism with the objection that they aren't asking people to think like a hawk, that ecocentrism merely objects to the "unwarranted, differential treatment of other beings on the basis that they do not belong to our *own* species."[50] This defense gives too much away, however; if ecocentrism merely means recognizing that differential treatment of animals requires justification, it's hardly a dramatic ideological change. Most advocates of ecocentrism use the language of *total conceptual transformation,* asking us to cultivate a wider sense of self through identification with other beings—to transcend our normal consciousness and develop an ecological self that merges with other species and even ecological processes. And surely only such a dramatic transformation can reasonably be expected to result in the profound social change they hope for. Thus they are calling, usually explicitly, not just for a new ethic but for a new religion.[51]

This is the sort of talk that Berry objects to. His point here, I think, is not simply that it's conceptually difficult to escape our human perspective, that we are obliged, in the sense of *unable* not, to think like humans. On this point, ecocentric philosophers can make a compelling case that we shouldn't underestimate our imaginations and capacity for conceptual transformation. But Berry sees a *moral* danger inherent in ecocentrism: The attempt to "rise above" our human perspective is unwarranted hubris—precisely the vice that ecocentrism is trying to cure. Thus we are *morally* obliged to think like humans. "Each creature," he points out, "does what is necessary in its own behalf."[52] Who are we to assume that we, alone among the species, are justified in adopting what amounts to a God's eye view of our place in the universe? Ecocentrism, even in many of its less extreme versions, is a heroic ethic, a dramatic rejection of that instrumental relationship to the world that constitutes so much of our everyday existence. To think like a thrush or hawk is simply another attempt to reach beyond our limits, to separate ourselves from nature and to deny our brotherhood with other limited, self-centered animals.

And it is also, he suggests, an attempt to deny our brotherhood with other humans. Berry is not the only one to suspect a deeply misanthropic element in ecocentrism, an implicit conviction that "man is everywhere a disturbing agent," that leads to hostility toward the activities of ordinary human life.[53] Misanthropy is not of course logically required by ecocentrism; humans are in theory as valuable as any other species. But it does seem to lead in that direction. For example, ecocentric activists tend to focus on preserving the wilderness rather than providing some workable ethic of land use—as though, Berry complains, "pristine wilderness is the only alternative to exploitation and abuse."[54] If we aren't supposed to view nature as useful, it's hard to construct an ethic that would justify even the environmentally sensitive use of nature for ordinary production to support the human community. "We cannot exempt ourselves from using the world," he argues, and "if we cannot exempt ourselves from use, then we must deal with the issues raised by use."[55] Although ecocentrism usually endorses the "necessary" exploitation of physical resources, it has so far failed to provide any criteria to determine what humans actually need.[56] Do we need, for example, a population exceeding five billion? Or three billion? Or even ten million? The logic of ecocentrism, rather than telling us how to use nature harmlessly, simply tells us that the most ethical course of action is to reduce the human population; this is, in the end, the best way to minimize our impact on nature.

In fact, there would be little lost from an ecocentric point of view if the human race died out altogether. Few ecocentric theorists take the logic that far, of course; when Gary Snyder, for example, contends that "there are too many human beings," he's not interested in changing their numbers but their nature: "Let's be animals or buddhas instead."[57] But changing human nature is arguably more drastic, and certainly more ambitious, than simply reducing the population.

Berry thus distances himself from both ecocentrism and many of his fellow survivalists (who also advocate population reduction) when he contends that "perhaps the greatest immediate danger lies in our dislike of ourselves as a species." This dislike, he fears, threatens "to justify further abuses of one another and the world."[58] Ecocentrism, he worries, fuels a dangerous contempt for ordinary human life, the life of everyday production and consumption. In reinforcing a problematic opposition between man and nature, it alienates us from both the natural and the man-made world: It instructs us to see ourselves as fundamentally different from other species in our inability to adapt gracefully to the environment, and to view with hostility our attempts to adapt the environment to our own needs. And it insists that the only way out of this dismal situation is a heroic self-transformation reminiscent of the spiritually ambitious projects of other world-denying faiths.

Berry's is a powerful criticism because it rests on the charge of hubris, which is central to most ecological critiques of modern society. But it also threatens to lead us too far in the other direction. If humans are like other animals in being self-interested and limited, why do we have all these moral duties that other animals don't have? To avoid a dangerous slide into amoralism, Berry has to recognize that humans *are* in some respects different from other animals. And he does, agreeing with George Perkins Marsh that humans are different because we have foresight, the ability to anticipate the long-term consequences of our actions. Thus we are uniquely *powerful*—which is why we have duties that other animals don't have, such as the duty to seek the good of other species even at our own expense. We encounter moral limits on our actions because of our technological capacity: "In the hierarchy of power among the earth's creatures, we are at the top. . . . And so it is more important than ever that we should have cultures capable of making us into humans—creatures capable of prudence, justice, fortitude, temperance, and the other virtues."[59]

However, Berry also worries that this line of reasoning may drastically overestimate our ability to anticipate the long-term consequences of our actions (as Marsh's *Man and Nature* amply proves). He shares the skepticism with which many environmentalists view exalted claims of human reason, knowledge, and control. Because we *can't* very well anticipate or control the long-term consequences of our actions, we should be wary of the ecocentric call for moral heroism on behalf of other species. It may simply lead us to further recklessly grand projects—such as the radical restructuring of our social, political, and economic relations, not to mention the complete transformation of our spiritual and intellectual traditions. So, he concludes, we should focus on the more limited and humble goal of saving our own necks. With a sufficiently sophisticated understanding of the importance of other species and complex biological relationships to human survival, our modest attempts at self-preservation should benefit the planet as a whole.

None of this is to suggest that Berry is hostile to typical ecocentric causes, such as the ethical treatment of animals or protection of the wilderness. On the contrary, he has actively pursued wilderness preservation, and his poetry (including his most well-known verse, "The Peace of Wild Things") displays a profound appreciation for wild nature.[60] And he is as severely critical of modern methods of raising livestock as any animal liberationist.[61] But he resists the suggestion that an ethical relationship with nature requires a noninstrumental stance toward it. Consider, for example, one of his favorite causes: encouraging the use of horses instead of tractors for farmwork. Berry uses horses on his Kentucky farm, he explains, not just because they're more practical than tractors but because he *likes* horses; working with them is for him a cooperative, social event. "Between a farmer and a team there exists a sort of fellow feeling that is impossible between a farmer and a tractor."[62] His characterization of their relationship poses a stark contrast to the language of domination with which most ecocentric theorists describe human/animal interactions. Animals, Berry implies, are sufficiently like people for their relationship to allow for various degrees of mutuality, even friendship. Thus he values his horses, not in the abstract as independent ethical beings working out their own evolutionary destiny, but in the particularity of their relationship to him. His interaction with and reliance on horses allows him to empathize with them and therefore care about their well-being.

This is an example of what Warwick Fox calls using "personal identification" as a basis for extending ethical concern to nonhumans. Fox criticizes this approach on the grounds that it fails to rescue us from egotism (Berry cares for *his* horses, not horsekind in general) and therefore leads to "possessiveness, greed, exploitation, war and ecological destruction."[63] (Fox advocates a transpersonal identification, resting on, for example, one's recognition of one's connection to the cosmos as a whole.) But for Berry, the fact that such personal identification "slips into attachment and proprietorship" (in Fox's words) is precisely its value. It is attachment and proprietorship that ensure *care;* transpersonal identification is more consistent with an attitude of letting things alone, which is precisely what farmers can't afford to do. Moreover, Berry's friendship with horses seems to reinforce his sense of membership in the biotic community. Farmers may have moral duties that their livestock don't, but those duties arise out of their *interdependence* with other animals. The farmer's instrumental view of nature, far from being an ethical obstacle, highlights and reinforces this sense of interdependence, which in turn supports an ethic of care for other species.

Berry's position, in sum, is unapologetically anthropocentric—but for the reasons that have less to do with philosophical consistency than with rhetorical, moral, and political concerns. The fragile planet thesis allows him to link our interest in self-preservation (a healthy interest based on a humble appreciation for our mortality and limits) to his specific environmental and political objectives. This lets him sidestep (temporarily, at least) many of the fundamental value conflicts that infect American politics and appeal to anyone interested in preserving the human race. At the same time, it challenges the moral and political ennui he sees in contemporary America—without, he thinks, fueling a destructive spiritual ambition that may ultimately become world- and life-renouncing. For Berry, the one value capable of uniting us, giving meaning to our lives, *and* providing a practical ethic for ordinary life is the life and health of the world.

But relying on this claim of the earth's fragility does have one drawback. It requires him to make a credible case that the planet really is fragile—that the problems environmentalists have identified represent a serious threat to human health and reproduction. Unfortunately, the factual debate has become deeply contentious, with consequences that aren't entirely consistent with Berry's agenda.

There are certainly plenty of facts to back up the fragile planet thesis. Environmental watchdog organizations regularly publish depressing reports on the state of the global environment; there is little good news. We are told that agricultural production is diminishing, irreplaceable resources are being used up, valuable ecosystems are being degraded and destroyed, population is increasing, and pollution is depleting the ozone layer, reducing the air, water, and land supply, and causing global warming.[64] The facts speak eloquently for themselves; they would thus seem to be a solid place to anchor environmental politics.

But all these facts are, of course, contested; critics claim that the problems aren't as serious as some contend, that solutions are readily available, or that progress toward solutions is being made.[65] These claims, if substantiated, would certainly weaken Berry's position—although they wouldn't undermine it completely. As I have pointed out, Berry is arguing not simply that reforming our agricultural practices would save the planet but that it would make possible a more fully human life. That claim relies only in part on the fragile planet thesis; that is, even if we *aren't* farming the planet to death, we may still be destroying the social and cultural resources necessary for human life. Nevertheless, to the extent he frames the problem as the fragility of the planet, his argument inevitably involves him in the scientific debates surrounding the extent and causes of environmental damage.

Unfortunately, those debates show no sign of being resolved—nor should we expect them to be. True, science holds out the promise of establishing reasonably certain knowledge about the causes of environmental damage. But environmental protection necessarily involves making decisions about risk—which are ultimately matters of value, not fact. Accordingly, there is no guarantee that debate over environmental protection will result in rational consensus on specific policies; it may continue just as endlessly as debate over abortion or public versus private education. Still, debates about environmental risks—at least risks that are widely shared—may not be as intractable as value conflicts that divide people along religious or partisan lines. And in any case, as suggested earlier, Berry's goal does not seem to be ending debate or guaranteeing a rational consensus. His goal is to focus debate on the right things, to bring to our politics a sense of common purpose and responsibility that could come from arguing over how best to care for the earth.

So conflict over the facts is not in itself the difficulty. The problem is that grounding the environmental debate in the facts gives the scientific community considerable weight in policy making—they are, after all, the authorities on matters of fact. This has antidemocratic implications because it makes policy debate more arcane, technical, and inaccessible to laymen. Scientific uncertainty plagues most environmental issues; our understanding of environmental processes just hasn't kept pace with our perception of environmental problems.[66] And the problem is complicated by the fact that the environmental movement has exposed the politics surrounding the production and use of scientific knowledge. Industry interests, many environmentalists contend, affect the values and commitments of the scientific community. The very industries under attack from environmentalists influence funding of scientific research, which allows them to shape (if not control) research agendas, the interpretation of data, and the dissemination of results.[67] As Berry puts it, "even such nominally altruistic sciences as medicine and plant-breeding have now become so deeply interpenetrated with economics and politics that their motives are at best mixed with, and at worst replaced by, the motives of corporations and governments."[68]

The perception that scientists may be serving industry interests tends to undermine their authority, so that their conclusions (when they reach conclusions) remain open to challenge. This situation creates endless scientific debate without bringing the level of debate within reach of the average layman—a problem of which Berry is acutely aware. His writing is littered with scathing attacks on the academic establishment and the agricultural "experts" who, in his view, obfuscate relatively straightforward issues with arcane jargon, questionable assumptions, obvious biases, and their remoteness from the problems they claim to be trying to solve.[69] Echoing a long Populist tradition of hostility to the intellectual elite, Berry embraces the thoroughly democratic conviction that the average man *must* have the intelligence to make sense of the information on which our policies are based. "It is certain," at any rate, "that as long as expert knowledge remains in the heads of experts it cannot become a solution."[70]

Berry's concern about the relationship between science and public policy focuses in part on the exclusivity and elitism of the educational establishment, particularly the land-grant universities whose original mission was to ensure the broad dissemination of scientific knowledge. But it also reflects a deeper concern about the values and mind-set that characterize scientists as a group. Importantly, this is not to suggest that he rejects science itself as a legitimate way of discovering truth. Indeed, it would be odd if he did, considering that his major influences include Wes Jackson, a plant geneticist and cofounder of the Land Institute. Jackson, he claims, has been "an indispensable source of instruction and a continuous testing of my thoughts."[71] And Jackson defends science in the strongest terms. Darwin's theory, he claims, is "a powerful one that holds at all levels of life all over our beautiful planet. It is coherent, it makes sense, it has no internal contradictions."[72] Scientific discoveries such as Mendel's laws of heredity "have positive results few us would oppose."[73] In fact, Jackson complains that the scientific establishment is not scientific *enough*. If our culture were more enlightened in an evolutionary and ecological sense, he contends, we would reject our harmful agricultural practices and take better care of the environment.[74] Berry seems to agree; he insists that good farming "involves both science and art."[75] In fact, he typically treats science as a discipline as demanding, creative, and valuable as writing poetry.

What Berry objects to is not science but "scientism," an ideology that has grown up alongside modern science and serves to justify its more ambitious projects.[76] The critique of scientism has long been central to environmentalism. Ecology itself developed as a holistic alternative to the nineteenth-century trend in the natural sciences toward reductionism, a central feature of scientism.[77] Scientific reductionism, the critique goes, can blind us to system effects and create the illusion of technical mastery. Scientism teaches that science can "know all things and solve all problems, whereupon the scientist may become an evangelist and go forth to save the world."[78] This evangelical fervor is in turn underwritten by a claim of epistemological privilege—a claim that the only beliefs that can be called "true" are those discoverable and verifiable through the scientific method. What art, religion, and other humanist disciplines teach is not truth but unprovable, unknowable "values." Thus proponents of scientism do not consider that "religious faith may be a way of knowing things that cannot otherwise be known."[79] Moreover, disciples of scientism contend that the scientific method is neutral with respect to most values—and therefore the humanities have little of relevance to say to scientists. In short, critics of scientism claim that the reductionism, materialism, and empiricism of modern science tend to narrow the mind and create warped, stunted intellects incapable of truly appreciating, much less realizing, liberal values.

There are of course more sophisticated defenses of the scientific method than scientism, and Berry himself agrees that it produces useful knowledge about the material world. But he insists that there are real limits—epistemological as well as social and political—to scientists' ability to discover truth, and that to the extent scientific research is directed at solving social problems, it is not value neutral. His complaint, then, is that scientism fosters an illusion of mastery and value neutrality that tends to blind scientists to both their limits and their responsibility for the effects of scientific research.[80]

Thus the dominance of scientists in environmental and agricultural policy is worrisome not only because it is inegalitarian but also because scientists are precisely the wrong sort of people to be making these decisions. Berry is particularly concerned about the impact of scientism on agricultural experts: "Modern American agriculture has made itself a 'science' and has preserved itself within its grandiose and destructive assumptions by cutting itself off from the moral tradition." It has thus "confin[ed] its vision and its thought."[81] As a result,

> it is still perfectly acceptable in land-grant universities for agricultural researchers to apply themselves to the development of more productive dairy cows without considering at all the fact that this development necessarily involves the failure of many thousands of dairies and dairy farmers—that it has already done so and will inevitably continue to do so.[82]

Furthermore, "such work is permitted to continue, I suspect, because it is reported in language that is unreadable and probably unintelligible to nearly everybody in the university, to nearly everybody who milks cows, and to nearly everybody who drinks milk."[83] In short, when scientists (or people who embrace scientism) dominate the policy process, policy making cannot be democratic and policies are unlikely to be humane.

Still, Berry admits that science is useful, even necessary, to good environmental policy. So how can we avoid its deleterious effects on the policy process? On this point he has little to offer. He merely suggests that a modern university should "provide a forum in which such researchers might be required to defend their work before colleagues in, say, philosophy or literature or history"—colleagues like himself, that is.[84] His reasoning is that those trained in the humanities will have a better sense of the values implicated by and cultural significance of the research. They could therefore raise questions such as whether we're justified in cooping up livestock and manipulating their genetic structure in order to increase productivity and put more small farmers out of work. But although this proposal may combat scientism to some extent, it is unlikely to cure it. Nor does it resolve the more fundamental problem of elitism. Rather than ensuring the dissemination of information to "everyone who drinks milk," it simply involves another segment of the intellectual elite in policy debate.

To engage the general public, we would need to rework our educational practices and institutions more dramatically, and Berry has little to say about such a project. But dealing with the informational demands of public policy in a way consistent with democratic values remains one of the most challenging problems in political theory, and it's hardly surprising that Berry, who is deeply skeptical of mass politics and government institutions, doesn't address it in more depth.[85] After all, the purpose of the fragile planet thesis is not to alert us to the deficiencies in our democratic institutions but to refocus our attention on the prepolitical, presocial conditions of democracy: the preservation of the natural world. For Berry, the fragile planet thesis takes the place of the Populists' rhetoric of social justice and diatribes against the concentration of wealth: It ties the interests of small farmers to the fate of the community, making their cause our common cause. It thus brings new relevance to the old claim that small farmers are essential to the health and welfare of the nation. The next chapter investigates that claim.

Chapter Four

Settling America

Given that the planet is fragile and needs stewardship, the problem is how to organize society to ensure such stewardship. Berry's social theory centers on this question. Much of it, however, has to be inferred from his explanation of why existing social arrangements *fail* to encourage stewardship. This part of his analysis rehearses the now-familiar litany of complaints by environmentalists about the culture of consumption and the pathologies of economic rationality. Berry gives this conventional environmentalist critique a Populist slant by focusing on the problems for land use created by the corporate form of ownership and on absentee and short-term ownership generally. The fusion of environmental concerns with a Populist sensibility forms the basis of his broader critique of American culture.

His solution, however, is an interesting departure from both conventional environmentalism and Populism: His case for an agrarian alternative to industrial capitalism rests critically on the role of *tradition*—as opposed to government regulation, the market, or individual reason—in supporting ecologically rational behavior. This emphasis on tradition seems to introduce a communal or organic element into his social theory that conflicts with his libertarianism. But the conflict is more apparent than real. Unlike many conservative social theorists, Berry offers a rationalist defense of tradition—a conception of tradition as an aid to rationality and defense against government regulation—that reinforces rather than undermines his democratic and libertarian principles.

As argued in chapter 3, Berry's defense of small farmers breaks with earlier agrarians by reformulating the farmer's role, which for him is not to produce wealth or secure democracy but to be stewards of the land's fertility. While Jefferson advocated small farms for political reasons, "there is also," he contends, "an ecological justification."

> If landed properties are democratically divided and properly scaled, and if family security in these properties can be preserved over a number of generations, then we will greatly increase the possibility of *authentic cultural adaptation* to local homelands. Not only will we make more apparent to successive generations the necessary identity between the health of the human communities and the health of local ecosystems but we will also give people the best motives for caretaking and we will call into service the necessary local intelligence and imagination. Such an arrangement would give us the fullest possible assurance that our forests and farmlands would be used by people who know them best and care the most about them.[1]

Thus his argument rests on two claims: that small family farmers would have the proper incentives to be good stewards and that they are able to acquire the knowledge and techniques necessary to proper ecosystem maintenance.

Neither claim is entirely original. Berry's arguments to some extent echo the ideas of nineteenth-century European agrarians that small farms are more productive than large estates. As mentioned in chapter 2, early socialist and anarchist agrarians offered a host of arguments and scientific studies supporting the efficiency, productivity, and sustainability of peasant (or yeoman) small farms over large-scale agriculture.[2] Berry also draws on this line of argument, but his targets are not the landed estates of the nineteenth-century aristocracy; they are the large agribusiness corporations of twentieth-century America. When he insists that small farmers are more likely to be good stewards, he means more likely than corporations geared toward large-scale industrial agriculture.

His reasoning, in a nutshell, is this: A family that has farmed the same piece of land for generations, and hopes to continue to do so, has an incentive to maintain soil fertility and generally act as a steward of the land. Two incentives, actually: self-interest (broadly construed to include one's interest in one's children's prosperity) and affection for the land. Corporations, in contrast, "will never be bound to the land by the sense of birthright and continuity, or by the love that enforces care."[3] Motivated solely by profit, they can't take into account moral or aesthetic values. In contrast, individual owners imbue the landscape with meaning. Long-term occupation of a place allows the owner to develop a web of associations and memories that he or she will wish to preserve. Thus the farm is more than an economic resource—it becomes a monument to the owner's life in that place. Such emotional attachments can serve as a powerful incentive to preserve the land in good condition.[4]

This argument draws much of its force from the invidious opposition between small, family (yeoman) farming and corporate agriculture—a familiar trope that echoes Populist assaults on corporations as well as the critiques of industrial agriculture developed during the 1940s and 1950s. Clearly Berry's early Populist-style attacks on coal companies helped to prepare him to take on agribusiness. But he also adopts a cross-cultural perspective very much in the ecological tradition.[5] In *The Gift of Good Land*, for example, Berry develops his case for sustainable agriculture by describing agricultural practices in Peru and among Native Americans.[6] Farmers in the Peruvian Andes have been growing potatoes for several centuries on steep mountainsides that few Americans would attempt to cultivate. Adapting to these inhospitable conditions, they have developed methods of plowing and weeding that reduce soil erosion, as well as creating hundreds of varieties of potatoes.[7] This agriculture isn't perfect; Berry points out that ecological problems have plagued this mountain civilization since the time of the Incas.[8] But he is nonetheless impressed by the extraordinary care and skill of the Peruvian farmers. Such care and skill, he believes, may offer a solution to our environmental problems—if only we can figure out how to produce it in American farmers.

Similarly, Berry praises the agriculture of the Papago of the Sonoran Desert, who, because they farmed "one of the most difficult human habitats in the world," developed both a culture and an agriculture that was "intricately respectful of the means of life, surpassingly careful of all the possibilities of survival."[9] Again, Berry emphasizes the creativity and adaptability of Papago farmers. Although traditional, he points out, their agriculture has not been static; it benefited from contact with the Spanish, who introduced new crops and work animals. "Perhaps any innovation must be in some way disruptive," Berry speculates, but the history of the Papago suggests that traditionalism can accommodate innovations, as long as they don't disrupt the community's basic relationship to the land.[10]

Such favorable accounts of non-Western cultures are common among environmentalists of all stripes, and have become a standard support for the ecocentric argument that it is the Western worldview that prevents us from achieving a similarly harmonious relationship to nature.[11] Importantly, however, Berry attributes the Peruvians' success not simply to their worldview but to their *traditions*—the practices they developed over centuries of trial and error and the conservative peasant culture that maintains them. This focus on what people are actually doing contrasts with the vaguer, often inaccurate accounts of non-Western ideology that ecocentric theorists sometimes rely on. But Berry is nonetheless playing the same game, drawing an invidious contrast between good, traditional, non-Western agriculture and bad, industrial, commercial, Western agriculture. Thus his descriptions of traditional practices are laced with critical attacks on American agribusiness: commercial agriculture, he warns, is making inroads in Peru. American corporations sell chemicals banned in the United States (such as DDT), and agricultural experts try to persuade farmers to adopt a different variety of potato that would be more suitable for commercial production—but, according to Berry, less suitable for eating.[12] If they succeed, the Peruvians might share the same fate as the Papagos: The government (Berry doesn't specify which government; presumably the Americans) encouraged them to raise cattle, which ruined the rangelands, and to dig individual wells, which undermined their customs of mutual dependence and sharing. The result was the wholly unnecessary disintegration of what had been a workable agriculture.[13]

This account of agricultural imperialism is also integral to his history of American farming. The same story, he suggests, could be told of Kentucky and other rural areas throughout the United States after World War II, as farming communities that had the potential to develop the skill and care that characterizes sustainable agriculture gave way to agribusiness.[14] Although he doesn't quite offer a conspiracy theory, he does emphasize that both corporate and government decision makers consciously and explicitly set out to "modernize" American agriculture by reducing the number of farmers, taking "marginal" lands out of production, and encouraging large, corporate farming (a policy he compares with the forced resettlement of villagers by communist regimes).[15] Thus the story of the Peruvians and the Papagos serves as a template for his history of American farming; his Kentucky neighbors are victims of the same force—namely, corporate agriculture or agribusiness—that is destroying native agricultures all over the world.

But all of this begs the question, what exactly is wrong with corporate farming? Behind Berry's criticism of corporate farming are hints of the Populists' resistance to the concentration of capital and their suspicion of distant eastern capitalists whose uninformed and irresponsible decisions disrupt local communities. But the heart of his case against agribusiness is its *insensitivity*, its inability to adapt to local conditions. Recall his emphasis on the importance of affection and aesthetic pleasure in countering market pressure to exploit the land; corporations are not supposed to respond to such incentives. They are creatures of the market, responding, ideally, only to economic incentives and government sanctions.

More specifically, Berry draws attention to the problems inherent in the corporate *form of ownership:* A corporate CEO might well cherish a deep appreciation and affection for the land, but because she's responsible to shareholders, she simply isn't free to forego short-term economic advantage in favor of long-term interests in soil fertility—not, at any rate, without the shareholders' consent. And shareholders are famously inattentive. Berry notes that in 1975 the *Los Angeles Times* reported that "some of our largest and most respected conservation organizations," including the Sierra Club, had, through careless decision making, acquired stock in Exxon, General Motors, Tenneco, and various strip-mining firms.[16] His worry is that the pressure to increase profits will foster this sort of carelessness, however well-intentioned the owners and managers. Unfortunately, inattentiveness is difficult to cure. Corporations, after all, are a way to distribute the risks of ownership, which means they also distribute the responsibilities. Corporate shareholders, multitudinous and mostly anonymous, can avoid the community-enforced norms and conventions that usually constrain owners in deciding how to use their property. The corporate form (and for economists, this is one of its chief virtues) allows them to act as pure profit seekers.

Obviously this critique isn't directed against farms that are managed by the corporate shareholders directly, as many family farms are. The problem results from the separation of ownership and management, the dispersal of responsibility among many unconnected individuals and the failure of owners to develop a strong connection with the land. In this respect, corporate agriculture is not simply a problem in itself; if it were, we might respond that, after all, very little farming in America is corporate (less than 4 percent in 1992).[17] Rather, corporate agriculture serves for Berry as a paradigm of what's wrong with American agriculture and American society in general: We don't in any meaningful sense live where we work.

"One of the peculiarities of the white race's presence in America," Berry argues, "is how little intention has been applied to it. As a people, wherever we have been, we have never really intended to be."[18] Echoing the earlier advocates of permanent agriculture, Berry reinterprets Frederick Jackson Turner's frontier thesis: In general, we have looked on America not as a homeland but as a place to exploit as quickly as possible and move on. Those who managed to establish the beginnings of a traditional and domestic culture have been ruthlessly expropriated; the exploiters "have always said that what was destroyed was outdated, provincial, and contemptible."[19] While Turner argued that the unsettling effect of the frontier produced socially desirable qualities such as egalitarianism, nationalism, and rugged individualism, Berry contends that our failure to settle the land prevented us from developing an intimate association with it.[20] Instead we have learned to cherish illusions of independence—from nature, from the past, and from each other. We have, he insists, traded conscious awareness of our dependence on neighbors and the land for a blind, unacknowledged dependence on specialists and experts and markets.[21]

This reasoning echoes Liberty Hyde Bailey's call for farmers to achieve an ethical relationship with the natural world through cultural adaptation and Bennett's account of the history of American agriculture. It has been echoed more recently by bioregionalists, who emphasize the ecological importance of domestic settlement and developing an intimate association— not just economic but emotional, spiritual, and historical—with the physical environment.[22] Ecological sensitivity, according to this view, depends critically on developing a "sense of place," a sense of its history and possibilities. Our failure to develop this sense of place accounts for our failure to protect the environment—or at least serves as evidence of a fundamentally unhealthy relationship to the land. Berry is a little vague on which is the cause and which the effect. He appears, like Turner, to be suggesting that an ideology developed out of the material and social conditions of American society, but that this ideology (of individualism, freedom, progress) has now taken on a life of its own and become a causal factor in social life.[23] Like the ecocentric critique of Western civilization, this theory drifts toward a monocausal explanation of all that is wrong with American society, and is vulnerable on that score (surely that's not all that's wrong with us; surely developing a sense of place wouldn't in itself be enough to fix things). But the more limited claim is still compelling: If a sense of place does contribute to environmentally sensitive farming, small family farms may be more likely to achieve it than large-scale corporate farms.

That's a big "if," though. Berry's "sense of place" may be too indeterminate and subjective to constitute an effective guide to ecologically rational behavior. My sense of place may include hydroelectric dams and ski lodges, while my neighbor envisions pristine forests and wild rivers. On the other hand, the demands of living in community with others may create some pressure toward achieving consensus on land use. In any case, living where one works has at least one environmental virtue: it addresses the problem of externalities. Berry's case against corporate farming and absentee ownership rests in part on the point that the failure to live where we work creates the incentive to externalize pollution costs. Farmers who live on their farms are less able to externalize the costs of the pollution; if they pollute the local water supply with pesticides or fertilizer, they must drink the polluted water or help pay to clean it up. Thus they have a personal incentive to act in ways consistent with the good of the local community.[24] They will also, of course, be more susceptible to pressure from their friends and neighbors not to poison the well—provided class, race, and other sorts of hierarchies don't insulate them from such community pressures (which is why social democracy is essential to his agrarianism). So domestic settlement, whatever its larger impact on American culture or the cultivation of a "sense of place," promises at least to correct some of the perverse incentives created by geographic mobility and absentee ownership.

Such arguments about the incentive structures that encourage environmentally destructive behavior by corporations are hardly unique to Berry. They've become standard fare among environmentalists, typically supporting calls for stricter environmental controls on big business and greater political power for local communities. But Berry pursues the reasoning further: He contends that it also counsels against public ownership of (productive) land. In stark contrast to the preservationist and conservationist traditions, both of which usually endorse government ownership of natural resources, Berry argues that "good use of property seems to require not only ownership but personal occupation and use by the owner."[25] Berry is not in general a strong advocate of private property rights.[26] But to the extent that public ownership disperses individual responsibility and involves absentee ownership, he reasons, it creates precisely the same disincentives to stewardship as large-scale corporate farming. Although he recognizes that such problems may not arise in communities with strong traditions of communal agriculture, he insists that we have no such traditions; no cultural pressures would work against the tendency to neglect and exploit publicly owned land.[27]

This insistence on the advantages of private, individual ownership reflects the Populist roots of Berry's environmentalism. He just doesn't trust the professionalization of government functions or the intellectual elites who staff the administrative apparatus. Thus he objects to our tradition of public ownership of forests—it "separate[s] forestry and forest conservation from the rural economy," he complains, and in any case,

if in order to protect our forest land we designate it as a commons or commonwealth separate from private ownership, then who will care for it? The absentee timber companies who see no reason to care about local consequences? The same government agencies and agents who are failing at present to take good care of our public forests?[28]

Private owners of forests don't have a particularly good record of stewardship either, but his point, I think, is that the failure of government agents to resist political and market pressures to exploit the forests demonstrates our lack of an effective tradition of communal ownership. Given this lack, public ownership of certain natural resources is not *in itself* sufficient to halt environmental degradation—it merely relieves the citizens of both a sense of personal responsibility for and effective control over those resources. Of course, in the society he envisions in which an ethic of stewardship has taken root, public ownership might work as well as private ownership. But if stewardship is a pervasive ideal, public ownership shouldn't be necessary—and it would still be undesirable to the extent it fostered the creation of a Washington-based elite corps of professional resource managers. There is, he suggests, a fundamental incompatibility between specialization of resource management and the sense of place that would characterize an ecologically rational society.

Thus Berry's attack on public ownership of natural resources parallels his critique of corporations. But it also reveals some of the weaknesses of that critique. What sounds like a valid criticism of heartless, profit-seeking corporations—that they have little incentive to respond to community pressure, that they diffuse responsibility and privilege economic values over other values—sounds more reactionary and less compelling when directed at public agencies. They, too, have little incentive to respond to local community pressure—but that is one of their *virtues*. They can serve larger, national interests. Similarly, public agencies like corporations bring economic rationality to bear on the management of public resources; again, from the progressive standpoint this is a virtue, not a vice. Importantly, if Berry's critique of public ownership is off-base, his critique of corporate ownership is vulnerable. To the extent corporations can rationalize environmental management and be made (through government sanctions and better incentive structures) to serve the public interest, they look considerably less sinister than Berry would have us believe.

True, thus far American corporations have proven stubbornly resistant to pressures from government, consumers, and workers to embrace green values. This resistance makes it difficult for committed environmentalists to entertain the idea that large corporations could become environmentally responsible; it tends instead to support Berry's view that something about the corporate form itself obstructs environmentally sensitive practices. But there are ways to overcome the separation of ownership and management, as well as the problem of scale. A large agricultural corporation needn't operate large farms, for example. It could instead operate many small farms, or secure production and marketing contracts with small farmers. Such contracts are standard in poultry and hog production, although admittedly neither farmers nor environmentalists are happy with the results. In standard production and marketing contracts, the contractor owns the commodity and supplies the inputs; the farmer is paid for production services only. Farmers and environmentalists both object that such contracts lead to standardized production processes that are environmentally insensitive and reduce the farmer's managerial discretion, leading to exploitation of the environment and the farmer.[29] But these problems may not be inherent in the contract system itself. Government regulation could encourage the adoption of more enlightened production techniques, and changes in contractual arrangements to give the farmers more managerial control could secure at least some of the economic benefits of corporate agriculture without sacrificing the cultural and environmental benefits of small-scale agriculture.[30] One benefit such an arrangement could not secure, of course, is standardization and the accompanying efficiency gains. Under Berry's view, standardization in production would have to be sacrificed in order to produce the flexible and innovative adaptation to local conditions he considers the hallmark of a sustainable agriculture.

With these reforms, corporate agriculture may not be as objectionable as Berry thinks. And private individual ownership looks considerably less appealing from an environmental standpoint when compared with enlightened public management. Berry's insistence on private individual ownership as a device to ensure care overlooks the fact that individual ownership can also *relieve* one of responsibility: If I own it, I can do what I like with it. Public agencies are formally, legally responsible to the community; private landholders are harder to monitor and sanction. And Berry may also underestimate the force of our traditions of communal ownership. Communities can and often do feel a strong sense of ownership of resources that have played an important role in civic life (consider the difficulty of moving sports teams to a new city). Indeed, the environmental movement draws much of its political efficacy from its success in arousing a sense of public ownership of and responsibility for natural resources. Finally, individual ownership can create insuperable problems in coordinating environmental management. Ecosystems don't respect property lines.

These are serious objections to Berry's theory, but they shouldn't blind us to the value of his insights into the cultural effects of widespread absentee ownership. His claim that environmental rationality requires authentic cultural adaptation to the land—a "sense of place" that imbues the landscape with meaning and value—remains an important innovation in traditional agrarianism. Berry's hope is that this sense of place, supported by memory, affection, taste, and community pressure, will soften the influence of market forces and allow farmers to pursue values other than profit maximization. It's hard to deny that government regulation would be less expensive and more effective if it were supported by social mores against destructive practices. Under this reasoning, rational use of natural resources requires that we strengthen the local community's ties to and long-term interests in the land—and stable farming communities composed of numerous small farms with long histories promise to do so. But, importantly, the value of such communities isn't just a matter of creating the right incentive structure for environmental stewardship; it depends critically on their *traditionalism*. This traditionalism sets Berry apart from both his Populist forebears and most of his environmentalist allies.

Berry contends that tradition is critical to stewardship in three respects. First, traditional communities create the right context for generating and maintaining the knowledge necessary for sustainable agriculture. Good farming, Berry insists (and he speaks from personal experience), is *hard*. It requires intimate knowledge of the land. Because local conditions vary dramatically, what works one place may be disastrous someplace else. A small, family-operated farm generates among the farmers the familiarity needed to work that *particular* piece of land properly.[31] This may take more than one generation; intergenerational continuity is important. Families have longer memories than individuals. "A family that has farmed land through two or three generations will possess not just the land but a remembered history of its own mistakes and of the remedies of those mistakes." Over the course of generations, both "knowledge and affection accumulate, and, in the long term, knowledge and affection pay."[32] Eventually, if the community remains stable, this local knowledge is preserved and passed on in its traditions, so that local culture becomes a resource. In Berry's words, "Culture preserves the map and the records of past journeys so that no generation will permanently destroy the route." Thus, "the more local and settled the culture, the better it stays put, the less the damage."[33]

Good traditions, then, are a kind of encyclopedia of agricultural information, a way to preserve workable agricultural methods—and such an encyclopedia is clearly essential if farmers are to deal effectively with the informational demands of enlightened stewardship. But beyond that, tradition helps to maintain long-term perspectives, to provide reasons for doing things of no immediate benefit. "The model figure of [sustainable] agriculture," Berry suggests, "is an old man planting a young tree that will live longer than a man, and that he himself may not live to see in its first bearing."[34] Such behavior may be economically irrational from an individual standpoint, but it is critical to long-term human survival. Only a traditional society, he argues, provides the context, the values and perspectives, in which such behavior makes sense to the individual.

This is an appealing argument for defenders of small farms, but unfortunately it threatens to undermine Berry's critique of corporate agriculture. Corporations, after all, wouldn't necessarily suffer from the information gap or short-term perspectives that trouble individual farmers. Corporations may lack a "sense of place," but they are probably better than families or communities at creating institutional memories; they would have the resources to amass and preserve the necessary local knowledge for good farming and to create long-term plans. Corporations are after all immortal, and aren't data banks in the end more reliable than family traditions?

Perhaps—but the critical point for Berry is that data banks also are inevitably unreliable. Insisting on the limits of human knowledge, he argues that we can't be certain that we know everything necessary to make the environmentally correct decisions.[35] Therefore, we need not only information, but people who know how to make decisions in the absence of information and certainty. And traditional societies, he claims, have an advantage in creating that sort of person, in shaping the right kind of *character*. Tradition is what ultimately produces good farmers. Good farming "grows not only out of factual knowledge but out of cultural tradition . . . and it requires not merely a competent knowledge of its facts and processes, but also a complex set of attitudes, a certain culturally evolved stance, in the face of the unexpected and the unknown."[36] Noting the stubborn conservatism of traditional societies (like those Peruvians who won't grow marketable potatoes), Berry hopes that tradition can help reign in the destructive energies that have been released by industrial capitalism, creating people who won't respond to the short-term economic incentives to engage in harmful agricultural practices. A society composed of stable, traditional agricultural communities, he believes, would generate the appropriate knowledge, create the proper incentives, and shape the kind of character necessary to sustainable agriculture.

In theory, at least. Berry is always quick to acknowledge that family farming can't guarantee good farming. Not all traditional societies achieve ideal farming techniques, and America itself has what might be called a tradition of small, family farms practicing abysmally bad agriculture—a practice that continues to this day.[37] But to answer Berry's argument simply by pointing to the poor stewardship of America's small farmers misses the point. Berry argues that the structure of incentives that has shaped American agriculture virtually guaranteed that even family farmers would be unable to be good stewards: Farmers were "never, in America, sufficiently thrifty or sufficiently careful of soil fertility." "It is tempting to suppose," he adds, "that, given certain critical historical and cultural differences, they might have developed sufficient thrift and care. As it happened, however, the development went in the opposite direction."[38] Market pressures and cheap, abundant land prevented the right kind of communities and traditions from taking root in America. Commercial agriculture creates precisely the wrong incentives—to increase profits by producing more (using chemical fertilizers and pesticides, and relying on machines so that one can farm more land). The availability of land has allowed farmers to mine the topsoil and move on when the soil is exhausted. Thus even his native Henry County, he acknowledges, "was not a perfect society. Its people had often been violent and wasteful in their use of the land and of each other." Nevertheless, "there were also good qualities indigenous to [its agricultural economy] that might have been cultivated and built upon." Instead, just as the frontier was closing and land becoming scarce, we turned to fossil fuels and adopted policies designed to move farmers off the land—missing our best opportunity to develop a truly sustainable agriculture.[39]

So Berry's turn to tradition is directed in large part against the influence of market forces in shaping the character and practices of American farmers. He does not share in the celebration of free enterprise characteristic of many early agrarians. For them, the market, when protected from monopolies and the concentration of capital, was an arena for the free play of creative intelligence; it was the place where economic liberty was realized and economic virtues rewarded. Berry's social theory echoes a darker—or perhaps simply more aristocratic—strain of agrarianism, a suspicion of the values represented and rewarded by markets. The free enterprise system, he insists, is *not* synonymous with personal liberty.[40] On the contrary, beneath Berry's endorsement of tradition lies the fear that the market subjects farmers to an almost irresistible—and so far unresisted—temptation to exploit the land. It privileges short-term financial incentives over any other value, even a long-term economic interest in environmental integrity. The market is both insidious and pervasive. So Berry would marshal against it every possible incentive—not only affection, aesthetic pleasure, and long-term interest, but tradition, community pressure, and even perhaps government regulation.

Berry's call for family farming is aimed at changing this whole structure of incentives and practices, to make stewardship at least minimally profitable, but also to minimize the profit motive in farming generally—to make farming less like a mere business and more like a calling.[41] Thus his point is not that family farms necessarily practice good stewardship, but that without such farms and farming communities, good agriculture is probably impossible. "Most people who move from place to place every few years will never learn to care well for any place, nor will most people who are long alienated from all responsibility for usable property." "A people as a whole can learn good care," he insists, "only by long experience of living and working, learning and remembering, in the same places generation after generation, experiencing and correcting the results of bad care, and enjoying the benefits of good care."[42]

In short, Berry is not defending family farming as it is currently practiced in the United States, but a vision of a kind of community that was never fully realized here, except in a few insular communities such as the Amish. The key feature of this ideal community is its traditionalism, its focus on maintaining a set of practices inherited from the past and passed on to future generations. It is this traditionalism that most sharply distinguishes Berry's ideal from the actual state of American agrarian communities, and his philosophy from that of earlier democratic agrarians. It's tempting, in fact, to see him as one of the new breed of communitarians who want to defend the value of community against the rampant liberal individualism of American society.[43] One might even suspect that an organic conception of community lies behind his endorsement of tradition and the importance of cultural controls. But Berry's reliance on tradition is somewhat idiosyncratic, and needs to be carefully delineated.

For example, he doesn't seem to consider traditionalism to be inconsistent with libertarianism. On the contrary, he relies on tradition and custom as forms of social control in order to *reduce* the need for government regulation and control. Like many conservatives, Berry hopes that strong behavioral controls at the community level will increase our sense of individual freedom by decreasing the intrusion of federal (and presumably state) bureaucracies in everyday life.[44] Tradition, under this reasoning, should be conducive to liberty. Of course, critics would point out that communal forms of social control—noninstitutionalized censure and coercion—can be a more serious threat to individual liberty than the publicly legitimated, institutionalized procedures of the state; indeed, Berry's beloved Amish have been well and thoroughly criticized on precisely those grounds.[45] Berry doesn't address this problem directly, but it's important to recognize that he is not an anarchist. While he is suspicious of central government, he doesn't object to the state per se. Rather, his defense of tradition is closer to the civic republican argument that free, constitutional government depends on civic virtues, including self-restraint. He simply emphasizes the role of tradition and vital local communities as opposed to laws and institutions in cultivating such virtues.

A more perplexing aspect of his traditionalism is his persistent *criticism* of America's traditions. For an advocate of tradition, Berry is quite free in his selection, rejection, and reformulation of his own political and intellectual traditions. Of course, one can advocate tradition in general without endorsing particular traditions. But how do we maintain both a traditional society and a critical stance toward particular traditions? For this is what Berry intends: "Tradition too," he insists, "must be used with care." Our traditions "obviously involve errors and mistakes, damages and tragedies. . . . [Tradition] is properly subject to critical intelligence and is just as properly subject to helps and influences from other traditions."[46] What kind of traditionalism is it that subjects traditions to critical intelligence, borrowing where it pleases, rejecting what it doesn't like?

Perhaps we should first ask what Berry means by "tradition." Despite its centrality to his social theory (or maybe because of it), he doesn't give a precise definition. Instead I suggest we turn to Eric Hobsbawm, who offers a useful typology, identifying three concepts often conflated in the term. A "tradition," for Hobsbawm, is

> a set of practices, normally governed by overtly or tacitly accepted rules and of a ritual or symbolic nature, which seek to inculcate certain values and norms of behavior by repetition, which automatically implies continuity with the past.

Tradition is characterized by invariance and formalization. "Custom," in contrast, is both "motor and flywheel" of traditional societies:

It does not preclude innovation and change up to a point, though . . . the requirement that it must appear compatible or even identical with precedent imposes substantial limitations on it. What it does is to give any desired change . . . the sanction of precedent, social continuity and natural law as expressed in history.

Finally, Hobsbawm distinguishes "convention," which has no symbolic or ritual significance, but is justified purely pragmatically:

It is evident that any social practice that needs to be carried out repeatedly will tend, for convenience and efficiency, to develop a set of such conventions and routines, which may be de facto or de jure formalized for the purposes of imparting the practice to new practitioners.

Hobsbawm suggests that convention and tradition are inversely related; where a pragmatic justification for a practice exists, it loses its symbolic and ritual power. Thus the discovery of pragmatic reasons for a tradition (like a hygienic justification for the Jewish prohibition on eating pork) indicates a loss of tradition.[47]

Berry's analysis, however, suggests that Hobsbawm has misunderstood the relationships among these meanings of "tradition." What Berry likes in traditional societies is their conventionalism—convention is what "can be bequeathed and inherited, . . . it can be taught, not as an instance (a relic), but as a way *still usable*."[48] But, as Berry recognizes, the pragmatic justifications for conventions don't necessarily reduce their symbolic power. The symbolic and pragmatic meaning of the practice may well be intertwined—just as custom (the changing substance of a set of rules) and tradition (the formal adherence to precedent that gives custom its authority) are typically intertwined. In other words, the "because" behind the farmer's actions is a complex, often unarticulated combination of pragmatic (because it works) and ideological (because this is the way we do it) justifications. Indeed, Berry's account of the Papago's decline suggests that agricultural practices *must* work in both senses: They must produce food reliably and also support the social and cultural cohesion necessary to maintain a group of individuals as a community.

Indeed, a practice that had a pragmatic justification but violated fundamental cultural understandings probably wouldn't take hold; consider the difficulty of persuading caretakers to use cost-benefit analysis to decide whether to continue caring for a terminal patient. Similarly, the fact that a practice has a pragmatic justification may be integral to its symbolic function;

it may represent an ideological commitment to rationality and efficiency. Indeed, if a convention is to have the powerful influence on individual behavior that Berry is counting on, it may have to be supported by both pragmatic and ideological justifications.

But it must also, paradoxically, be flexible, in the way custom is flexible—adapting an inherited body of rules or norms to ever-changing situations. "Things are obviously wrong with the past," Berry acknowledges; so the past must "be judged and corrected," and "the work of judgment and correction is endless."[49] This demand that we constantly evaluate and modify traditional practices raises doubts about whether what Berry is advocating is really traditionalism at all. After all, we usually encounter traditionalism in the context of attacks on what Michael Oakeshott dubs "Rationalism": the conviction that tradition, along with custom, prejudice, authority, and habit, must be subjected to critical evaluation and, if they fail the test, summarily rejected.[50] It was rationalism that Burke, for example, thought the most dangerous part of French revolutionary doctrine. A government whose authority was based solely on the rationality of it laws, he insisted, would ultimately have to rely on terror to secure obedience. "On the scheme of this barbarous philosophy," he warns, "laws are to be supported only by their own terrors, and by the concern, which each individual may find in them, from his own private speculations, or can spare to them from his own private interests."[51] In contrast, a government whose authority was traditional could forego raw force and win the deference of the masses through habit and custom, and "all the pleasing illusions, which made power gentle, and obedience liberal."[52]

Burke thus endorses what Hobsbawm has in mind by "tradition"—a set of rituals designed to inculcate values and norms (in this case, to legitimize authority). But the conservative defense of tradition isn't entirely antirational. Burke also suggests that tradition could be an aid to *collective* rationality: "We are afraid to put men to live and trade each on his own private stock of reason; because we suspect that this stock in each man is small, and that the individuals would do better to avail themselves of the general bank and capital of nations and of ages." Rather than "exploding general prejudices," he counsels us

> to discover the latent wisdom which prevails in them . . . because prejudice, with its reason, has a motive to give action to that reason, and an affection which will give it permanence. Prejudice is of ready application in the emergency; it previously engages the mind in a steady course

of wisdom and virtue, and does not leave the man hesitating in the moment of decision.[53]

This argument works, of course, only if the prejudices in question contain "latent wisdom"; Burke doesn't justify his assumption that most prejudices do. But it was a common view among Burke's intellectual predecessors, such as Sir Edward Coke, that customs "have been by the wisdom of the most excellent men, in many succession of ages, by long and continual experience, (the trial of light and truth) fined and refined."[54] In other words, a sort of natural selection is at work, so that thoroughly irrational habits die out—or are weeded out by "excellent men." Berry's defense of tradition seems to rest in part on the same logic. True, one reason he likes traditional societies is that respecting tradition makes it more likely that projects begun by one generation are likely to be completed by future generations. A rational person is more likely to plant a tree in a society where patterns of settlement and land use don't change much from one generation to the next. Traditional societies thus cultivate in their members a long view, which also encourages ecologically sound behavior. But his other, more Burkean rationale for traditionalism is that traditional (which for him implies long-standing)[55] practices, whatever their defects, at least *work;* in the context of agriculture, this means they are sustainable. Sustainability isn't the only criterion against which we want to evaluate social practices, of course, but it is necessarily an essential feature of an ecologically sound agriculture.

But herein lies the difficulty: Clearly the Burkean defense of tradition is actually defending custom, that protean creature whose virtue is precisely that it is always *changing,* adapting itself to new conditions. Berry's defense of tradition thus seems to assume that traditional practices are long-standing and therefore must be sustainable, but also that they are always changing and adapting to new conditions. This is a familiar problem with the defense of custom, and the usual response is that an institution composed of customary practices (like the classic example, the common law) may remain the same in its general form even as minute changes and adjustments are occurring. What is sustainable, then, is not the specific set of practices but the broad characteristics of the agriculture as a whole and the basic principles by which it undergoes change. The fact remains, however, that these minute changes may result, over the centuries, in something that looks quite different from the original custom. The Peruvian and Papago agriculture Berry calls "traditional" may in fact have been of recent origin, and for all we know they may not be sustainable at all.

Nevertheless, there is certainly some sense in which the Peruvian and Papago cultures are properly considered more traditional than modern Western cultures. Surely the greater authority of tradition and custom in such societies encourages a cautious, conservative approach to change, which in turn is likely to result in an agriculture composed of relatively long-standing practices. The key point for our purposes is that such traditionalism does not require the members of the society to view specific traditions uncritically. On the contrary, Berry assumes that a critical intelligence will investigate and approve the reasons for supporting good traditions.

For example, the Peruvian potato farmers Berry approves of practice "an agriculture of extraordinary craftsmanship and ecological intelligence." But they have difficulty explaining their methods and reasons to outsiders, because the methods "were worked out over a long time, long ago; learned so well, one might say, that they are forgotten." This much sounds like Burke; Berry even suggests that the only kind of culture that works is

> thought sufficiently complex, but submerged or embodied in traditional acts. It is at least as unconscious as it is conscious—and so is available to all levels of intelligence. Two people, one highly intelligent, the other unintelligent, will work fields on the same slope, and both will farm well, keeping the ways that keep the land.[56]

The virtue of traditionalism is that the farmers don't have to understand thoroughly the reasons for farming as they do (it's enough that "this is the way we do things"), which is why the unintelligent can farm as well as the intelligent. But it's important to Berry that the intelligent, if they investigate, will discover that there *are* reasons for doing so. In fact, Berry speculates that the traditional culture, far from being intellectually moribund, was one "astir with profound originations" and that "works of genius were accomplished in the development of cropping systems and systems of soil conservation, in plant and animal domestication and selection, in the invention and refinement of tools."[57] Collective rationality depends on individual rationality, on creativity and experimentation. Good traditions don't develop simply through random mutation; someone has to have a good idea first. Berry even worries that the disintegration of traditionalism *hampers* such creativity by depriving people of the cultural intelligence embodied in traditions. "With us," he worries, "it grows harder and harder even for intelligent people to behave intelligently, and the unintelligent are condemned to a stupidity probably unknown in traditional cultures."[58]

So Berry's traditionalism isn't antirational or elitist; it includes critical evaluation and adaptation, and the source of innovations isn't a ruling class or intellectual elite, but those actually working the land. But he does share with conservative social theorists (and most modern liberal theorists) a reluctance to rely on *individual* rationality as the primary means of social control. As Burke pointed out, consistently rational behavior is in large part a matter of habit. Just as a rational person cultivates habits like wearing a seat belt, a rational society cultivates traditions like respecting freedom of speech—in both cases, the habit serves to guard against inattention, emotionality, stupidity, and other potentially fatal failures of reason. Tradition in this way can be an aid to rationality, rather than an alternative. Similarly, tradition can correct the pathologies of individual rationality. We have a wealth of theoretical literature explaining why even reliable and habitual individual rationality doesn't always lead to socially beneficial behavior. The prisoner's dilemma, the problems of collective action, the externalization of costs—environmentalists have argued for years that these can lead a group of rational individuals to ecological disaster. As Burke implied, the usual liberal solution to such problems is government regulation, backed ultimately by the threat of government coercion. Berry, in contrast, shares with Burke the hope that tradition and custom will serve as an effective alternative to government coercion as a means of ensuring collective rationality.

In short, for Berry, tradition and reason are mutually supportive; critical, creative rationality is the source of good traditions and justifications for maintaining them, while tradition serves to cultivate good habits and encourage collective rationality where individual calculations of costs and benefits would lead to the tragedy of the commons. Thus neither the value of tradition nor its authority rests on its being accepted uncritically by the masses. Nor does maintaining traditions mean simply resisting change. Rather, Berry's is a creative, participatory traditionalism, in which each generation develops and enriches the traditions they inherit. It's similar, in fact, to Ronald Dworkin's idea of a chain novel (his model for the development of common law), in which each succeeding writer attempts to stay faithful to what was written before but also to develop creatively the possibilities implicit in the received text.[59]

Berry's own engagement with the agrarian tradition illustrates the critical and creative stance that he is advocating. Consider, for example, his treatment of slavery and racism, explored in *The Hidden Wound*. The essay is a critical evaluation of the legacy of slavery and racism in his own community and family (which once owned slaves). Berry presents slavery as part of America's history of bad agricultural practices that we rightly rejected. The question, then, is how does he decide which practices to embrace and which ones to reject? One might expect a traditionalist to deal with this problem by offering an interpretation of American history in which racism figures as a deviation, a mistake that was fundamentally inconsistent with the basic principles and general trends of the political culture. Interestingly, Berry doesn't take this fundamentalist approach, which would require a constant return to those problematic "basic principles."[60] His interpretation of American history consistently recognizes the presence of different, often conflicting, trends and impulses. The content and direction of American political development isn't determined; each generation has to pick and choose from this inheritance according to some external standard of rightness.

Berry instead tries to support his intuitions about the wrongfulness of racism, first, by what amounts to an appeal to natural right or an innate moral sense. Reaching back to his childhood memories, he describes the free and open relationship he enjoyed with black servants on his grandparents' farm before he learned the social conventions that would make such relationships impossible later in life.[61] It's a familiar strategy, demonstrating the conventionality of conventions by reminding us that they must be learned. His appreciative and loving relationship with Nick and Aunt Georgie demonstrates that racism isn't natural but acquired. The implication is that the natural innocence of childhood can serve as a source of critical standards for evaluating our traditions. "To me," he says, "the great power that children possess is candor; they see the world clear eyed, without prejudice."[62] This appeal to an innate moral sense is problematic, however. Surely the fact that children aren't born racists doesn't in itself prove that racism is wrong. Children have to be taught not to steal and lie as well. Morality (Berry himself usually insists on this point) is conventional, not natural.

Berry offers another critique of slavery and racism, however, that fits more consistently with his social theory. Echoing arguments that have been in play since Tocqueville, he contends that slavery had a corrosive impact on American culture and agriculture by degrading manual labor and separating it from ownership:

As the white man has withheld from the black man the positions of responsibility toward the land, and consequently the sense of a legally permanent relationship to it, so he has assigned to him as his proper role the labor, the thousands of menial small acts by which the land is maintained, and by which men develop a closeness to the land and the wisdom of that closeness.[63]

Racism, or any social hierarchy, is problematic to the extent it insulates the elites from labor, and thus contributes to the separation of ownership and management endemic in our rootless, unsettled nation. Domestic settlement requires that we work where we live, that we interact with the physical environment directly. Measured against this standard of sustainability and ecological rationality, slavery and racial hierarchy fail the test. Like corporate farming, they alienate us from the land.

The Hidden Wound suggests that Berry's creative traditionalism allows for some pruning; bad traditions must be abandoned as we go. But it also demonstrates the care and thoughtfulness that should go into the decision to reject a tradition. The application of critical intelligence should increase the possibilities for future development, and a society with a long and rich set of traditions has greater creative potential than a society that has lost or rejected such traditions. This point helps to make sense of Berry's resistance to ecocentrism. As discussed in chapter 3, he worries that ecocentric critiques not only oversimplify the rich intellectual heritage of the West but also blindly reject much that is valuable in that heritage. Ecocentric philosophers, of course, would respond that their analyses are precisely the kind of critical engagement with tradition that Berry advocates.[64] This debate about what parts of our heritage need pruning, however, simply underscores the fact that this sort of creative traditionalism is a collective task of cultural maintenance rather than an individual duty of cultural rebellion. According to Berry, arguments about the value of specific traditions are precisely the sort of debates we should be having.

With all the qualifications in place, then, Berry's traditionalism turns out to be pretty relaxed—less a rigid set of social controls than a general orientation toward the past and preference for stability over change. But that merely begs the question: Can tradition (especially in a community governed by a critical, innovative traditionalism) serve as an effective source of social control? It's long been a complaint of progressives that tradition *is* a powerful influence on individual behavior, inhibiting even short-term, self-interested behavior. Peasants, for example, are famous for their resistance to innovation and market pressures. Tradition, however, seldom works alone. Berry wants to endorse tradition primarily as an *alternative* to government regulation. But surely the rulers have an important role to play in maintaining traditions as well. Just as tradition and reason may be mutually supportive, tradition and government coercion may be (indeed, usually are) complementary. Government coercion may be particularly important to Berry's project of creating an ecologically rational society, since it involves significant changes in mass behavior.

Certainly the right traditions won't develop simply by encouraging family farming through persuasive essays, however eloquent. Although good farmland is no longer cheap and abundant in the United States, it's still economically feasible to mine the land, sell it, and move one's capital into other enterprises. And the incentives created by our system of commercial agriculture still encourage unsustainable practices.[65] Berry tends to elide this point, but the agricultural system he envisions—small farmers producing primarily for controlled, local markets—would require a good deal of government regulation to prevent competitive pressures from forcing farmers into bad practices. Both market regulation and strict controls on land use—perhaps even on land alienation—would be necessary to create and support the kind of communities he wants.[66] Eventually some of these regulations may become unnecessary, as unsustainable practices become unthinkable. But the government coercion will probably have to come first, just as slavery had to be explicitly outlawed before it became archaic.

Reliance on government to make government unnecessary isn't inconsistent with the agrarian tradition, of course. Despite their distrust of politics and government, agrarians have more often advocated than resisted government regulation. But in Berry's case, the need for government regulation threatens to undermine his argument in key respects. If softening market pressures and creating counterincentives aren't sufficient to lead small farmers to ecologically sound practices, then we may in fact do better (ecologically, if not culturally) to abandon family farming altogether and encourage the development of a small number of large, vertically integrated agricultural corporations. Corporations, after all, may be more easily regulated than millions of small farmers, being both fewer in number and (by virtue of that despised short-term economic rationality) more responsive to regulatory tools like tax breaks and fines.

Admittedly, our experiences with regulating large corporations hardly justify that conclusion. Large corporations have the resources to fight regulation and the incentives to seek short-term gains rather than pursuing long-term strategies; their political and economic power remains a profound challenge to effective regulation. And Berry is undoubtedly right to worry that the concentration of capital and separation of ownership and management create obstacles to changing our farming practices. But they also create opportunities that shouldn't be overlooked. That Berry does overlook them reflects both his libertarian and his Populist heritages. His ideal, in which cultural controls take the place of government regulation and the primary agricultural producers are independent family farmers, may appeal less because of its logic and more because it plays to deep-rooted (and for environmentalists deeply problematic) American biases against big business and big government.

Berry's vision doesn't appeal to everyone, however. I want to conclude this chapter by examining an important source of resistance to Berry's traditionalism: the worry that (as Susan Okin put it) "reliance on tradition simply cannot be sustained in the face of feminist challenges."[67] Feminists are justifiably suspicious of tradition. Patriarchy, after all, is one of the most enduring traditions in human history. Berry's traditionalism does allow for critical evaluation and rejection of particular traditions, but feminists have ample reason to suspect that such critical evaluation, in an agrarian society, will stop short of a full-scale critique of patriarchy. Agrarian societies, many have charged, are based on the patrimonial ideal—the desire to pass the farm down from father to son. This desire for intergenerational continuity is what creates the long-term perspective, the incentive to stewardship, that Berry is counting on to inhibit ecologically destructive practices. And this ideal, they contend, fosters and feeds on the oppression of women.

Specifically, some feminists charge that the social and ideological pressure to maintain family solidarity in order to achieve intergenerational continuity has prevented women from taking steps to protect themselves from abusive husbands and fathers. They have been trained, pressured, and coerced into subordinating their individual desires and interests to the good of the family enterprise. The result is a situation in which women are particularly vulnerable to abuse and exploitation.[68] Studies from the 1920s on suggest that farm life is more lonesome and less rewarding for women than for men—that they have less control over their labor and fewer economic opportunities, and that the demands of traditional agriculture are simply physically overwhelming.[69]

The reality of agrarian life is actually more complex than this picture suggests, though. Many women find farming fulfilling and describe themselves as equal partners in the family enterprise. They object to being characterized as victims; on the contrary, as Sarah Elbert puts it, "women in agriculture have not been self-sacrificing so much as they have been self-actualizing through the sense of 'us' and 'ours' that characterizes family farms."[70] But the fact that not all women are exploited doesn't diminish the force of the feminist complaint. The conventional formulation of the patrimonial ideal does seem to render those subject to it more vulnerable than women in families with more individualistic values.[71] Berry's understanding of the patrimonial ideal, however, is far from conventional. His treatment of this subject is worth close examination because it touches on a theme central to his ecological and social ethics—the limited and problematic nature of any sort of human control of biological forces.

What exactly is the status of the patrimonial ideal in Berry's agrarian society? He undoubtedly recognizes it as an important part of agrarian life, a desire that animates many of the farmers he lives among and describes in his novels. But, significantly, few of the characters in his novels actually succeed in passing their farms down to their (biological) children. One might see in that failure a critique of the socioeconomic system that disrupts rural families. But in fact for Berry it seems to stem, not from economic or social dislocation, but from a more basic problem: the failure of sentiment to follow biology. It stems, in fact, from the problematic nature of the biological notion of family.

Consider Jack Beechum, the patriarch of Berry's fictional farming community[72]—patriarch only in a symbolic sense, however. He has no sons and his daughter is uninterested in farming. Jack's true heir is his tenant, Elton Penn, who lives on and wants to keep the farm. Caught between the obligations of paternity and his desire to leave the farm to someone who wants it, Jack devises a complicated legal strategy that leaves Elton with the farm, but deeply in debt. A second would-be patriarch, Jarratt Coulter, manages to alienate both of his sons in his quest for domination and control—hardly an endorsement of patriarchy. His brother, Burley (a much freer spirit), ends up serving as a surrogate father to the younger son, Nathan. But the patrimonial ideal complicates this relationship as well. Burley decides late in life to acknowledge his illegitimate son, so he leaves the boy his half of the Coulter family farm—thus dividing Nathan's expected inheritance and forcing him into partnership with his cousin. Then there is Mat Feltner, a better candidate for patriarch than either Jack or Jarratt. But his only son is killed in World War II, so he must work out a paternal relationship with his daughter-in-law and her second husband. This arrangement seems to work; Berry even implies that such makeshift families are *preferable* to biological ones. In his stories, neither sentiment, sympathy, nor property follow biology. The best fathers, as well as the best sons, turn out to be the ones that are chosen rather than merely inherited.

The persistent failure of patrimony follows logically from Berry's view of marriage and family as conventional (rather than natural) forms invented to impose order on biology. This disciplining of biology is necessary; humans (by virtue of their extraordinary power) need cultural constraints to achieve a way of life that isn't destructive of their natural or social worlds. Thus the institutions of marriage and family serve "to reduce the volatility and the danger of sex—to preserve its energy, its beauty, and its pleasure."[73] Nevertheless, they frequently fail, or at least succeed only partially. That's to be expected; nature—and this point is the heart of his environmental ethic—resists domination and ordering.

Berry elaborates the point by arguing that attempts to breed better domestic animals can succeed only up to a point; improvements in size and productivity eventually result in the loss of health, vigor, or reproductive ability. "Humans," he concludes, "are intelligent enough to select for a type of creature; they are not intelligent enough to *make* a creature." Domestic animals must retain some of their wild characteristics, or they become useless. And efforts to make an "entirely domesticated human" are equally doomed to failure:

> The effort to make plants, animals, and humans ever more governable by human intentions is continuing with more determination and more violence than ever, but that does not mean that it is nearer to success. It means only that we are increasing the violence and magnitude of the expectable reactions.[74]

We must create social forms to domesticate our biological natures—the concept of stewardship implies this—but we must also allow for wildness, for the tendency of biological energies to escape these social forms and go their own, unpredictable way. Domesticity, in animals, communities, or the landscape itself, must be complemented by margins of wilderness—places, people, and relationships undisciplined by conventional social forms.[75]

Clearly this libertarian notion greatly qualifies Berry's endorsement of tradition and community. Any too-stringent form of social control (including, presumably, customary forms that undergird organic conceptions of community) is doomed to end not only in failure but in violence and disorder. Thus it would be hubris to assume we could *make* the world conform to our neat plans of familial inheritance. The patrimonial ideal is, for Berry, simply another example of Americans' desire to master the world. Although he recognizes the hold it has on the imaginations of his farmers, and even counts on it as a motivation to take care of the land, in the end it's clear that the *biological* ideal of patrimony won't work. The land should be left to the person who will best take care of it, who can establish a meaningful and productive relationship with it—a criterion that, because it is based on ability, is properly gender neutral. Stewardship, a role equally available to men and women, supersedes the patrimonial ideal. Biology isn't destiny; families and farms alike must be chosen before they can be inherited.

Under this reading, Berry's patrimonial ideal is less oppressive than its traditional formulation. The desire to leave the farm to one's children becomes simply the desire to leave the farm to someone who will love and care for it, someone with whom you have been able to achieve a parental relationship based on a common love for the land. It isn't necessary to keep the farm in the biological family, or even to keep the biological family intact, to achieve this sort of intergenerational continuity (which is not to say that marriages and families can be simply dispensed with; conventional forms are valuable, just not perfect). So while feminists may have other reservations concerning Berry's agrarianism (some of which I'll discuss in chapter 6), his version of the patrimonial ideal shouldn't be problematic. It could, in fact, help to empower farm women by supporting their right to ownership and control of the land they help to care for.

In fact, the most problematic part of Berry's social theory isn't his reliance on tradition, but his contention that a community of small family farmers, by virtue of their knowledge, affections, and interests, would take care of the land better than a progressive partnership between corporations and government. Such communities have achieved sustainable agriculture in the Sonoran Desert, the Peruvian Andes, China, and even northern Europe. Berry's analysis of why such communities work may be a useful corrective to the tendency of Americans to discount the value of such forms of agriculture. But his insistence that this is the *only* way to achieve sustainability is less compelling. Berry underestimates the flexibility, adaptability, and practicality of corporate and public administration; the corporate form, for example, has proven a useful device for family farmers, and federal programs can help empower local initiatives to protect the environment and reign in powerful corporations. Clearly, there are a host of complexities here that Berry fails to recognize. His contrast between American society and the ideal society of small family farmers raises more questions than it answers about the respective roles of government, business, and local custom in an ecologically rational society.

But there is another way to make sense of Berry's argument: Even if the small farmers in the agrarian society he envisions wouldn't necessarily be good stewards, the point remains that good stewards would act like the farmers he envisions. In other words, he is not just providing a practical blueprint for an ecologically sound agriculture but a model of stewardship that could inform action even in our contemporary, ecologically unsound society. Berry himself, recognizing that not everyone can be a farmer, nevertheless recommends that we all keep some sort of garden, in order to learn the art of stewardship.[76] The ideal of stewardship, then, is not only a goal of social policy but a moral principle that can infuse our everyday activities with ethical content, thus giving shape to a more meaningful, more fully human life. This moral argument constitutes Berry's most extensive revision of democratic agrarianism.

Before turning to that argument, however, we must address a final reservation about Berry's social theory: For all his insistence on the practical necessity of reforming our agricultural practices, it's still tempting to dismiss his envisioned alternative as hopelessly unrealistic. Isn't he asking us to turn back the clock, to halt the ineluctable forces of technological and economic progress? In short, isn't Berry's agrarianism in the end mere utopianism?

Chapter Five

A Place on Earth?

Berry's novel *Remembering* ends with a utopian vision. Andy Catlett, having lost his hand in a farm accident, returns home to Port William after a journey of healing and self-discovery. Port William is the same as it was when he left, but Andy has changed: He is now able to envision another Port William, "corrected and clarified." In his vision, the fields and town are

> as he never saw or dreamed them, the signs everywhere upon them of the care of a longer love than any who have lived there have ever imagined. The houses are clean and white, and great trees stand among them and spread over them. The fields lie around the town, divided by rows of such trees as stand in the town and in the woods, each field more beautiful than all the rest. . . . And in the fields and the town, walking, standing, or sitting under the trees, resting and talking together in the peace of a sabbath profound and bright, are people of such beauty that he weeps to see them. He sees that these are the membership of one another and of the place and of the song or light in which they live and move.[1]

Such passages make it tempting to dismiss Berry's agrarianism as nostalgic or utopian, lamenting a way of life that never existed or envisioning one that never could. That view is reinforced by the fact that most of his novels are set in an imagined past, recounting the history of the fictional farming community of Port William. In them, Berry describes and honors a way of life that is rapidly disappearing: the life of a small farmer in a predominately rural, agricultural community. So it's understandable that critics would charge Berry with wanting to escape from the realities of modern life, to "turn back the clock." Nevertheless, I would argue that such charges are misguided. Berry's fiction is not mere nostalgia; it is an attempt to persuade us of the *practicality* of his program for reform.

To explain that (admittedly) counterintuitive claim, I must turn from the substance of Berry's arguments to his method of justification—that is, what sort of reasons he gives us to embrace his ecological agrarianism and how he hopes to make those reasons persuasive. As outlined in the previous chapters, many of Berry's reasons refer to the consequences of reform: he claims that an agrarian society would better preserve the fragile planet—a claim that can be adequately supported or refuted with scientific and sociological arguments. But, as I suggested in chapter 3, Berry is not merely concerned with preserving the ecosystem; what he wants to preserve is the possibility of a certain kind of human existence. Thus he also offers a nonconsequentialist argument for his agrarian society: Self-restraint in the use of resources isn't just a practical necessity; knowledge of our limits and how to live within them is "the most comely and graceful knowledge that we have."[2] His agrarian society is desirable, he contends, simply because it realizes an ideal human life, because it exhibits certain virtues that are admirable in their own right. Obviously, this claim isn't amenable to scientific investigation; on the contrary, it seems to put us back in the mire of moral relativism. Surely there are many visions of the good life. Why should we embrace Berry's? How is Berry's conception of virtue and the good life better justified than anyone else's?

My purpose in this chapter is to explain how the allegedly utopian or nostalgic aspects of Berry's work—particularly his novels and stories— address that problem of justification. Berry's fiction, I contend, attempts to win converts to his vision of the good life by demonstrating its *relative* value. Under this reading, he is claiming not that his is the only philosophically justifiable conception of the good life but merely that it is considerably better than the vision currently dominating American society. To support that claim, he describes a world (the fictional world of Port William) in which people do embrace his values, and asks us to consider whether it isn't better than the one we currently live in—not a utopia, to be sure, but more sustainable, more fulfilling, and more fully human. Thus his novels are not an escape from the realities of modern life. Rather, they suggest an *alternative* to those realities. They offer a vision of a life more rewarding, and in some ways more practical, than the one we are currently living.

Berry's aim is not simply to sharpen our critical faculties but to educate our moral imaginations—to suggest a richer conception of the good life toward which we might strive and the virtues that would help us to achieve it. The following chapters will explore that moral vision; here I want to focus on the methodological problem—the problem of justification—raised by his project. Berry's form of moral reasoning belongs to a branch of philosophy known as virtue ethics, so called because it asks not only which actions are justified but what sort of persons we should strive to be, what virtues we should seek to cultivate. Berry is one of a growing number of environmentalists who find virtue ethics attractive.[3] Unfortunately, reliance on this sort of reasoning creates a number of difficulties for green theorists—including, most prominently, the problem of moral relativism.

Berry's interest in the virtues, perhaps coincidentally, parallels a general trend in moral philosophy stemming from Elizabeth Anscombe's 1958 article, "Modern Moral Philosophy." Anscombe's article criticizes the notion of moral duty lying at the heart of the two dominant branches of moral philosophy, utilitarianism and deontology.[4] She points out that both branches approach ethics as a matter of fulfilling duties, utilitarians arguing that an action is justified when it contributes to the sum of human happiness and deontologists contending it is justified when it conforms to some general principle of right. Such a conception of ethics, she argues, captures only a very small part of our moral experience. Basic judgments in ethics are not typically about the rightness of particular actions but about character. In other words, we often evaluate actions by asking whether they exhibit certain virtues, not whether they fulfill certain obligations. Therefore, right action is not simply a matter of following rules; it is a matter of developing good character.

This shift in focus from duties to the good life and the character traits necessary for it has a number of consequences of interest to philosophers. But for our purposes, the most important is that instead of trying to divine some set of transcendent or fundamental principles from which to derive our moral duties, we should investigate how culture shapes our moral characters. Moral education, according to virtue ethicists, is a matter of imitating culturally defined moral exemplars rather than learning rules.[5] The good life (according to John Cottingham, for example) can be conceived as a structured pattern of living rooted in a civic culture in which "right pathways of emotion and action have been laid down in infancy and fostered by long habits of training and upbringing."[6] Virtue ethics thus foregrounds culture and its relationship to individual behavior—an issue that Berry, like many environmentalists, is centrally concerned with.

Nevertheless, the compatibility between virtue ethics and environmentalism is far from obvious. One difficulty is that, unlike deontological and utilitarian ethics, virtue ethics isn't aimed at formulating general rules. It therefore seems to give us little guidance in framing or justifying legislation. It's not clear, for example, how a virtue ethicist would evaluate a proposal to require automobile manufacturers to reduce emissions by 10 percent over the next five years. She could perhaps focus on what sort of virtues one would exhibit by voting for such legislation: rationality, prudence, justice, or selflessness, for example. But surely to decide whether voting for the legislation is just (or even rational, prudent, or selfless), we need to know whether the legislation is *itself* a just law—a question most easily addressed by deontological or utilitarian ethics. This problem may not concern Berry very much, of course, because he doesn't put much stock in government regulation as a way to control individual behavior. But, as pointed out in chapter 4, even if we would ultimately like to rely on tradition and socialization as our primary means of social control, we are unlikely to realize Berry's environmental agenda without extensive regulation. Duty ethics would thus seem more immediately relevant to environmentalism than virtue ethics.

On the other hand, virtue ethics has advantages for environmentalists as well. Most importantly, it gives them more purchase on the problem of motivation, one of the weaknesses of duty-centered ethics. Duty ethics usually require that actors be motivated primarily by a desire to be moral, to do the right thing.[7] But philosophers have questioned both the moral value and the efficacy of such motivation. To visit a sick friend out of a sense of duty, for example, may seem less praiseworthy than to visit her out of friendship.[8] And less reliable as well, perhaps—the requirement that we act out of duty defies our normal understanding of human psychology. Virtue ethicists argue that people typically want to do the right thing not because they want to perform their duties but because such behavior is consistent with their image of an ideal character. An individual, they might argue, recycles not because she feels an obligation to increase the sum of human happiness but because she has an image of proper behavior that includes recycling. Of course, this account of motivation may also be too simplistic. But if the virtue ethicists are even partly correct, then instead of developing more and better rules of behavior we should offer attractive models of environmental virtues, and think about how to reform our practices to promote those virtues.

The problem of how to motivate consistently good behavior helps to account for Berry's interest in virtue ethics. Although virtue ethics typically do not focus on the rightness of particular acts as duty ethics do, virtue ethicists are concerned with how to orient a person toward the good, to cultivate her desire to act virtuously. As argued in chapter 4, it is this problem of motivation that leads Berry to discount the value of laws and institutions and concentrate instead on fundamental cultural values and practices. Virtue ethicists teach that good character evolves out of good cultures, a principle entirely consistent with Berry's interest in reforming American culture generally.

Virtue ethics would thus seem to fit neatly into Berry's ecological agrarianism. Nevertheless, it does present some difficulties for environmentalists, who are already (as pointed out in chapter 3) vulnerable to charges of illiberalism. Virtue ethics, like some environmental ethics, has been criticized as elitist. As Michael Slote complains, virtue ethics not only seems to lack an account of social justice, it has "a proven record of siding with anti-democratic social/political ideals."[9] Modern virtue ethicists, he notes, tend to draw heavily on Aristotle and an idealized vision of the Greek city-state, eliding the incompatibility of classic Greek social norms (including slavery and subordination of women) with modern democratic values. Moreover, the rich contextualism of virtue ethics makes it attractive to communitarian critics of liberalism. Virtue ethics therefore seems to be aligned with a conservative political stance that favors ancient republics over modern liberal democracies.

But one can defend community without being elitist. In fact, Berry's endorsement of social equality derives directly from his communitarianism; social hierarchies, he fears, insulate people from community values and norms, and therefore defeat the purpose of encouraging strong communities in the first place. Virtue ethics may conflict with liberal individualism, of course, leading to calls for intrusive state action to promote virtue.[10] But it doesn't have to. Berry, as we have seen, is positively libertarian—maybe *too* libertarian—on the question of the government's role in controlling individual behavior. He endorses strong communities in order to *reduce* the need for government regulation. In short, despite his interest in the classical virtues, his vision for America is informed more by the Populists than by Pericles.

The most serious problem with virtue ethics, I suggest, is not its elitism. Rather, it is that virtue ethics raises in a particularly challenging way the issue of moral relativism. Virtue ethicists usually justify the virtues in terms of their essential role in the well-being of the agent; virtues are conceived as traits essential to human flourishing.[11] But, as Gary Watson explains, "Whether we are flourishing depends on who (what) we are by nature." And "such evaluational essentialism does not sit well with modern notions. Just as God is dead . . . so the concept of human nature has ceased to be normative."[12] If Berry's moral theory rests on a particular conception of human nature and the good life, those foundations would seem to be vulnerable to interminable value conflict. Moral relativists would contend that we can generate any number of plausible accounts of human nature. Why should we accept Berry's as correct, or normative? And if Berry is wrong about human nature doesn't his whole moral theory, and much of his case for social reform, collapse?

Clearly, Berry's project requires him to explain why the understanding of human nature underlying his virtue ethics is persuasive—or why his case for social and moral reform is persuasive even if one disagrees with his understanding of human nature. Berry's method of justification, however, is somewhat opaque. While he spends a great deal of time explaining what's wrong with our conventional values, his claims about what humans really are and how we should live are more asserted than argued. For example, he tells us that human nature includes "our animal nature" as well as our "cultural patterns and restraints that keep us from acting like animals." He further suggests that "the best human cultures" have a certain kind of unity; "their concerns and enterprises are not fragmented, scattered out, at variance or in contention with one another."[13] As we will see, these claims are integral to his general moral theory; many of his moral arguments seem to depend on them. But rather than explaining to us why we should accept them, he simply describes a world—his fictional Port William—in which they're taken for granted. What sort of argument is that?

To answer that question, we must first consider how social and moral philosophers usually justify their claims. Don Herzog's discussion in *Without Foundations* is a helpful guide. Herzog begins by explaining the most familiar and intuitive approach to justification, which he calls foundationalism: the belief that the best, most certain method of justifying our beliefs is to reason from self-evident axioms in a disciplined way to our conclusions—like proving a theorem in geometry.[14] More precisely, foundationalism demands that justification be grounded on principles that are (1) undeniable and immune to revision, and (2) located outside politics and society. Depending on what one believes is "outside politics and society," one could appeal "to unalterable facts of human nature, to language, to theology and principles of rationality."[15] To take a familiar example, we might justify the state by beginning from the premise that humans are by nature self-interested and resources are always limited; these are our foundational principles. We could then argue that self-interested actors in a world of limited resources inevitably come into conflict. Therefore, if we want to avoid the war of all against all, we need some sort of political authority to resolve conflict. *Quod erat demonstrandum.* The appeal of foundationalism, according to Herzog, is that it promises to give us conclusions that hold despite cultural differences. Because it rests on universal, self-evident principles, it results in conclusions that demand assent from any human being (or rational, or moral, actor).

Foundationalism, however, is not the only, and not even the best, way to justify our beliefs. As Herzog points out, it has a poor track record.[16] Nothing is simpler than challenging either the foundational principles (perhaps humans are not self-interested by nature) or the minor premises (perhaps there are other ways to resolve conflicts, or maybe avoiding the war of all against all isn't worth the price). Raise doubts about any step in the chain of reasoning and the argument collapses.

Rather than relying on this strategy, then, Herzog suggests a different approach, which he calls "contextual justification." Contextual justification proceeds by demonstrating that the institution, practice, tradition, or whatever you want to defend is better than the alternatives.[17] It starts not from foundational principles but from the problems and possibilities of a given social context. It then looks for alternative institutions or practices, which it evaluates by considering their concrete implications. Under this approach, "that an institution is justified . . . means not that it has been certified by some airtight philosophical theory as inherently correct, but that it is the best available option."[18] A contextual argument for political obligation, for example, would start not from the assertion that all humans are self-interested and have limited resources, but that *we* (humans living right now, in this place) tend to be self-interested and *our* resources are limited. These are the problems of our given social context. It is experience, not deductive logic based on problematic assumptions about human nature, that teaches us that we frequently run into conflict over those resources. We can then assert that the government we have is able to resolve such conflicts, and to do so better than any alternative we can think of. To bolster this conclusion, of course, we would have to consider in detail what the alternatives would look like, and draw comparisons with our current system. The state would be justified if we couldn't think of a better alternative to the specific problems we face.

Admittedly, contextual justification is messier than foundationalism; it doesn't offer neat and tidy proofs, but rich descriptions of social practices and invidious comparisons among them. But it has a key advantage: it can proceed in the face of disagreement about fundamental values. We don't need to start with a consensus on what humans, in some metaphysical sense, *are* by nature. We can start with a consensus on how a particular set of humans tends to behave, or what kinds of problems we typically face. Granted, a political theory of this sort "will draw on our moral and political beliefs to help rank what is better."[19] But those starting values are only tentative: "Our values will guide us to explore other possibilities" but "describing the possibilities . . . will force us to criticize and refine our values."[20] A contextual justification starts with a set of values that one would expect most people to endorse (like preserving the planet, for example). In the process of considering alternative social arrangements, we may reconsider what we mean by preserving the planet, or ask (as ecocentrics do) for whom we are preserving it. It is a dialectic process; considering alternative institutions may lead us to reevaluate the values we began with. This process may not lead us to consensus, but it doesn't require us to start at consensus either. As Herzog says, "A satisfactory justification need not put an end to all disagreements in politics." Contextual justification provides not certainty but a "preponderance of good reasons."[21]

I suggest we read Berry's novels and essays as offering contextual justifications for his moral and social theories. Perhaps because he recognizes that we disagree about fundamental values, he does not take the foundationalist approach of starting from a particular conception of human nature and deducing from that premise how we should live. Indeed, it is significant that his claims about human nature are buried deep inside his essays rather than offered as a starting point for his arguments. His starting point is always our current social and political situation: a complex combination of cultural, ecological, and economic practices and institutions that are, he claims, resulting in ecological and cultural decay. He compares this state of affairs with his own richly imagined alternative, a set of social practices that embody a different moral vision, most fully drawn in his novels about the fictional Port William. He then suggests that his alternative is preferable to our current state of affairs—once we consider more thoughtfully what it is we really want.

Under this reading, when Berry does make assertions about human nature and the good life, we should not read them as foundational principles we must accept because they're unassailably true. Rather, we should interpret them as alternatives to our current conceptions that we should embrace *because they work better given our situation*. In other words, Berry seems to be claiming no more than that our lives will be richer and more sustainable if we adopt his view of human nature and the good life. This is not to deny that Berry may believe his conceptions are not just practical or better but *true* in some foundationalist sense.[22] But his argument does not depend on that stronger position. All he needs to demonstrate is that, given our current situation, his conceptions of human nature and the good life are valuable in that they illuminate dimensions of human experience obscured by contemporary social practices—and also that their consequences are much better for the human community. His novels, in which people do adopt and act on these values, demonstrate his point; they advocate his particular conceptions of human nature and the good life by showing us what the world might look like if such conceptions held sway. We might of course disagree with him about any of this; contextual justification does not promise to put an end to debate. But our debates would have to center on whether ecological decay is really a problem, whether his solutions would work, or whether some other solution might not work better—not on what humans *really* are by nature. Thus Berry deals with the problem of moral relativism by asking us to concentrate on the concrete, practical question of how we can make our lives better rather than attempting to create consensus on some abstract, metaphysical foundational principles.

This account of Berry's method of justification should forestall the complaint that, because all values are relative, his theory lacks objective foundations. If Herzog is right, it doesn't need foundations. What it does need is a rich and compelling description of human flourishing and the good life—precisely the sort of description offered in his novels about the fictional community of Port William.

Nevertheless, we might still complain that Berry's fictional Port William isn't a compelling description of the good life but a mere utopia—an unrealistic, idealized vision of life that we could never actually achieve. Contextual justification would seem to invite such charges, relying as it does on descriptions of a better life that we have not yet realized. And it's a reasonable complaint; it's hard to see why a skeptical reader would be persuaded by a wholly unrealistic vision of the good life. It is therefore important to consider more carefully the claim that Berry's Port William is a utopian community.

Port William, a farming community dispersed along a river and over the hilly countryside of northern Kentucky, is based on Berry's native Henry County. We know little about its economic, political, or social structure, except what we can infer from its resemblance to Henry County. We do know that the town has been there a long time; its inhabitants no longer remember "why it was built where it was, or when, or how."[23] Its remembered history

goes back only two or three generations, about a century. Before that, presumably, pioneers came and cut down the forests, broke the black earth, and
established farms and homesteads along the river. Sometime toward the end
of the nineteenth century, they began growing tobacco. By the end of the
twentieth century, Port William looks much like the rest of north central
Kentucky: the farms are small, the farmers are struggling, and tobacco is
still the primary cash crop. Farming in Port William is changing, but slowly.
Like much of rural America, it is a community poised between modernization and extinction.

Berry's novels cover the century of Port William's remembered history,
recounting the fortunes and misfortunes of a set of characters Berry refers
to as the "Port William membership." The membership begins (as far as anyone can remember) with people like Ptolemy Proudfoot and his wife, Minnie, of the extensive Proudfoot clan. Tol is a hardworking farmer, successful
enough for early twentieth-century Kentucky, and Minnie is a schoolteacher
who occasionally dabbles in politics (she's against drinking and for women's
suffrage). The stories of Tol and Minnie have the flavor of folktales, humor-
ous stories remembered and recounted for generations. But the characters
aren't mere legend; they have a real connection to the modern Port William.
Although Tol and Minnie have no children of their own, they serve as men-
tors and surrogate parents to the young Elton Penn, an important character
in the later history of Port William.

Elton Penn will become the tenant, and eventually the owner, of Jack
Beechum's farm.[24] Jack, one of Berry's most developed characters, is a tough,
independent farmer who serves as role model and mentor to the younger
farmers in the community: Elton Penn, Mat Feltner, Wheeler Catlett, Jarrat
and Burley Coulter. Most of Berry's fiction concerns these latter characters
and their families. They are Berry's contemporaries, witnessing the changes
he lived through, and their stories are not on the whole happy ones.
Wheeler's brother is murdered; Mat also loses his father to a senseless act of
violence, and his son Virgil is killed in World War II. Nathan, Jarrat Coulter's son, watches family conflict drive his brother away; he himself is torn
over the decision to leave Port William for college. Andy Catlett tries to adapt
to the mechanized world of modern farming and loses his hand as a result.
Other characters include Jayber Crow, the town's barber, who spends his life
in silent devotion to a married woman; Gideon and Ida Crop, who lose their
daughter Annie in a flood; Mary Penn, Elton's wife, who struggles with the
loneliness and hardships of rural life; and Hannah, Virgil's wife and widow.

So much for Berry's allegedly romantic depiction of rural life. Even a casual reader of his novels should notice their bleak tone and pervasive air of tragedy. Most of his plots revolve around death or depression: sons and husbands are killed in war, children are lost in floods, limbs are mutilated by farm machinery, lives are disrupted by murder or suicide, economic security is almost nonexistent, and personal relationships are difficult, confused, and sometimes violent. The community he depicts is far from idyllic, much less utopian. On the contrary, Berry owes more than most critics have recognized to such unromantic writers as Hamlin Garland and Sinclair Lewis. It is significant that when Berry decided to settle in Kentucky, many of his friends and colleagues warned him of "the village virus" and the lessons of Lewis's *Main Street*.[25] In a sense, his project was from the start a critical engagement with Lewis's realist vision of rural life.

Main Street itself is part of a tradition of literary realism that includes Laura Ingalls Wilder and many more obscure (mostly female) novelists. These writers countered the ubiquitous nineteenth-century glorification of the pioneer by depicting the hardships and rewards of life on the frontier from a woman's point of view.[26] Annette Kolodny traces this genre back to Caroline Kirkland, whose classic 1839 work *A New Home—Who'll Follow* challenged the sentimental picture of frontier life typical of nineteenth-century literature. Kirkland's son, Joseph, carried on this tradition of realism in his own novels and encouraged Hamlin Garland, author of the bleak "middle border" stories, in the same direction. Kirkland's other progeny include early twentieth-century novelists such as Willa Cather, Bess Streeter Aldrich, Susan Glaspell, Rose Wilder Lane, and Edith Summers Kelley—who was, not coincidentally, a friend of Sinclair Lewis.[27] In contrast to the more pastoral, Virgilian strain of American agrarianism, these novels emphasized the loneliness, self-denial, and hard work that characterized rural life for most farm women. The genre's gendered perspective was aimed at bringing greater realism to the depiction of rural life by introducing the experiences of a more dependent, more vulnerable class of pioneers.

Berry's novels fall squarely within this tradition. Berry's rural folk, male and female, share the characteristics earlier novels attributed to female pioneers: resilient but vulnerable, dependent and often oppressed by social forces beyond their control. True, Berry departs from the conventions of this tradition in that his protagonists are seldom women.[28] Since his work is mostly semiautobiographical, he usually adopts an unapologetically masculine point of view. Nevertheless, his personalized, autobiographical account of growing up in a rural Kentucky farm community is explicitly aimed at dispelling the romance that pervades southern historical literature.

Consider for example his critique of George Dallas Mosgrove's history, *Kentucky Cavaliers in Dixie*. Berry complains that, like much southern history, it was "written under the spell of chivalry and medieval romance." Mosgrove describes the Civil War as "a pageant of gallantry, tournaments, and jousts."[29] Berry challenges that romanticism by drawing on his own history and memories. For example, one of Mosgrove's heroes, Bart Jenkins, was a slave buyer well known to Berry's family. Berry contrasts Mosgrove's laudatory sketch of the dashing and gallant Jenkins with his grandfather's memory:

> My father's father remembered that when he was a boy he once saw Bart Jenkins in a heated argument with another man. . . . As the argument went on, he worked delicately at the fingertips of one of [his] gloves, as though preparing to remove it. Looking the other man levelly in the eye, not raising his voice but speaking slowly and with precise emphasis, working at the fingers of that glove, he said: "I wish I had a shovel full of shit. I would throw it in your God-damned face."[30]

Far from falling under the sway of romanticism, Berry mines his own experience and the memories of his family and neighbors in order to counter this romantic tradition with realism.[31] Like Kirkland and Lewis, he is trying to give us a clearer vision of rural life.

Admittedly, Berry presents this difficult life in its best light, highlighting the resources rural folk have to deal with hardship. He even acknowledges a utopian element in his writing; although the world he describes is hardly ideal, his characters are occasionally visited by visions of a utopian world—Port William "corrected and clarified." But surely to criticize him for this utopian theme is to misunderstand the purpose of utopian literature. Utopian writers strive to stimulate our political imaginations and to provide a critical standard against which our current social relations can be measured. Berry reasons that unless one believes in prophecy, such utopian visions are the only guide to the future. He agrees that idealistic visions must be informed with an "accurate sense of the real"—if only to avoid feeding self-righteousness and overconfidence in our capacity to create a perfect world. Our ideal world should be consistent with the sort of creatures we are, and the sort of place the world is. But without ideals, he maintains, our sense of the real becomes pervaded with sentimentality, morbidity or cynicism—in other words, without critical standards, we tend to accept existing conditions as inevitable, the "best of all possible worlds."[32] His utopianism, then, is aimed at *avoiding* sentimentality and encouraging progressive reform. To the extent Berry describes rural life positively, his intent is not to mislead us but to shake us out of our unthinking acceptance of the problems, deficiencies, and benefits of industrial society—to point out that there are other ideals to strive for.

Granted, that argument is unlikely to convince the most skeptical of Berry's critics. They would claim that the forces of modernization are unstoppable, that global economic forces and the direction of technological change, not to mention the inevitable growth of the human population, have already determined the future of American agriculture and the American economy generally. There is no point in imagining an alternative—at least, an alternative along the lines Berry suggests—because for better or worse, the genie of progress is out of the bottle; this *is* the best of all possible worlds. In its extreme form, of course, that position implies that we have no power at all to manage the economy, technological change, or the population—which would make most domestic and international policy, and much individual political activism, pointless. A more limited claim might be persuasive, though: Although perhaps not impossible, it would be extremely difficult and expensive to counter the forces of modernization. It might simply be a waste of resources to try to turn such a powerful tide. We would do better to simply accept the benefits of industrialization and globalization—the material abundance, the economic opportunities, the technological advancements— and resign ourselves to their costs. Indeed, Berry himself sometimes seems to counsel resignation, despairing of the prospects for any significant social change.

But the impracticality of social reform is hardly a reason to dismiss Berry's critique of American society. Those persuaded by his arguments would point out that, while extensive social reform may seem daunting, our unrestrained exploitation of natural and social resources is hardly practical either, over the long term. There are serious difficulties facing us whichever path we choose. And in any case, as long as we think we *have* a choice—as long as we are going to take responsibility for creating the future—we need to think clearly about what we want that future to look like. Surely we can't think clearly unless we free ourselves from our superstitious belief in the inevitability of "modernization." Of course the future will look different from the present; of course we will call that future "modern." But that does not mean that the choices we make now have no bearing on the specific shape and texture of modernization. For example, economists have been predicting for many years that family farms would go extinct; so far, they haven't. Instead, small, family-operated farms have sought government policies protecting them from unstable markets, as well as exploring new ways to adapt to market forces—such as increasing reliance on off-farm income and creating new markets for products (organic crops, for example) that small farms can produce efficiently. As a result, the future of family farming looks less obvious today than it did in 1970.

Even if we could be confident about economists' predictions about the long-term future of American agriculture, though, we still need to make choices for the short term. Although we may doubt our ability to achieve the society Berry desires, his vision might still serve as a useful guide for those choices, orienting us toward values that we want our agricultural policies to realize, at least to some degree. Thus the question we must answer is not whether Berry's agrarian society is possible but whether it is *desirable*. And to answer that question, we must consider carefully what it is we really want–in other words, what really constitutes the good life. That is the subject of the following chapters.

It is worth noting—because Berry himself notes it—that the utopian vision in *Remembering* is temporary. Andy understands that he can't dwell in this unreality. "He is not to stay. Grieved as he may be to leave them, he must leave. He *wants* to leave. He must go back with his help, such as it is, and offer it."[33] The purpose of the vision is to show him what he should be working toward, what possibilities are inherent in the less-than-perfect world he lives in. That is Berry's project as well. His novels may recount the passing of a way of life, but they are also meant to demonstrate its value and to encourage its revival. He would persuade us to embrace his program for social and moral reform by juxtaposing his dystopian critique of American society—our present reality—to his vision of a better alternative. It is not a perfect world he envisions, nor is it underwritten by fundamental principles concerning human nature. It is simply better than the world we currently live in—or so Berry would have us believe. What he understands, perhaps better than his critics, is that whether we *do* believe him will not depend solely on the quality of his evidence or the rigor of his reasoning. It will depend also on how we respond to his stories of Port William—stories that describe a way of life achieved, at least partially, temporarily, and imperfectly, in a certain place on earth.

Chapter Six

Beyond Individualism

One of Berry's early essays opens with a description of an Appalachian furniture maker. The scene appears at first to be a charming pastoral idyll: The carpenter sits outside his small house in the shade of some box elders, working patiently and skillfully with his few primitive tools, while his children play happily under the trees. It could be a glimpse of "some happily simple time in the past." But a wider focus reveals the bleak conditions of Appalachian coal country in 1965. The furniture maker lives in inadequate housing on a landscape ruined by strip mining; his children are poorly clothed, and only one attends school. A skilled craftsman, he nevertheless depends on welfare, which is decreased by the amount of money he makes selling furniture.[1]

The essay echoes similar accounts of Appalachian poverty in the works of Harry Caudill.[2] But Berry's perspective on the problem differs from Caudill's in important ways. An enthusiastic supporter of the New Deal and the TVA, Caudill saw federal government as the savior of the region. A progressive administration, he hoped, would support conservation, economic development, and programs to facilitate the transition from an agricultural to an industrial economy. He even suggested that Appalachians should give up farming and move to town where friendly federal bureaucrats could service them more effectively. According to Caudill, much of the Cumberland plateau would be improved by being flooded and turned into a playground for the working class.[3]

In contrast, Berry argues that federal government is a chief culprit in the decline of Appalachia. Federal welfare, he complains, only increases dependence on government, opening the door to government oppression. "If a man continues long in direct and absolute dependence on the government for the necessities of life, he ceases to be a citizen and becomes a slave."[4] Worse, the welfare system fails to value workers for their industry and art. Government bureaucracies don't exercise taste, judgment, or compassion. Their "help" is impersonal; they treat human beings as abstractions, not individuals. Welfare thus contradicts American ideals of human worth and dignity, which rest on the notion of making a living in the work of one's own choice, by one's own gifts. Government's proper role is to create and protect the conditions under which personal effort is meaningful—and thus far the federal government (the TVA in particular) has singularly failed to do so.[5]

This much sounds like a standard conservative paean to self-reliance and autonomy, decrying the evils of big government and income support. A more careful reading of the essay, however, reveals a different message. Berry's complaint about welfare is not simply that it makes the craftsman dependent but that it makes him dependent on the *wrong things:* He depends on an impersonal bureaucracy instead of on his family and neighbors, the teachers who instilled in him the values and disciplines necessary to his craft, and the local community that might serve as a market for his products. "The truth is that the furniture maker is the dependent of his region in a more meaningful and crucial way than he ever will be the dependent of any government."[6] The language of slavery and independence is deceptive; the essay is about not the value of autonomy but the inescapable fact of *dependence.* Berry's point is that even with all the federal programs to help him as an individual, the furniture maker's fortunes still depend, fundamentally, on the fortunes of the region as a whole.

This insight leads to a critical transformation in the moral core of democratic agrarianism. Individual independence, Berry concludes, is not the chief value of agrarian life. Dependence is the central fact of our existence; dependence must accordingly become "the beginning of a new moral vision."[7] Berry's moral theory offers just such a vision. In place of the rugged individualism celebrated in both the agrarian and environmental traditions, he emphasizes communal and environmental virtues cultivated by our interactions with nature—most importantly, the virtue of understanding our limits and our place in the order of Creation. In the process, he reinterprets the meaning of both agriculture and the wilderness.

Appropriately, perhaps, Berry develops his moral vision by taking on that icon of American individualism, Huck Finn. It's not that he doesn't like *Huckleberry Finn,* he assures us: "*Huckleberry Finn* made my boyhood imaginable to me in a way that it otherwise would not have been." In it "we feel a young intelligence breaking the confines of convention and expectation to confront the world itself."[8] But something goes wrong with the story toward the end: "We are asked to believe—or to believe that Huck believes—that there are no choices between the 'civilization' represented by pious slave owners like Miss Watson . . . and lighting out for the territory."[9] That failure to imagine a third alternative, he worries, is more than a personal failing on Mark Twain's part:

> It is arguable that our country's culture is still suspended as if at the end of *Huckleberry Finn*, assuming that its only choices are either a deadly "civilization" of piety and violence or an escape into some "Territory" where we may remain free of adulthood and community obligation. We want to be free; we want to have rights; we want to have power; we do not yet want much to do with responsibility.[10]

The charge appears repeatedly throughout Berry's essays. "It has become increasingly fashionable . . . to advocate . . . a strict and solitary adherence to principle in simple defiance of other people," he complains. "'I don't care what they think' has become public currency with us; saying it, we always mean to imply that we are persons solemnly devoted to high principle—rugged individuals in the somewhat fictional sense Americans usually give to that term." Such bids for personal autonomy are no more than "a rhetorical fossil from our frontier experience." Thinking perhaps of Edward Abbey, he claims that "once it meant that if our neighbors' opinions were repugnant to us, we were prepared either to kill our neighbors or to move west."[11] Now, fortunately, it's simply "adolescent bluster." Autonomy itself is an "illusory condition, suggesting that the self can be self-determining and independent without regard for any determining circumstance or any of the obvious dependences. . . . There is, in practice, no such thing as autonomy. Practically, there is only responsible and irresponsible dependence."[12]

Such reservations about the meaning and value of autonomy are commonplace among social critics worried about the atomism of modern liberal societies. But they sound a little odd coming from Berry—a democratic agrarian, avowed admirer of Thomas Jefferson, and direct descendant of the Populists. The concept of autonomy is central to that tradition; in fact, it's intimately connected to most of our received understandings of freedom, free will, rights, individualism, even personhood. Berry appears to be rejecting a value integral not only to American politics but to Western philosophy generally—not the stance one would expect from a champion of tradition!

But Berry's project isn't quite that radical; his casual use of the term "autonomy" can be misleading. As we have seen, even within American agrarian and environmental thought, autonomy can mean quite different things, from the political and economic independence prominent in the agrarian tradition to the spiritual autonomy and freedom from social obligation endorsed by preservationists. The same problem plagues moral philosophy generally, where autonomy might imply any combination of critical reflection, rational self-control, self-legislation, moral independence, self-creation, individuality and authenticity, or initiative and the capacity for action.[13] This conceptual richness makes the task of critical analysis tricky; an apparent attack on autonomy may be doing no more than criticizing one kind of autonomy as impairing some other type of autonomy, or as failing to realize autonomy in its fullest sense. This, for example, is the charge Thoreau leveled at the agrarians: the economic and political independence they celebrate, he claimed, do little to enhance true intellectual and spiritual autonomy.

This is not Berry's line of attack—but neither is his position that autonomy has no practical relevance for human life. While his most extreme rhetoric implies that we shouldn't seek *any* sort of autonomy, he probably doesn't intend to go that far. We can, after all, criticize a moral ideal centered on achieving individual independence without rejecting the notion that some minimum level of autonomy is a precondition for moral agency. And Berry's criticisms are clearly aimed at an ideal, a more-than-ordinary level of independence and self-sufficiency achieved only by some heroic individuals. He gives us no reason to believe he is taking the more radical position that a basic level of autonomy—the capacity for independent thought and action—isn't necessary for moral personhood. On the contrary, the subjects of Berry's criticisms—Huck Finn, Hemingway's Nick Adams, those mythic frontiersmen who either killed their neighbors or moved west[14]—suggest that what he means to criticize is the "somewhat fictional" ideal represented by rugged individualism. Surely this is a more acceptable target.

On the other hand, it may be *too* good a target. After all, what serious philosopher would endorse an ethic that allows you to kill your neighbor and get away with it? If that's what rugged individualism means, it's just a straw man, and hardly worth Berry's attention. Between basic autonomy and this extreme version of rugged individualism, however, lies a conception of individual independence and self-reliance that is closer to what we usually mean by American individualism—and this is the moral ideal Berry is truly interested in. His major critique of rugged individualism is aimed not at some frontier legend like Daniel Boone but at one of his own carefully nuanced characters, the eponymous hero of *The Memory of Old Jack*. In contrast to the superhuman ruggedness of the stock action hero or mythic frontiersman, Old Jack's self-reliant individualism could well serve as a realistic and appealing ideal for many Americans. Jack's story is therefore the best illustration of the deficiencies of that ideal.

The Memory of Old Jack introduces us to Jack Beechum on the last day of his life. Even at the age of ninety-two, he is stubbornly independent; his every action seems inspired by a prickly, uncompromising sense of personal autonomy. In the opening scene he pointedly sets aside his cane and, standing alone "like a statue" in the early morning light, lets his mind roam freely over the town and back over the decades, unconstrained by his physical immobility. Significantly, his memory settles immediately on his first team of mules, bought when he had nearly cleared his farm of debt. Buying the expensive mules was an act of not only independence but almost reckless self-confidence: "He was going to clear [the farm]. There was no longer any doubt in him about his ability to do that. It had become plain to him that he was equal to what would be required of him, and to what he would require of himself."[15] This joyful pride in his self-sufficiency is Jack's most dominant character trait, finding its best expression in his (usually solitary) operation of his farm.

Ironically, though, Jack is not, and perhaps never has been, equal to what was required of him. On the contrary, as the memory of his successes and failures gradually makes clear, his struggle for self-reliance and independence limited him. Just as setting aside his cane impairs his mobility, Jack's reluctance to depend on others constantly diminished his possibilities. His self-sufficiency is in fact an illusion; he was able to buy his farm only with the help of a friend, and took many years to free it from debt. A single accident, a fire in the barn, destroyed his fragile financial independence, which took many years to regain. And now, at the end of his life, his physical frailty has forced him to leave his farm and move into a boarding house in town, where his friends can take care of him. Moreover, Jack's inability to see through the illusion of self-sufficiency had tragic consequences for his closest relationships. His marriage failed because both partners were unable to accept their interdependence; his fellowship with his hired hand also dissolved because Jack resented his dependence on the other man.[16] His life, as he remembers it, is actually a series of failures. What redemption he receives comes in realizing that "he could do nothing sufficient to his needs," that "he lives by a bounty not his own."[17]

Jack is a tragic figure, then—but he's not a foolish one. The conception of rugged individualism he embodies is in many ways admirable. He is strong-willed, competent, and disciplined. He aims for freedom of action, for the ability to overcome external constraints. The touchstone of Jack's individualism is self-reliance, including physical toughness and even aggressiveness. This perhaps accounts for its appeal to farmers, whose work puts a premium on physical abilities like strength and endurance. But Jack's individualism also encompasses freedom from social obligations, including family—a much more problematic point for farmers. Jack's independence interfered with precisely those relationships, his marriage and his friendship with his hired hand, that were critical to the success of the farm. Freedom from social obligations, Berry constantly reminds us, is hard to reconcile with the communalism and interdependence of farm life.

Nor is this sort of individualism conducive to spiritual and intellectual virtues. Self-realization and authenticity are at best marginal considerations for Jack. Such virtues are generally more prominent in the preservationist than the agrarian tradition; as discussed in chapter 2, one value of the wilderness is that it allows one to realize one's true, authentic self, free from the distortions and masks of social life. Jack is no Thoreau; he is untroubled by concerns about authenticity. Similarly, critical reflection and other intellectual virtues are conspicuously absent from Jack's rugged individualism. Like many agrarians, Berry does highlight cleverness and common sense, traits that allow one to run a business and avoid being manipulated by parasitic city folk. But intelligent as Jack is, he lacks self-awareness and enjoys only a limited understanding of the social, political, and economic forces shaping his world.

In sum, the rugged individual Berry envisions is competent, physically tough, self-reliant, and clever if not well educated. He is self-confident but not psychologically complex, a loner who doesn't want or seem to need a supportive community. A rare breed, perhaps, but hardly a straw man or illusory ideal. Jack is one of the most admired characters in Berry's fictional Port William. Even before his death he has become a "public statue," a monument to his own patriarchal status in the community. Berry's sympathy for Jack and the ideals he embodies permeates the novel. Nevertheless, the story makes clear that the foundations of Jack's individualism—his insistence on self-sufficiency, freedom of action, and economic and emotional independence—are morally suspect.

Of course, any moral ideal, if pursued to extremes, can become problematic. Berry's complaint about Jack's quest for self-sufficiency and freedom is not simply that it can have unhappy consequences, however, but that it is driven by a particularly dangerous fantasy: a seductive but ecologically destructive image of infinite human *power*. The rugged individual is appealing because he is unrestrained by natural and social obstacles. His sphere of action is potentially limitless. Clearly this search for limitless power is problematic for community solidarity; the conflict between individuality and communal values troubles Jack throughout his life. But, interestingly, this doesn't seem to be Berry's chief concern; as I will argue later, he considers such tensions an inescapable part of social life. Rather, his primary complaint is that this desire for individual power and freedom works to justify the industrial regime that he holds responsible for our ecological and cultural decay. "The knowledge that purports to be leading us to transcendence of our limits has been with us a long time. It thrives by offering material means of fulfilling a spiritual . . . craving: we would all very much like to be immortal, infallible, free of doubt, at rest."[18] Unfortunately, "as much as we long for infinities of power and duration, we have no evidence that these lie within our reach, much less within our responsibility."[19] Replaying a theme prominent in moral discourse since Sophocles, he suggests that our search for individual power and freedom is a dangerous attempt to transcend the human condition: "We will have either to live within our limits, within the human definition," he warns, "or not live at all."[20]

The essence of his critique, then, is that rugged individualism as a moral ideal represents a hubristic quest for individual freedom and power, an attempt to deny the fundamental fact of the human condition: that we are limited, dependent creatures. And this ideal in turn leads to ecologically destructive practices. It is the desire for freedom and power, he contends, that fuels our ever-increasing reliance on machines and nonrenewable energy sources. "This mechanically derived energy is supposed to have set people free from work and other difficulties once considered native to the human condition." Unfortunately, "this liberation of the machine is illusory. Mechanical technology is based on quantities of materials and fuels that are finite." He continues: "The problem with mechanically extractable energy is that so far we have been unable to make it available without serious geological and ecological damage, or to effectively restrain its use, or to use or even neutralize its wastes."[21] The quest for limitless power, for freedom from limits, is not only hopeless but dangerous, both morally and ecologically.

In Berry's view, then, the freedom and power sought by Jack Beechum— the ability to overcome physical obstacles and accomplish one's goals without help from others—leads directly to reliance on machines, fossil fuels, and all the environmentally destructive practices that characterize the industrial regime. Jack Beechum's spiritual heir is not the small organic farmer living close to the land but the agribusinessman, cultivating his vast wheat fields all by himself in a shiny new air-conditioned tractor. The irony is that our desire for this sort of independence is precisely what has led us to a host of dangerous dependencies: on machines, corporations, creditors, and government agencies. The tragedy is that—caught as we are at the end of *Huckleberry Finn*—we can't seem to imagine any alternative.

Berry does imagine an alternative, though. Specifically, in place of our celebration of rugged individualism, Berry would like to see a revival of the classical virtues. This classical turn is hinted at throughout his essays, but suggested most forcefully by *The Memory of Old Jack*. Over the course of the novel, Jack is transformed from an American hero into a Greek one; instead of a rugged individual, we see at the end a great man brought down by the fatal flaw of hubris. And if hubris is our problem, the solution may well be a return to the classical virtue of sophrosyne.

Granted, Berry never mentions sophrosyne by name. Much neglected by modern moral philosophy, it may be unfamiliar to many readers as well. Sophrosyne is the virtue that prevents hubristic overreaching. Although sometimes interpreted simply as humility, its meaning in Greek and Roman thought was much richer and more complex than that.[22] Often denoting self-control, it was frequently represented by the charioteer who piloted those spirited horses, the appetites and the passions. Thus it could be translated as temperance or moderation. In addition, however, it carried the connotation of prudence, pragmatism (even Odysseus's sort of cunning), or good management—which made it a virtue associated with domesticity. In fact, Cicero and Horace identified sophrosyne as the virtue proper to the good husbandman and *vita rustica,* which gives it an important place in the agrarian tradition. Carrying this connotation further, Plato associated sophrosyne with order and harmony generally, thus linking it to justice. And, of course, sophrosyne was also summed up in the Gnostic command to "know thyself"—in other words, to know one's proper place in the cosmic order, to know what it means to be human as opposed to divine or bestial.

Sophrosyne would thus seem to be a good alternative to the ideal of rugged individualism embodied by Old Jack. Not that sophrosyne is incompatible with individualism; temperance (self-control) is typically an important element of autonomy, and the cleverness and pragmatism implied by sophrosyne plays into some images of rugged individualism. In fact, the agrarian concept of rugged individualism seems to be rooted in the classical virtue of sophrosyne at least as much as it is rooted in a more modern concern for economic and political independence. But emphasizing sophrosyne rather than self-sufficiency and freedom of action changes the moral core of agrarianism in important ways: The moral value of farming becomes not its promise of freedom and power but its tendency to teach self-restraint and prudence. The farmer's dependence on nature, from this perspective, is valuable because it is a constant lesson in human limits and fallibility.

Berry returns repeatedly to this theme. One of his more revealing poems tells the story of his failed attempt to build a pond. Poorly designed, the earthwork slumped and fell into the pond. "The trouble was the familiar one: too much power, too little knowledge."[23] The work of farming, Berry constantly reminds us, is difficult. It is usually too much for one person, and mistakes are lasting and sometimes deadly. The only safe way to approach this difficult labor is carefully, with humility and prudence rather than an overconfident sense of self-sufficiency. Clearly the same lesson applies to environmental stewardship generally. If our chief ecological fault is that we do not respect limits on consumption and exploitation of resources—that we constantly try to overreach ourselves—then sophrosyne (prudence, moderation, good management) is not only the chief virtue of good farmers, it is the virtue most necessary to preserve the planet. Sophrosyne, then, is central to Berry's ecological agrarianism; good farmers can serve as models of environmental stewardship because good farming tends to cultivate moderation, self-control, and an understanding of our limits.

To this extent Berry's reliance on sophrosyne should be relatively uncontroversial. Few moral philosophers, after all, are against moderation and prudence. But sophrosyne implies a good deal more. The concept in classical thought was inextricably tied to fundamental beliefs about the good life.[24] To "know thyself" is to know what it means to be human, to live a fully human life. In echoing this command, Berry raises the question of what people are for—or, to put it another way, what our place is: "People are not gods. They must not act like gods or assume godly authority. If they do, terrible retributions are in store. In this warning we have the root of the idea of propriety, of *proper* human purposes and ends."[25] To be sophrosyne is to understand what humans' proper ends are, which in turn is to understand where we fit in the order of Creation.

And Creation does, according to Berry, have an order. One of the more intriguing elements of his moral theory is his attempt to revive the notion of the Great Chain of Being—revised, however, almost beyond recognition. For Berry, the order of Creation is not a chain rising from animals to angels but a series of concentric circles: The individual is part of a family, which is part of a community, which is part of an "agriculture" (a traditional pattern of interaction between the human community and the physical environment), which is contained within nature (the biological forces that regulate all living things).[26] Wisdom consists in knowing one's place in this system and not trying to seize power above one's place—to control the forces of nature, for example, or to live outside of community, completely autonomous and free.

Such claims about the good life and the moral order of the universe help us make sense of what Berry means by "living within our limits." Clearly, they also raise the problem of moral relativism: What makes his conception of the moral order of the universe persuasive? As argued in the previous chapter, though, all he needs to do is persuade us that his view of humans' proper place and ends in the moral order of the universe is better than the vision of limitless capacities under which we are currently laboring. The more serious problem with sophrosyne is that it may not be a politically desirable trait. Berry, we might object, is counseling humility, a virtue that seems incompatible with political action aimed at improving the status of oppressed groups—including small farmers. As I argued in chapter 1, the Populists and W. E. B. DuBois downplayed humility for just this reason. Temperance and moderation hardly look like desirable character traits for activists aiming at challenging oppressive social arrangements.

Importantly, though, for Berry sophrosyne is not aimed at reinforcing any *social* hierarchy. On the contrary, Berry's Great Chain of Being keeps all human beings at the same level, forcefully reminding them of their common dependence on each other and on nature.[27] Nor does this sort of humility necessarily imply political passivity. To be sure, Berry is suspicious of politics and politicians. Significantly, one of his favorite exemplars of sophrosyne is Odysseus, who moves from "the battlefields of Troy . . . and the values of that world" (glory and heroism) to "the terraced fields of Ithaka" and "the values of domesticity and peace." Odysseus's sophrosyne is exhibited not only in his pragmatic cleverness but in his desire to return home, to make the transition from warrior to farmer—suggesting that there is virtue in his ability to disengage from the affairs of the larger world.[28] On the other hand, Berry also finds evidence of sophrosyne in—of all people—Malcolm X. Berry points to the passage in the *Autobiography* in which Malcolm talks about growing peas in his mother's garden:

Part of the strength of that passage is that it is probably the only really serene and happy moment in the whole book. . . . It is hard for me to avoid the suspicion that the experience—lying there as low as he could get, against the earth, his mind free—filled him with a rich sense of the possibilities of life in this world that never left him.[29]

The reading is more than a little strained, but the point, I think, is that sophrosyne is not inherently incompatible with political activism. On the contrary: if sophrosyne teaches us that we shouldn't aspire to be gods, it teaches also that we *should* aspire to be fully human. Thus resisting oppression could be seen as involving the exercise of sophrosyne: the recognition of what it means to be human.

Nevertheless, as a practical matter Berry's focus on sophrosyne could be problematic for those concerned with challenging oppressive social structures. The quest for individual freedom and power may seem hubristic, but it has proven an effective basis for the politics of status—more effective, at any rate, than a quest for sophrosyne promises to be. The problem is illustrated by the feminist debate over the value of autonomy as a political goal. Many feminists argue that the concept of autonomy usually deployed in political debate emphasizes freedom of action, power, and emotional independence—and that this concept is derived from and justifies men's experience and development rather than women's. Some would go so far as to suggest that autonomy ought to be abandoned altogether, or at least reformulated to reflect our condition of connectedness, the dependence of one's sense of self on one's position in a web of relationships.[30] Others, however, counter that such a concept of autonomy derives from the recognition that individuality and the full development of one's individual capacities are central to the good life.[31] Autonomy, this camp argues, is politically valuable because it can serve as a normative standard of mature selfhood and emancipation, thus providing a critical perspective on and program for reform of patriarchal social institutions.[32]

Berry's attack on rugged individualism closely tracks the feminist critique of autonomy. Like many ecofeminists, Berry worries that a problematic conception of autonomy, centering on self-reliance, emotional independence, and individual freedom and power, permeates American notions of masculinity and helps to legitimate violent and exploitative actions toward nature. He argued as early as 1971 that "there is an historical parallel, in white American history, between the treatment of the land and the treatment of women. The frontier, for instance, was notoriously exploitative of both."[33] He thus anticipated the ecofeminist argument that gender ideology is deeply implicated in our relationship to the natural world.[34] And he shares their concern that a liberal feminist movement aimed at achieving autonomy for women might simply end up reinforcing a patriarchal, and ecologically destructive, ideology. But a movement that abandons autonomy as a goal may do little to improve women's subservient position; telling an oppressed group to cultivate humility, temperance, and moderation doesn't look like a good program for social change.

I have no solution to this dilemma, except to point out that one may endorse autonomy as a political goal without endorsing the destructive ideology of rugged individualism. In fact, as I will argue later, Berry is keenly aware of the value of autonomy at certain times and in certain situations, which suggests he may recognize the value of autonomy as a subordinate political goal, if not an ultimate moral ideal. Before exploring his limited endorsements of autonomy, however, we need to address a third, more complicated problem raised by his critique of rugged individualism. I've argued that focusing on sophrosyne rather than the freedom and power sought by rugged individualists is the key to Berry's attempt to create an ecological agrarianism, which is supposed to serve as a bridge between environmentalists and farmers. But rugged individualism is also central to the preservationist tradition. Doesn't Berry's critique simply deepen the gulf between agrarianism and preservationism? If we don't value the quest for individual freedom and power, why do we need the wilderness?

Preservationists have offered a host of other reasons to preserve the wilderness, from anthropocentric interests in ecosystem maintenance and natural beauty to an ecocentric concern for the rights of animals and other living beings. I don't want to oversimplify this rich tradition, but (as I argued in chapter 2) those arguments have typically been subordinate to the notion that what makes the wilderness such a critical value to Americans is its ability to cultivate independent, self-reliant individuals.[35] The wilderness is timeless, eternal; entering it allows one to leave behind social roles and the claims of history and custom, and discover one's "true" unmediated self. Society, in contrast, is the "unnatural" domain of custom, tradition, history, and community—all of which impose constraints on the individual. Under this conceptual framework, the wilderness is valuable because it has no history and no rules, and is therefore the proper place to realize individual freedom and autonomy.[36] Preservationists can thus argue that by protecting the wilderness, we preserve the conditions for cultivating rugged individualism and maintaining our distinctive American character. As Wallace Stegner put it, "Something will have gone out of us as a people if we ever let the remaining wilderness be destroyed." Never again would "we have the chance to see ourselves single, separate, vertical, and individual in the world."[37]

As powerful as it has proved to be at justifying wilderness protection, however, this interpretive framework creates problems for Berry. On one hand, it values the wilderness at the expense of community, making it difficult to defend agriculture (which diminishes wilderness and ties one to the community). On the other hand, if he simply reverses these values and asserts the importance of community over individualism, he leaves the wilderness—the domain of the rugged individual—defenseless. To defend *both* domestic and wild nature, then, he has to reformulate this conceptual scheme. He does so by rejecting the idea that the wilderness makes possible an unmediated relationship between the individual and nature. Berry argues instead that individuals relate to nature primarily by *participating* in a community and a history. Making a dramatic break with traditional preservationism, Berry uncouples autonomy and wilderness and emphasizes instead the communal and ecological virtues cultivated by interacting with nature, both domestic and wild.

He begins by defining nature in a way that includes man and his activities. "The defenders of nature and wilderness," he complains, "sometimes sound as if the natural and the human were two separate estates, radically different and radically divided." In fact, "what we call nature is . . . the sum of the changes made by all the various creatures and natural forces in their intricate actions and influences upon each other and upon their places."[38] Man is included among these creatures, which is precisely why man must respect the limits that "natural forces" (the laws of physics, biology, etc.) impose on his actions. "Unlike other creatures, humans must make a choice as to the kind and scale of the difference they make," he argues. "If they choose to make too small a difference, they diminish their humanity. If they choose to make too great a difference, they diminish nature, and narrow their subsequent choices; ultimately, they diminish or destroy themselves."[39] Humans are not opposed to nature, then, but embedded in it and subject to its biological and physical laws.

This general principle, however, tells us little about how individuals and societies relate to their natural world in practice. Like many other environmentalists concerned with issues of responsible use, Berry's thinking about this question relies heavily on the concept of *place*.[40] As argued in chapter 4,

Berry contends that ecologically sound use of the land depends on cultivating a "sense of place." Places accordingly figure prominently in the thoughts and affections of his characters, and his novels are centrally concerned with "how a place and person can come to belong to each other—or, rather, how a person can come to belong to a place."[41] But what is a place, exactly, and how does it mediate our relationship to nature?

When Old Jack Beechum investigated his new farm, he "walked over it, looking at it, loosening the earth in the rows of the crop ground with his heel, picking it up and crumbling it in his fingers" until "the new place claimed an ample space in his mind."[42] Berry's other characters, encountering new places, go through the same process: examining them at length, drinking from their wells and springs, inspecting their fences and buildings, learning their possibilities. Belonging to a place, it seems, has something to do with getting to know its particularity—how it is different, special. A place must therefore have a character distinct from the character of nature in general; it is a discrete, unique, *knowable* part of nature. Places thus give nature both its diversity and familiarity. It is through our association with a particular place, by becoming familiar with its unique character, that we relate to nature in general.[43]

Places are not, however, merely discrete parts of nature. Berry does not follow those bioregionalists who conceive of places as wholly natural phenomena. Kirkpatrick Sale, for example, contends that the world is divided into natural places (watersheds, for example), and that human culture should adapt to these natural configurations—an argument that tends to reinforce the problematic division between nature and society.[44] Berry's places, in contrast, are more complex. On one hand, the land endures while men come and go, so places must have some existence apart from man. The places Berry describes in his novels often have an eternal quality, like nature itself. One of Berry's characters, remembering a place he first saw fifteen years ago, notes that it has become "mythified," so that "it seems to him that he came here first, not fifteen years ago, but generations ago beyond memory."[45] Places seem to have existed "since evening and morning were the third day."[46]

On the other hand, places are marked out or recognized by people—sometimes quite literally, as when a newly wed couple in *A Place on Earth* claim their place by marking out the walls of their house.[47] Such acts suggest that places are in fact socially constructed, that they're made by people—but obviously not in the sense that roads and bridges are. Berry typically describes a place as representing a ritualistic union, a *marriage,* between people and nature.[48] Jack Beechum's decision to buy a farm, for example, is a "betrothal," his desire for the land almost sexual: it "would have carried him across the sea in a wooden ship, or through the Cumberland Gap on foot. . . . What he sought . . . was the yearly unfolding of the flower and fruit of the land."[49] It is not that Jack (or anyone else) literally *creates* the place, then. Rather, the place is defined, marked out from nature in general, as individuals (or communities) interact with nature. Clearly, the physical attributes of nature have as much influence on the quality and character of that interaction as the ideas, histories, and desires of the people. A place is therefore neither wholly natural nor wholly social; it is the product of a relationship between people and nature, coming into being as individuals interact and come to terms with the objective conditions presented by the physical (and social) world.

This relationship brings nature within the realm of human conventions. Far from being the domain of freedom, places always have their own rules and requirements; they make demands on us. Thus Berry criticizes tourists on the Kentucky River who seem to think that because a river is a public and wild place, it is "a *free* place," with no bosses or responsibility or restrictions. On the contrary, he insists that there is a right way to experience the river—there are rules that the tourists are violating by racing through on noisy powerboats, casting litter carelessly into the woods.[50] Such behavior isn't just irrational (because it destroys the place they've traveled so far to see), it's *inappropriate*. The river, he reminds us, is in someone's backyard, as are most "wilderness" places. "*All* of Kentucky is inhabited. . . . The wild country is gone. . . . Kentucky is inhabited all right," even if "for the most part the inhabitants have treated it as if it were uninhabited, or soon would be."[51] The tourist is thus violating a host of social conventions in his thoughtless use of the river. He "came to a natural place to be free of responsibility, only to receive from it the intimation that he cannot be free, that his life is surrounded by more demands and considerations than he can bear to admit."[52]

This conception of place as conventional helps us think about, if not fully resolve, the problem we touched on in chapter 4: How can environmental stewardship depend on a "sense of place" if different inhabitants have a different sense of the place and its possibilities? Unlike those bioregionalists who want to rely on the objective natural features of the place to determine its proper uses, Berry recognizes that any given place has many (although not limitless) possibilities. It is not entirely up to the individual, however, to choose among those possibilities. Because one's use of a place will be constrained by the conventions and expectations of the larger community, determining proper use will necessarily be a community project.

Disputes about place therefore cannot be resolved by a simple assertion of individual property rights. They are, inescapably, disputes about the nature and meaning of the community.

And they are also about history—if places have a social dimension, they also have a temporal dimension. The place may like nature itself be eternal, but it is not innocent of human history. The former inhabitants of a place are a vital part of it. "We may deeply affect a place we own for good or ill, but our lives are nevertheless included in its life; it will survive us, bearing the results. Each of us is a part of a succession."[53] Thus Berry's characters are conscious of their connection to a genealogical (although, keeping in mind Berry's conception of patrimony, not necessarily biological) chain that is rooted in a place. This connection can become almost organic; of one farmer, Berry says "his thought [became] indistinguishable from [the land], so that when he came to die his intelligence would subside into it like its own spirit."[54] The history of a place, the record of a community's interaction with it through the generations, links transient mortals to eternal nature. This history in turn survives in a communal memory, through the traditions and stories that evolve out of living together in a common place. The tie between generations, then, is the physical space they inhabit, the place. Likewise, participation in the community links the individual to the place. As Berry puts it, people can have "no devotion to each other that they [do] not give at the same time to the place they [have] in common."[55] That devotion he calls fidelity, which joins sophrosyne in his list of agrarian virtues. To be devoted to nature is to be faithful to a place, which means embracing a community and its history.

In sum, the individual relates to nature through participating in a community and a collective history, both of which are defined by, and define, a place. The value of interacting with nature is not that it helps the individual to achieve freedom and independence, then; rather, its value is that it connects the individual to a community. The opposition between nature and the individual on one hand and community and history on the other breaks down, and we return to those concentric circles in which the individual is embedded in a community and the community is embedded in a culture and in nature.

Under this view, wilderness is best conceived as a place to which one is a stranger.[56] Others may, probably have, lived there; it may have a history and its own rules, but these are unknown to the stranger. One's task upon entering the wilderness is not to learn how to act autonomously, any more than one seeks to act autonomously in a neighbor's living room. Rather, one should seek to act with *propriety,* to learn the rules—in other words, to understand the nature of this new place and the people who live (or lived) there. The goal is to turn the wilderness into a place—not so much to domesticate it but to become domestic to it. But this does not mean that wilderness qua wilderness—undomesticated, untamed—is without moral value. On the contrary, Berry does value pure wilderness, and not only for ecological reasons: "If we are to be properly humble in our use of the world, we need places that we do not use at all. We need the experience of leaving something alone."[57] Respecting pristine wilderness—*refusing* to use it or domesticate it—is a practical lesson in sophrosyne (temperance, humility, observing one's limits).

Berry's attitude toward wilderness is illustrated in his perspective on the traditional American solitary journey into the wilderness. On one hand, he rejects Edward Abbey's case for the wilderness journey, insisting that "there is a bad reason to go to the wilderness. We must not go there to escape the ugliness and the dangers of the present human economy." He objects that such an escape is illusory, and only serves to reinforce the false dichotomy between nature and society—"the estrangement of the wild and the domestic."[58] On the other hand, he suggests that there is something to be learned from such journeys, as he explains in his account of his expedition into the Red River Gorge in 1967.

Like Thoreau and Abbey, Berry began his journey with the goal of reaching "the vital reality of a place such as this." The wilderness, he tells us, strips away "the human façade that usually stands between me and the universe," so that "I see more clearly where I am."[59] Such rhetoric echoes the standard tropes of wilderness enthusiasts seeking spiritual autonomy and insight by leaving society. But this language soon gives way to a humbler and more tentative voice. Berry feels uneasy, out of place, lonesome, *naked*.[60] Confronting his first big rapids, he abandons any pretense to ruggedness: "The river was defeating me, and what is more it was making me glad to accept defeat."[61] Rather than trying to overcome or deny his vulnerability, however, he embraces it. This vulnerability, it turns out, is what opens one to change. If entering wilderness brings you to your "irreducible self," it does so through "a kind of death." His journey is thus a ritual enactment of human loneliness and humility. The value of the wilderness is that it forces him to accept a truer, *humbler* view of himself.[62]

The wilderness journey does provide an ethical education, then. But its purpose is not to become a rugged individual; rather, the point is to scare oneself into humility, to learn one's limits. The grandeur of the wilderness, rather than inspiring Berry with a sense of purpose and desire for mastery, merely impressed on him his vulnerability and dependence on society. What we learn by going into the wilderness is that we don't really belong there, that we are social creatures: vulnerable, needy, dependent on one another. Like farming, the wilderness schools us in our limits and our proper place; it offers a practical lesson in sophrosyne.

The moral value of both agriculture and wilderness, in sum, is their ability to cultivate sophrosyne. For Berry, sophrosyne, along with propriety and fidelity, become the key virtues of the small farmer—the virtues that promise to make the farmer a reliable defender of both wild and domestic nature. This transformation of the moral core of agrarianism and preservationism thus unites the two traditions. By abandoning rugged individualism, Berry is able to sidestep the intractable debate between farmers advocating an individualism centered on economic and political independence and preservationists advocating an individualism centered on intellectual and spiritual independence. As it turns out, they've both missed the point. What makes farmers and wilderness lovers valuable to the republic is not their respective versions of rugged individualism but their common understanding of human limitations.

Despite his rejection of rugged individualism, however, Berry is unwilling, or unable, to abandon the ideal of independence so central to the agrarian tradition:

> Even today, against overpowering odds and prohibitive costs, one does not have to go far in any part of the country to hear voiced the old hopes that stirred millions of immigrants, freed slaves, westward movers, young couples starting out: a little farm, a little shop, a little store— some kind of place and enterprise of one's own, within and by which one's family could achieve a proper measure of independence, not only of economy, but of satisfaction, thought, and character.[63]

He is more than sympathetic to this dream. "I do not mean to deny the value or the virtue of a *proper* degree of independence in the character and economy of an individual."[64] But that independence is limited; individuals are defined in part by their membership in a community, so that "a part of [an individual's] properly realizable potential [lies] in its community, not in itself."[65] To be sure, conflicts between the individual and the community are inevitable, but "the conflicts are not everything. . . . A part of our definition is our common ground, and a part of it is sharing and mutually enjoying our common ground."[66]

The difficulty, of course, is defining our proper degree of independence and negotiating those boundaries between the individual and the community. Berry's most illuminating exploration of this problem is a short story entitled "It Wasn't Me." The story is particularly interesting because it revolves around what has historically been a central preoccupation of the democratic agrarian tradition: debt. For many decades it has been nearly impossible to acquire a farm without going into debt, and even in the nineteenth century, debt was an inescapable fact of life for most farmers.[67] It's not too much of an exaggeration to say that in the agrarian tradition the struggle for independence has been synonymous with the struggle to avoid or get out of debt. Berry's treatment of that struggle therefore goes to the heart of the agrarian tradition.

"It Wasn't Me" tells the story of Elton Penn's failed attempt to acquire a farm without going into debt. Penn had been working Jack Beechum's farm for years, and Old Jack wanted him to inherit the farm. The problem was that Jack had a daughter. Clara had long since married and moved to the city, and had no interest in farming. But Jack nevertheless felt an obligation to her. She was his daughter and, according to his notions, she ought to inherit the farm. He therefore left Clara the farm and left Elton what he thought would be half the purchase price. His plan, jotted down on a note to his lawyer Wheeler Catlett but never recorded in his will, was that Clara should sell the farm to Elton for twice the amount he left to Elton.

Unfortunately, Old Jack underestimated the value of the farm and overestimated the character of his daughter. Clara, informed of her father's wishes, decided that she could do better. So she auctioned off the farm, and Elton Penn—at Wheeler's urging—submitted the winning bid: one-hundred dollars an acre more than he expected and could afford to pay. Unfortunately, his success put Elton in an awkward position. He was nervous about having inherited anything from Old Jack in the first place. "Nothing in his experience had prepared him for a benefit that was unasked, unearned, and unexpected. Nothing in his character prepared him to be comfortable with an obligation he could not repay."[68] Now he had committed himself to buying the farm for more money than he expected; in addition to his debt to Old Jack he has to decide whether to incur an additional debt to Wheeler, who has offered to lend him the money.

The ensuing conversation between Wheeler and Elton revolves around the ideal of independence. One might expect the scene to replay the conventional agrarian theme of the virtuous farmer falling into the clutches of the greedy, manipulative lawyer. But it is Wheeler who shows the better moral judgment:

> Elton complains, "But, damn it, Wheeler, don't you think I *ought* to lose it [the farm] if I can't make it on my own?"
>
> "No," Wheeler says. "I *don't* think that. I can see how a person *might* think that. It seems to me I thought something like that myself once. But I don't think it anymore."
>
> "It's the obligation. . . . If it hadn't been for you, Wheeler, I'd have lost that farm today. . . . Why should you have felt obliged to help me get into a problem that now you feel obliged to help me get out of?"
>
> Wheeler knows this longing for independence in Elton because he knows it in himself. . . . But he is amused too and is trying not to show it.
>
> "It wasn't me," Wheeler says. . . . "It wasn't me. If I had stood back and let you lose that farm, or let it lose you, that old man [Old Jack] would have talked to me in the dark for the rest of my life."[69]

The conversation is taking place in Wheeler's office, but by this point "the office has faded away around them. They might as well be in a barn, or in an open field. They are meeting in the world . . . striving to determine how they will continue in it. Both of them are still wearing their hats and coats."[70] They are in the original situation, the state of nature: two free and independent men deciding whether to enter into society with one another.

Elton expresses a typically American attitude:

> "I want to make it on my own. I don't want a soul to thank."
>
> Wheeler thinks, "Too late," but he does not say it. He grins. That he knows the futility of that particular program does not prevent him from liking it. "Well," he says, "putting aside whatever Mary Penn [Elton's wife] might have to say about that, and putting aside what it means in the first place just to be a living human, I don't think your old friend has left you in shape to live thankless. . . .
>
> "[Y]ou're indebted to a dead man. So am I. So was he. . . . Back of you is Jack Beechum. Back of him was Ben Feltner. Back of him was, I think, his own daddy. And back of him somebody else."

Elton objects:

> "The line of succession I'm in says you've got to make it on your own. I'm in the line of succession of root, hog, or die."
>
> "That may have been the line of succession you were in, but it's not the one you're in now. The one you're in now is different."
>
> "Well, how did I get in it?" Elton says almost in a sigh, as if longing to be out of it.
>
> "The way you got in it, I guess, was by being chosen. The way you stay in it is by choice."[71]

The point, which Elton eventually, reluctantly, acknowledges, is that he can't be a farmer without incurring debts that may never be repaid. The fact of his marriage (which he keeps trying to overlook) ought to have taught him that. If it hasn't, buying a farm surely will.

Nor is this reason to be depressed; on the contrary, Wheeler is downright cheerful about it. After all, these unpaid debts are the essence of community:

> "The life of a neighborhood is a gift. I know that if you bought a calf from Nathan Coulter you'd pay him for it, and that's right. But aside from that, you're friends and neighbors, you work together, and so there's lots of giving and taking without a price. . . . You don't send a bill. You don't, if you can help it, keep an account. Once the account is kept and the bill presented, the friendship ends, the neighborhood is finished, and you're back where you started. The starting place doesn't have anybody in it but you."[72]

Independence as Elton imagines it—the ability to live thankless—is illusory. The original situation is merely a hypothetical (or at most temporary) state that one enters in order to see more clearly where one's obligations lie—and choose accordingly.[73] Thus the goal is not to avoid or escape ties of dependence and responsibility; the best an autonomous agent can do is to make those connections one's own, to affirm them through a conscious act of choice. In this way, "chance disappears into choice."[74]

This much is consistent with the critique of individualism already discussed. But Elton's situation suggests that the question isn't just whether some state of perfect independence is possible or desirable. Elton might be indebted to Old Jack, but he could have chosen to give up the farm to avoid being further indebted to Wheeler. Or he might have borrowed the money from a bank to avoid burdening their friendship. Our inability to achieve perfect independence doesn't make the ideal irrelevant, it just directs our attention to a new set of questions: First, when is seeking more independence an appropriate goal? Second, if perfect independence is impossible, on whom should we depend?

In addressing the first question, Berry acknowledges that individual independence is an important goal, but only at certain times and in certain situations. Determining its proper time and place depends on having a story about the proper course of individual growth and development, which Berry offers: Human life is best conceived as a cycle marked by a series of transitions between dependence, independence, and responsibility. "Throughout most of our literature," he notes, "the normal thing was for the generations to succeed one another in place."[75] At some point (Berry suggests it was a nineteenth-century development) this norm changed; the theme of the child returning home became "only a desire and a memory."[76] This he considers a deviation from the normal and desirable state of affairs. Of course, children do need to grow up and leave home. The struggle for this sort of autonomy remains a valuable part of individual development.[77] But ideally they should *come back,* and take on the responsibilities of family, community, and their own personal history. If returning diminishes individual freedom to some extent, that shouldn't be counted as a loss. Dependence and responsibility— particularly when ratified by conscious choice—are fulfilling in their own way. Moreover, they constitute the glue that holds communities together, making possible ways of life a completely "independent" person could never achieve.[78]

Clearly this argument rests on Berry's larger critique of American society as being too restless, too ready to light out for the territories. If we reject the larger critique, then his view of leaving and returning as normative is vulnerable; no doubt it's possible to tell a number of different stories about the "normal" pattern of human life. Nevertheless, we can separate his concern about geographic mobility from his point about the limited importance of the search for autonomy. Whatever the normal pattern of human life, it's unlikely that such a goal is appropriate to every stage of it.

Of course, Berry is not unique in suggesting that our understanding of autonomy ought to be more sensitive to the patterns of human life.[79] But we must distinguish Berry's position from that of theorists who talk about autonomy as a *global* property, a property of a complete life. Robert Young, for example, suggests that the heart of autonomy is "to exercise one's freedom in such a way as to order one's life according to a plan or conception which fully expresses one's own choices."[80] Under this view, one's life may be called autonomous even if one voluntarily sacrifices some autonomy at times to fulfill one's life plan (by entering a monastery, for example, or by getting married). Under this conception of autonomy, Elton Penn can be said to be living autonomously to the extent he lives the life he chose—even if that life involves some dependencies.

Berry's use of the life cycle concept has somewhat different implications. The life cycle is not under our control; it is a natural condition to which we must adapt our life plans. Its significance is that the decision to sacrifice some independence isn't always ours. Most people will move *involuntarily* from a youthful independence to states of complex interdependence, responsibility, and even a childlike dependence (in sickness or old age) over the course of their lives. The problem for an actor attempting to live autonomously is that those involuntary stages of dependence may interfere with her ability to fulfill a life plan—and therefore seem to rob her of something morally desirable.[81] From Berry's perspective, however, the point is not simply to order one's life according to a plan that fully expresses one's own choices, but to seek the degree of autonomy *appropriate* to one's age, experience, and place in the community. Under this view, involuntary stages of dependence are morally desirable precisely because they require us to acknowledge that we cannot achieve perfect independence and freedom. Virtue (sophrosyne) lies in recognizing the limited scope of our autonomy, in being willing to depend on others when appropriate *given the nature of the human condition* (rather than merely when appropriate given the nature of one's life plans).

For Berry, then, independence is a proper goal mostly for teens and young adults (or, importantly, for slaves and other oppressed groups). In most cases it will be inappropriate for a mature adult to seek independence and freedom the way that adolescents do; community life demands that adults enter into a web of interdependencies, just as old age demands that we accept a greater degree of dependence as an appropriate condition. Elton Penn's desire for independence is amusing to Wheeler not because it's inherently wrong, but because it's childlike. Elton has simply outgrown that particular goal.

The view that states of dependence are sometimes normative and morally desirable leads us to the second question: Given the limited scope of our autonomy, on whom or what should we depend? Children of course have little choice about their dependencies; adults have a great deal more, and their choices accordingly carry more moral significance. Elton might have chosen to go to a bank or the government for help, instead of to his friend Wheeler. The story suggests that these options are not morally equivalent. Elton is a better man for having chosen to depend on a friend: dependence on the right people, or things, improves character.[82] For example, people who depend directly on the land are more likely to be responsible and responsive to its needs. Nature, Berry points out, doesn't allow freedom from responsibility. Farms demand more from you than impersonal markets; poor decisions and actions are recorded indelibly in the earth, in the loss of topsoil, fertility, and viable ecosystems.[83] Elton's dependence on Wheeler will also undoubtedly demand more from him than dependence on an impersonal bank. That is precisely why he is better off accepting Wheeler's help.

Moreover, the community is better off for it. These choices of dependencies not only shape one's own life, they influence the character of the community. (Imagine, for example, the consequences for the community of a business owner seeking help from organized crime.) Not surprisingly, Berry favors dependence on family, friends, and neighbors over organizations, particularly nonlocal organizations like large corporations and federal government. Personal interdependence is, in his view, critical to building strong communities. "When people are no longer useful to each other, then the centripetal force of family and community fails, and people fall into dependence on exterior economies and organizations."[84] Thus the breakdown of family and community, a favorite conservative complaint, is to Berry a function of home economics: "In the present economy . . . where individual dependences are so much exterior to both household and community, family members often have no practical need or use for one another."[85] His solution is to encourage family members to work together, to make the household a center of economic production rather than simply consumption. "By elaborating household chores and obligations, we hope to strengthen the bonds of interest, loyalty, affection, and cooperation that keep families together."[86] Happily, family farms do just that.

Berry's analysis of the causes of family and community breakdown takes the familiar conservative complaint and turns it against the corporate capitalism that conservatives usually support.[87] Communities, he points out, would be stronger if they were composed of small family businesses and if children had little incentive to leave home to seek greener pastures. This is not, of course, what most conservatives have in mind for America. Nor, for that matter, do most liberals. Berry's vision not only raises conservative fears about restrictions on free markets and the erosion of economic competitiveness, it raises liberal fears about oppressive conformity and limited opportunities for individual development. After all, dependence on family and neighbors sounds appealing only if your family and neighbors are dependable. If they're uncaring, controlling, cruel, stupid, or violent, the individual may be better off depending on those large, impersonal organizations.

But Berry insists that depending on family is generally less threatening to liberty than depending on corporations: "If you are dependent on people who do not know you, who control the value of your necessities, you are not free, and you are not safe."[88] A woman who chooses to work at home and depend on her husband for cash is not, in his view, necessarily worse off than a woman who accepts "subordination to bosses."[89] Better off than either is the couple that doesn't need to participate in the cash economy at all, that depend solely on the land—and each other—for sustenance. But his main point, I think, is not that family members and neighbors are invariably more dependable and caring than bureaucracies. It is simply that such interdependencies are essential to community. And the problems attendant on living in community with others are preferable to the problems attendant on living isolated, alienated lives in the shadow of large-scale bureaucracies—perhaps precisely *because* living in community is so troublesome, and demands so much more of us.[90]

As for the problems attendant on large-scale bureaucracy, we need to bear in mind that for Berry they are largely, if not exclusively, ecological. Strong communities and traditions are integral to Berry's program for improving agricultural practices and cultivating environmental stewardship. If his critique of corporations—their ecological irresponsibility and insensitivity to local conditions—is persuasive, it provides further reason to encourage family and community dependencies, even at the risk to individual welfare. In weighing that risk, however, we should not take rugged individualism as our moral ideal. A good human life, for Berry, is characterized by the combination of autonomy, dependence, and responsibility appropriate to one's place in the natural and social world. That vision, both more complicated and more demanding than rugged individualism, is the ideal we should aim for.

Old Jack was in the habit of saying, "Son, do you owe anybody anything? Well, you won't amount to a damn until you do."[91] It's an ambiguous remark; coming from Jack, we should perhaps read it as an endorsement of independence, implying that the struggle to get out of debt teaches one the value of self-reliance. Coming from Berry, however, we should read into it a recognition that dependence is not only our natural condition but the source of our character and value. This insight takes aim at what Berry considers the moral foundations of industrial capitalism. Others may point to a utilitarian concern with efficiency and a desire to better the lives of the have-nots as the primary justifications for our ever-expanding consumption and exploitation of natural resources. Berry is apparently skeptical of such other-regarding motives; in his view, the emotional force behind our economic system is our longing to be independent of nature and each other, to be free from constraints on action and master our own destiny. That desire, although understandable and even in some situations admirable, constitutes a major barrier to living a full, and fully human, life.

But we are still far from understanding what this ideal human life would look like. Once we give up our restless striving for autonomy and power, what are we to do with ourselves? How will Berry's agrarian republic allow us to realize our potential as humans? The next chapter takes up that question, exploring Berry's alternative to the "deadly civilization of piety and violence" and the imaginary territory of freedom and irresponsibility.

Chapter Seven

A Secular Grace

One of the recurrent scenes in Berry's novels, constantly returning us to the fundamentals of agrarian life, is the tobacco harvest. Here, Nathan Coulter remembers bringing in the crop:

> Daddy picked up the first stick in his row and stuck it in the ground. "Take a row, boys. Move fast, but be careful." . . .
>
> I watched him out of the corner of my eye, working himself into the motion of it, his shoulders swaying in the row ahead of us. He worked without waste or strain, bending over his movement. . . .
>
> The afternoon went on, hot and clear, the ground soaking up the heat and throwing it back in our faces. We cut one row and went back and started another. When we ran out of water Grandpa took the jug to the house and filled it. We stopped to drink, and worked again. The rows were long, and the tiredness wore down into our shoulders and backs and legs. . . .
>
> By five o'clock we could see it was the best day's work we'd done since we started. That made us feel good, and we worked faster, looking forward to quitting time when we could talk about what we'd done and brag to ourselves a little.[1]

It's not exactly an idyllic vision of farm life; no one really welcomes this kind of work. But neither is it plaintive. This is just what farming is: hard, grueling work. The sweat, the heat, the aches in the back and shoulder and legs, are definitive of the farmer's life, shaping his character and outlook. This—believe it or not—is the good life.

The question is, what on earth is good about it? Berry's conception of the good life centers on the moral value of *labor,* an enduring theme in agrarian thought. But Berry's account of why labor is morally enriching goes beyond that of earlier agrarians. Labor in traditional agrarian thought is tied to wealth creation as well as character formation; labor makes the nation wealthy as well as cultivating politically desirable virtues, such as self-sufficiency. For Berry, in contrast, labor is morally significant not because it creates wealth but because labor is our primary means of relating to the physical and social world: It mediates our relationship to nature (by working the land) and to our community (to the extent we work together or for each other). Labor forces us to confront reality, to learn what it is and is not possible for us to do, to understand our limits. In this way, labor helps us to realize our ultimate end or *telos,* the good toward which an ideal human life aims. Berry's term for this good is grace—a richly developed concept that takes the place of autonomy in Berry's "new moral vision." The relationship between labor and grace thus lies at the heart of his moral theory.

Berry's case for the moral value of labor begins with an attack on the dangers of consumerism. Americans, he complains, have been raised on the ideals of freedom and limitless "self-development" to become, not extraordinary human beings, but shallow, unhappy, wasteful consumers. The average American, he asserts, "is probably the most unhappy average citizen in the history of the world."

> He has not the power to provide himself with anything but money. . . . From morning to night he does not touch anything that he has produced himself, in which he can take pride. For all his leisure and recreation, he feels bad, he looks bad, he is overweight, and his health is poor.[2]

Such complaints about the meaninglessness of a life oriented toward consumption are a long-standing theme in agrarianism (among other things that make farmers virtuous, recall, are their industry and frugality). But Berry doesn't simply replay the anticonsumer ideology of the Populists. His has an ecological slant:

> A more realistic and creative vision of ourselves would teach us that our ecological obligations are to use, not to use up; to use by the standard of real need, not of fashion or whim; and then to relinquish what we have used in a way that returns it to the common ecological fund from which it came.[3]

Rather than thinking of ourselves as the end point of a process that begins with (hard, undesirable) production and ends with (fulfilling, limitless) consumption, we should see ourselves as part of a cyclical process characterized by production geared toward consumption, and vice versa. As on a subsistence farm, one eats in order to work and works in order to eat.

And the working part is clearly, for Berry, the more important part: "It has become almost a heresy to speak of hard work, especially manual work, as an inescapable human necessity" much less as "good and ennobling, a source of pleasure and joy."[4] But that is how he speaks of it. "Work is necessary to us, as much a part of our condition as mortality. . . . We have tried to escape the sweat and sorrow promised in Genesis—only to find that, in order to do so, we must foreswear love and excellence, health and joy."[5] Without work—particularly physical labor directed at satisfying real needs—our body becomes obsolescent, merely "a diverting pet . . . that must be taken out for air and exercise."[6] It is work, then, that gives us dignity. Under this view, sophrosyne—the ability to moderate our desires—is merely a starting point; it leads us out of a culture shaped and driven by consumerism and toward a more fulfilling, more human life, shaped and driven by labor.

But why labor? What is uniquely valuable and fulfilling about hard work? As an initial approach to this question, it's helpful to contrast his praise of work with his more ambivalent view of craftsmanship. Berry's craftsmen do not typically lead the fulfilling lives that hard work is supposed to offer. On the contrary, craft is often associated in Berry's works with physical deformity, silence, and death. Consider for example the carpenter Ernest Finley, whose story is told in *A Place on Earth*. Ernest takes up his craft after having been crippled in the war. He's a good worker, but hardly a happy or healthy one; withdrawn into his work, he cuts himself off from the social world. He works alone, keeps himself hidden, and perfects his silence.[7] His isolation and impotence are represented by his love for a married woman who remains oblivious to his passion. Cut off from the world of marriage and productive relationships, he finally commits suicide.[8] A similar, if less tragic, example is Jayber Crow, the town's barber. Like Ernest he is a craftsman of sorts, and like Ernest, he is a solitary man and a victim of unrequited (or at least unconsummated) love.[9] Work did not redeem either Ernest or Jayber; on the contrary, it served instead as an inadequate substitute for a more rewarding engagement in social life. Rather than connecting them to the world, their work provided a way for them to keep themselves separate and alone.

The stories of Ernest and Jayber contrast with Berry's descriptions of harvesting tobacco, which is always a communal activity, an opportunity for cooperation with and connection to others (even if only with one's horse). The harvest may be difficult, painful, and rife with tensions—but it's never lonely, and it usually ends up improving one's character. These conflicting visions of the rewards of work suggest that Berry would distinguish among kinds of work; indeed, his contrast between agricultural labor and craftsmanship seems to map Hannah Arendt's categories of work and labor. According to Arendt, this distinction is common in Western thought (underlying, for example, the more familiar distinction between skilled and unskilled labor).[10] Labor, she contends, is concerned with biological processes that produce the necessities of life. It is "primarily concerned with the means of its own reproduction" but "it never 'produces' anything but life."[11] Labor (such as harvesting crops) is thus continuous and cyclical; its end is the life process itself, the cycle of producing and consuming. Moreover, labor tends to underscore our commonalities with others; we typically labor in the same way for the same reasons. Work, in contrast, is the fabrication of things, a linear activity with a definite end—building a house, writing a poem.[12] Because work produces an object, it can serve as a vehicle by which the worker expresses his unique personality. It is therefore more individualistic, and often more solitary, than labor.

Arendt contends that work has traditionally been, and should be, valued more highly than labor because it expresses one's personality. Moreover, work produces something that we can hold in common; it makes the world a home. According to Arendt, "the presence of others who see what we see and hear what we hear assures us of the reality of the world and ourselves."[13] Thus "to live together in the world means essentially that a world of things is between those who have it in common, as a table is located between those who sit around it."[14] To be in community with others, we need physical objects that we hold in common. Berry would of course agree, but Arendt insists that the earth, the products of nature, cannot serve as the thing we have in common. It is human artifacts—the products of work—that make up our common world.

Arendt doesn't explicitly defend her claim that the earth cannot constitute our common ground, but it appears to rest in part on the fact that we hold nature in common not only with each other but also with animals. Her understanding of labor and work reflects an anthropocentrism that values humans precisely to the extent they are *not* like animals. Thus Arendt devalues labor because it is directed toward satisfying our common biological needs (our animal natures) rather than transcending them. Even worse, collective labor—like harvesting a crop—requires us all to behave the same, to become identical and (ominously) interchangeable. In Arendt's view, labor causes people to relate to each other as animals, not as meaningful actors. In her vision, labor "indicates the unity of the species with regard to which every single member is the same and exchangeable."[15] Laborers, in short, are fit subjects for a totalitarian regime.

Berry's concerns about industrialization, however, are quite different from Arendt's anxiety about totalitarianism. Thus he reverses Arendt's evaluation, suggesting that the traditionally disfavored labor should be valued over work. He consistently describes labor such as planting and harvesting as ennobling, activities through which one can realize the best of human virtues. Work can also promote important virtues, of course, but it is nonetheless dangerous. As much as Berry admires good craftsmanship, he contends that work tends to be solitary, individualistic, solipsistic. Work is aimed not at participating in natural processes but transcending them; it is an attempt to create an artificial world, a world that reflects one's individual personality. Although work is clearly necessary—Berry agrees that we are not animals, that we need to create an artificial world to live in—he would warn us of the dangers of this project. Ernest's work led him to a false sense of independence, a hubristic belief that he could extract himself from the ties of social life. And it ended in suicide, the ultimate rejection of social bonds, the final hubristic attempt to control one's fate. Labor, in contrast, keeps us constantly aware of our dependence and vulnerability, our need for one another. Thus labor more so than work teaches sophrosyne and sociability.

For Berry, then, labor is more valuable than work in part because labor is a better expression of sophrosyne. But Berry's case for labor goes beyond its relationship to sophrosyne. Sophrosyne is, in a sense, a negative virtue, counseling one as to what not to do. Berry's aim is higher; he wants to elaborate a larger moral framework within which it makes sense to strive for sophrosyne—to outline an alternative to the seductive ideals of limitless self-development, power, and freedom. To understand the full value of labor, we have to understand this alternative goal: a moral ideal he calls grace.

The best expression of this ideal comes, not from Berry, but from Norman MacLean's novel *A River Runs Through It*. Berry quotes this passage, in which the narrator is explaining why, in his family, "there was no clear line between fishing and religion":

> As a Scot and a Presbyterian, my father believed that man by nature was a mess and had fallen from an original state of grace. . . . I never knew whether he believed God was a mathematician but he certainly believed God could count and that only by picking up God's rhythms were we able to regain power and beauty.[16]

In MacLean's novel, the characters "pick up God's rhythms" through the art of fly-fishing; Berry picks them up by cutting tobacco. He describes a consummate tobacco cutter thus:

> In the rhythms of that difficult work Elton moves like a dancer, seemingly without effort, lightly. . . . swaying, bending and rising in the ripe row in the rich evening light—that unsparing man, so careful in his ways—his blade striking lightly as he bends, the golden plants turning to rest upon the stick, the row lengthening rapidly behind him, shortening ahead of him. With increasing distance the figure loses personality; it becomes a lyrical embodiment of youth and strength and grace.[17]

This isn't grace in the Christian sense, but a secular grace revealed in physical action. Grace turns demanding physical tasks into a beautiful dance. Ernest Finley, for example, was able to achieve a measure of grace in his work by virtue of his sophrosyne: He had "quickly developed the judgment necessary to his lameness, which enabled him to estimate accurately what he could and could not do." As a result, he could "lift and carry and climb" better than people expected.[18] Nevertheless, his lameness (not to mention his suicide) suggests the limits of his gracefulness; the repetitive, rhythmic aspect of labor, and the fact that it has no end except the life cycle itself, makes it a better vehicle than work for achieving grace. For Berry, the laborer is the paradigm of gracefulness; it is grace that transforms him or her from a mere drudge into a kind of artist.

In its core sense, then, grace is skill or technical competence—it is virtuosity, the ideal sought by the laborer, athlete, or dancer. Construed more broadly, grace is the ability to move effortlessly and beautifully, in harmony with one's physical and social environment. It is less an intellectual virtue than a physical awareness—a sensitivity to the situation combined with a sense, below the conscious level of thought, of what to do—and what one *can* do—in this context. Importantly, the concept of grace assumes that the context presents obstacles and poses limits; grace is achieved by responding to these challenges. Just as a dancer must know the limits of the stage, a graceful actor must know the limits of her range of action. A graceful person knows the right thing to do in this particular place and time; she exhibits the virtue of propriety. This virtue allows her to perform the action easily and naturally, without awkwardness, strain, or hesitancy. Thus Berry's most admirable characters exhibit a natural capacity for physical activity that manifests itself as grace.

But grace is more than just another virtue like sophrosyne or propriety. Grace is what one achieves when one practices *all* of the virtues well; it is the good toward which a virtuous person aims. "A purposeless virtue," Berry insists, "is a contradiction in terms. . . . A virtue must lead to harmony between one creature and another"[19]—that is, to grace. Grace is not a good in the utilitarian or consequentialist sense, however; one does not practice the virtues to achieve grace in the sense that one might play the violin to make money. Rather, grace resembles what Alasdair MacIntyre describes as a good internal to a practice. A practice, according to MacIntyre, is "any coherent and complex form of socially established cooperative human activity through which goods internal to that form of activity are realized in the course of trying to achieve those standards of excellence which are appropriate to, and partially definitive of, that form of activity."[20] He uses chess as an example: While we may acquire external and contingent goods (like money) by playing chess, there are goods that "cannot be had any way except by playing chess or some other game of that specific kind," such as "a certain highly particular kind of analytical skill, strategic imagination and competitive intensity."[21] The ability to achieve these internal goods is what we call virtuosity, the core sense of grace. A specific virtue, in contrast, is "an acquired human quality the possession and exercise of which tends to enable us to achieve these goods which are internal to practices and the lack of which effectively prevents us from achieving any such goods."[22] Practices and virtues are thus mutually constitutive. And grace is best understood as the achievement of the virtues appropriate to the practice in question.

Clearly the concept of a practice (or discipline, to use Berry's term)[23] is important to understanding both virtue and grace. Berry, like MacIntyre, uses specific practices (cutting tobacco, riding a horse) to illustrate the concept. But he also uses grace as a *general* moral ideal, suggesting that living itself is a practice, an activity through which we realize certain internal goods and aim for standards of excellence that are partially definitive of living. Under this view, one must have some understanding of the practice of living to understand what virtues such as sophrosyne, propriety, and fidelity require of us, just as we need some understanding of those virtues to understand what "living" in its truest sense—living gracefully—really is. In Berry's vision, the life of a small farmer in a stable agrarian community serves as a model of a life in which we can realize the key virtues (sophrosyne, propriety, fidelity), and thus achieve grace. This vision of a graceful life thus brings the virtues together and orders them.

Grace therefore serves as a moral ideal for individuals, a vision of the good life based on the ideal of the good farmer but to which even nonfarmers may aspire. It also, however, has cultural and ecological implications.[24] For example, grace facilitates collective labor. Cooperative labor can create an almost organic bond among the workers: skilled tobacco cutters "cooperate like the two hands of a single body, anticipating each other's moves like partners in a dance."[25] Arendt worried about the totalitarian implications of those organic bonds, but Berry reminds us that such cooperation is critical to community. As I argued in chapter 6, Berry emphasizes the importance of working together to strengthen families and communities. Economic interdependence leads to collective labor, which (if done properly, gracefully) produces a host of social benefits. The tobacco harvest, for example, "is the most protracted social occasion of our year. Neighbors work together; they are together all day every day for weeks." It is an occasion for talk, and telling old stories; it therefore becomes "a sort of ritual of remembrance"[26] Through this common work we achieve both grace and community—or, more properly, we achieve community to the extent we achieve collective grace.

Moreover, graceful work creates order and enriches the world, both materially and spiritually. It allows the actor almost magically to use resources without diminishing them. As an example Berry points to the Menominee Indians in northern Wisconsin, who practice a forest economy:

> In 1854, when logging was begun, the forest contained an estimated billion and a half board feet of standing timber. . . . From 1865 to 1988 the forest yielded two billion board feet. And today, after 140 years of continuous logging, the forest still is believed to contain a billion and a half board feet of standing timber. Over those 140 years, the average diameter of the trees has been reduced by only one half of one inch—and that by design.[27]

This is a graceful economy, an economy that leaves the forest in better condition today than it was when the Menominees started cultivating it. In addition, the forest "is the basis of a culture" and "home not only to its wild inhabitants but also to its human community."[28] So the forest has also been enriched in meaning by virtue of the Menominees' activity there.

Conversely, the absence of grace is evidenced by disorder and impoverishment—precisely the features of modern agriculture that Berry indicts. "In general," he tells us, "the better the land, the neater the farm looks." Industrial farms, however, look "monotonous" and "sterile."[29] Of course, one might well ask, by whose standards? Surely by some criteria, industrial farms are quite neat—even aesthetically interesting, in their stark geometry and dramatic dimensions. To make sense of Berry's claim, I think, we have to assume that our aesthetic judgments about land use are often influenced by our judgments about the quality of the life lived in that place. Formal aesthetic standards notwithstanding, a diversified farm looks better to most of us because it seems to most of us like a better place to live. "Orderly" environments look orderly to us for the same reason they are good: because they arise out of a characteristically human life (just as a lion's den would look orderly to a lion because it is created by and makes sense in terms of a lion's life).

Moreover, industrial farms aren't just aesthetically unappealing; they generate a string of increasingly complicated problems. Traditional diversified farms conforming to ancient patterns wasted nothing; farmers raised grain, fed it to livestock, and used the manure from the livestock to fertilize the field. Industrial agriculture specializes, growing great fields of grain in one part of the country and giant herds of livestock in another. The result is that wheat and corn farmers must use chemical fertilizers (whose only advantage over manure is that they're easier to transport), and cattle ranchers are faced with mounting piles of manure to dispose of. The system, as Berry puts it, "take[s] a solution and divide[s] it neatly into two problems."[30] More than two problems, if you include the difficulty of disease control among the cattle and the soil erosion and compaction endemic to our grain monoculture.

A graceful solution solves a number of problems at the same time rather than creating a host of new ones—like the Menominees' forest economy, which provides a livelihood, maintains the forest in good condition, and makes the wilderness a home. Berry calls this "solving for pattern," the pattern being a joint product of nature and culture. In general, he argues, a good solution, instead of doing violence to natural processes of growth and decay, works within those processes and turns them to human advantage. The best, most graceful, agriculture is that which comes closest to the processes at work in the prairie and the forest; usually this will be a traditional agriculture, conforming to a pattern of human interaction with nature that has evolved in that place over centuries.[31] Lives directed toward grace, living harmlessly and enriching the world, should generate such patterns rather than disrupt them.

In sum, for Berry the good life is characterized by grace, by a responsive adaptation to the constraints of the physical and social environment. And grace in turn is achieved only through activity—particularly physical labor. Grace is what ennobles labor and therefore justifies Berry's anticonsumerism and producer-oriented ideology. In MacLean's words, "all good things . . . come by grace and grace comes by art and art does not come easy."[32] If you're trying to harvest a field of tobacco, you will be motivated to acquire that competence that makes the labor feel effortless and pleasurable. In the process of acquiring such competence, you should also acquire the virtues that will allow you to continue living gracefully when you leave the field. It is in the context of a life full of hard work—such as the life of a traditional farmer—that we learn the value of discipline, self-restraint, and acceptance of human limits. And it is in this context, perhaps not exclusively but certainly most forcefully, that the ideal of grace makes sense. The concept of grace thus completes Berry's moral vision—a more attractive vision, he hopes, than the promise of freedom and power offered by our industrial regime.

But is it? How does grace compare with individualism as a moral ideal? Interestingly, both grace and individualism (as described in chapter 6) aim at increasing individual power by enhancing one's ability to act, to cope with obstacles to or constraints on action. Of course, it is precisely this desire for power that Berry identified as the chief *defect* of individualism. Exercising power gracefully, however, is different from the more combative and violent way that rugged individualists exercise power. Grace is more restrained, disciplined, and responsive; in acting gracefully, one accepts and responds to the physical features of the world, rather than attempting to change or overcome those features. Grace allows one to adapt to the world, rather than force the world to conform to one's own will. It therefore shouldn't create the ecological and cultural problems that a quest for "limitless" power does.

On the other hand, this same feature of grace would seem to make it an unsuitable basis for social criticism. Individualism puts a premium on individual autonomy—and, as discussed in chapter 6, the concept of autonomy has played an important role in social reform. We can criticize our institutions for failing to allow individuals to live autonomously, and we can count on individuals seeking autonomy to challenge institutions that get in their way. If grace requires adapting to the social as well as physical world, then how can it serve as a critical standard for evaluating our social arrangements? Would individuals seeking to live gracefully ever challenge existing institutions?

Berry himself is perhaps the best response to this objection. He does in fact use grace as a critical standard: he contends that our current social arrangements are not graceful in themselves (they are disorderly and wasteful) and that they do not allow us to live gracefully. "To live undestructively in an economy that is overwhelmingly destructive would require of any of us, or of any small group of us, a great deal more work than we have yet been able to do," he complains. "How could we divorce ourselves completely and yet responsibly from the technologies and powers that are destroying our planet?"[33] Our social arrangements don't even allow for consistency, much less grace. So an individual seeking to live gracefully, it seems, would have to support social reform aimed at achieving a better harmony with the natural world. As Berry's discussion of Malcolm X suggests,[34] even small moments of grace can suggest to us a rich sense of the possibilities of life in this world, which can in turn inspire political action.

Thus a life oriented toward grace might well include activity, political and otherwise, in behalf of the environment.[35] In fact, the ideal of grace expresses what many environmentalists seem to be groping toward in their desire for a healthier, richer, more harmonious relationship to the natural world. Still, we may have reservations. Even to a committed environmentalist, Berry's account of the good life seems to be missing some important elements. Most notably, his focus on labor leads him, at least apparently, to devalue both art and spirituality—both of which have been critical supports for the environmental cause. Surely we value nature not only for its ability to teach us how to work but for its beauty and its ability to bring us into contact with a higher spiritual reality. An environmental philosophy that failed to recognize those values would cut itself off from the long and rich tradition of nature writing that has proved both morally enriching and politically useful. Before we endorse Berry's vision, then, we should consider whether his agrarian utopia would have a place for the aesthetic and spiritual practices so deeply intertwined with Americans' love for the natural landscape.

The best way to address this question is by comparing Berry to his agrarian predecessors, the Twelve Southerners. I argued in chapter 1 that *I'll Take My*

Stand is concerned primarily with defending leisure and the humane values against the soul-killing forces of industrialization. This interest in cultivating the mind arguably makes the Southerners' aristocratic agrarianism a better vehicle for an environmental sensibility than democratic agrarianism, because it gives us reason to value nature for its aesthetic and "humanizing" qualities. The question, then, is to what extent Berry shares the Southerners' interest in leisure and in cultivating the mind and spirit.

Although some commentators, and apparently Berry himself, consider him an intellectual descendant of the Twelve Southerners, there are subtle but important differences in their respective critiques of industrialization.[36] For the Twelve Southerners, the problem with industrial capitalism was that it destabilizes social hierarchy, undermines traditional values, and leads to the triumph of instrumental rationality. Berry's complaints about industrial society, in contrast, focus on its misguided reliance on nonrenewable resources and its ability to make unimaginable power available to very fallible humans. Like the Twelve Southerners, he worries about the loss of community and meaning in modern society—but only secondarily. His fear is that the loss of community controls leaves us free to exploit our natural resources beyond all reasonable bounds, and the loss of meaning fuels our endless hunger for greater power and material abundance. In short, where the Agrarians wanted to preserve the conditions for humane civilization, Berry is equally concerned about the conditions for human *existence*.

True, Berry does praise the Twelve Southerners for their "defense of human civilization." He draws attention to a passage from the introduction to *I'll Take My Stand:*

The regular act of applied science is to introduce into labor a labor-saving device or machine. Whether this is a benefit depends on how far it is advisable to save the labor. The philosophy of applied science is generally quite sure that the saving of labor is a pure gain, and that the more of it the better. This is to assume that labor is an evil, that only the end of labor or the material product is good. . . . The act of labor as one of the happy functions of human life has been in effect abandoned. . . .

Turning to consumption, as the grand end which justifies the evils of modern labor, we find that we have been deceived. We have more time in which to consume, and many more products to be consumed. But the tempo of our labors communicates itself to our satisfactions, and these also become brutal and hurried. The constitution of the natural man probably does not permit him to shorten his labor-time and enlarge his consuming-time indefinitely. He has to pay the penalty in satiety and aimlessness.[37]

The quote reflects the Twelve Southerners' leisure ethic: Even work should be leisurely, so that it can be enjoyed. Consumption is not bad in itself; it becomes bad only when it is hurried—turned into work, as it were—or when consumption is unguided by standards of restraint and good taste. Both work and consumption should be done with an unhurried, gentlemanly air divorced from any sense of urgency or need. Life is an art to be enjoyed, not a hardship to be endured.

Berry also objects to mechanizing work with labor-saving devices and points out the empty, unsatisfying nature of modern consumerism. But his reliance on *I'll Take My Stand* is misleading. Although he agrees that industrialization has taken much of the joy out of work, he has little to say about the "brutal, hurried" nature of consumption—or the masses' bad taste. Rather, the problem with our approach to consumption is that we consume merely to stave off the "loneliness and fear" created by the loss of meaningful work.[38] We've bought into the sales pitch; we believe we can cure our deep dissatisfaction with our lives by buying yet another glittering toy. Thus consumption comes to fill that empty space in our moral universe, our lack of a sense of what life is for.[39] In contrast to the Twelve Southerners, Berry argues that consumption divorced from real need, and real work, simply isn't meaningful or enjoyable. Even our "consumption" of nature should be a natural outgrowth of our work and life in a place, rather than a leisure activity.[40] Consumption should always be disciplined by work and need. Thus Berry's case for frugality is quite different from the aristocratic sensibility that drives the Twelve Southerners' contempt for mass consumerism.

In fact, for all his talk about the pleasures of the agrarian life, Berry seems to have little interest in leisure. To be sure, leisure is part of the scheme; one works to rest and rests to work. But Berry worries that a strong leisure ethic is problematic in that it teaches us that *only* leisure is enjoyable: "More and more," he complains, "we take for granted that work must be destitute of pleasure. More and more, we assume that if we want to be pleased we must wait until evening, or the weekend, or vacation, or retirement."[41] It is the importance and pleasure of work rather than leisure that impresses Berry. After all, it is "the use only of our bodies" that teaches us what can be done in the world without causing damage.[42] It takes a lifetime of physical work to learn how to live harmlessly in the world. Leisure, it seems, does very little to advance us toward this ideal.

Neither Berry's anticonsumerism nor his attack on the mechanization of agriculture is really comparable to that of the Twelve Southerners, then. On the other hand, he does share their concern with preserving the humanities—and, like them, he seems to think an agrarian society has a better chance of doing so than an industrial society. It's significant, however, that he never provides a really compelling explanation of *how* agrarianism is linked to humanism. The Southerners, for all their faults, had a coherent account of what was needed to preserve humanism—a leisure *class*. Berry takes the opposite position: An agrarian society, he contends, would support the liberal arts precisely because it *wouldn't* have a leisure class. This proves to be a hard case to make.

Berry claims that the liberal arts cannot thrive if they are separated from the actual work that ordinary people engage in. Industrialization, he charges, has resulted in this very situation. It has freed large segments of the population from manual labor, which in turn allows some people to become professional intellectuals. Thus the humanities are pursued almost entirely by academic specialists—and to the extent the study of literature, poetry, and philosophy are separated from the way we actually live, they become irrelevant and meaningless. Poets, for example, no longer write for a general public; they write for other poets, or more properly, for literary critics whose reviews will affect the poet's academic career.[43] The problem here isn't that industrialization robs us of leisure time, but that the people involved in intellectual pursuits have *too much* leisure, too little contact with the "real world" of ordinary production and reproduction. Writing should not be a way to remove oneself from the world but "an instrument by which a man may arrive in his place and maintain himself there." A man is most a poet "when he is most humanely and exactingly a man."[44] Berry sets an example for other poets by living on and working his own farm; his philosophical and literary work is grounded in his day-to-day experience of being a farmer and a member of a community.

Clearly this line of criticism is part of Berry's larger attack on the academic establishment. His defense of the humanities is a Populist call for keeping knowledge accessible to the masses and imposing public accountability on the intellectual elite. It is not, however, an argument for agrarianism. Berry never explains how, exactly, an agrarian society would prevent specialization or erosion of the humanities. True, according to Berry an agrarian society, because it would be more stable than industrial society, would better preserve traditions—including humanist traditions. But would yeomen farmers actually value the humanities? Surely the aristocratic agrarians had a point in insisting that intellectual pursuits call for a certain amount of leisure. It's significant, I think, that none of the farmers in Berry's copious body of fiction is an artist; most aren't even particularly well educated.[45] They certainly don't spend their free time reading Homer.

Still, the fact remains that Berry *does* value art, literature, and philosophy; indeed, his life has been dedicated to these pursuits as much as it has been dedicated to farming. Thus we should be able to draw out of his writings a defense, if not of leisure, at least of art and other humane pursuits. One possibility is to pursue Berry's recognition that intellectual production is, in fact, a legitimate kind of work. To the extent that art or writing can be characterized as disciplines, they require many of the same virtues as farming: awareness of one's place within an ongoing tradition, acceptance of one's limits, fidelity to the craft.[46] Berry frequently characterizes art as work; he describes writing, for example, as comparable in some respects to building a house. "At first glance, writing may seem not nearly so much an art of the body as, say, dancing or gardening or carpentry. And yet language is the most intimately physical of all the artistic means. We have it palpably in our mouths; it is our *langue,* our tongue."[47] Such language suggests that a poet, like a tobacco cutter, might achieve a kind of grace in the performance of her craft.

But the fact remains that most intellectual production is not "so insistently tangible an act as the act of building a house or playing a violin."[48] Those more physically challenging activities would seem to be a better means to grace than writing poetry or painting a picture. Moreover, we must not forget the reservations about craftsmanship represented by Ernest Finley; while such artistic work may be admirable, it still poses the dangers of social isolation and hubris (problems to which artists seem particularly vulnerable). Fortunately, Berry has other arguments for valuing artists. A poem, for example, "has the power to remind the poet and reader alike of things they have read and heard" and of things others have read and heard. Poets help to create and maintain the community's collective memory. They remind us what ought to be remembered.[49]

Further, works of art can result in a greater awareness of and appreciation for the world we live in. Consider Berry's celebration of Harlan Hubbard's paintings: "Harlan's principle motive," he reports, "was the preservation of the world's 'radiant beauty,' its blessedness or sanctity." His scenes are suffused with "a heavenly or blessed light present in *this* world, in ordinary day."

And his "vocation as an artist" was to make this radiant beauty "visible to others."[50] For Berry, one of Hubbard's virtues was that he infused the familiar landscape of his own country with aesthetic and sacred value—and thus gave his audience a reason to care for it. The visual arts, literature, poetry, and even philosophy can thus be justified as increasing our understanding of and appreciation for the world we live in. They might even (as he suggests of the best nature poetry) "produce the moral effect of care and competence and frugality in our use of the world."[51] As suggested in chapter 2, language for Berry is a means of bringing us into contact with reality; so the language and visual arts can, like labor, help to bring us into a proper relationship to the material world.[52]

Artists and other intellectuals may therefore find a respected place in Berry's agrarian utopia, at least to the extent they help to seduce us into a healthier, more positive relationship with the world. But to perform their job properly, they will have to remain themselves deeply involved in this world, living and working in the community, not locked away in ivory towers trying to transcend it. So even here, labor remains central to Berry's vision—and the role of universities and professors remains uncertain. Berry may be right that the way we currently pursue the humanities tends to create an intellectual elite far removed from the concerns of the rest of the community. But what would happen to the humanities if we didn't support our intellectuals this way? I suspect few artists could live as Berry does, producing over thirty books while running a farm and raising a family. Specialization, as the Twelve Southerners recognized, has its virtues.

And so does leisure. If we take Berry at his word, we don't need much leisure to live the good life. Like Marx, he seems to assume that we'll find plenty of time and energy after work for cultural production. Thus he can give us no compelling reason either to support a leisure class (by preserving the humanities in the universities, for example) or to pursue such a lifestyle (by becoming a professor, for example). Importantly, the problem here is not, as Berry would have it, a question of agrarianism versus industrialism. If the values of industrial society are inimical to art and philosophy, so too are the traditional values of farmers—and an agrarian society may well be too poor and too labor-intensive to support professional intellectuals. Clearly, simply rejecting industrialism isn't sufficient to ensure artistic production. We also need to correct the overemphasis on work and productivity that infects both industrial and agrarian ideologies, and to elaborate a leisure ethic as vital as that of the aristocratic agrarians. Berry's view of art as a way to encourage affection for the world is, at best, merely a starting point for such an ethic. But it takes us, I think, in the right direction: toward a greater involvement in and love for the world.

If art leads us to greater involvement in the material world, spirituality would seem to lead us in the other direction. Thus one would expect spirituality to have at best a minor place in Berry's vision of the good life. This expectation is reinforced by Berry's claim that what drives our quest for freedom and power is essentially a spiritual desire. We want to be immortal, to make our lives meaningful by seizing the godlike power of industrialism. Under this view, the quest for limitless power is doing the critical psychological work of giving our individual lives a larger meaning. We build skyscrapers, hydroelectric dams, and space shuttles for much the same reason as the Egyptian pharaohs built the pyramids: as a way to ensure our continuing presence and importance after death. From this perspective, we might be better off (ecologically, at any rate) to ignore or suffocate our spiritual impulses. But that's hardly feasible; if they play such an important role in industrialization, they're unlikely to disappear in Berry's reconstituted agrarian republic. So if we abandon our dreams of an industrial paradise, as Berry recommends, how are we to satisfy that spiritual hunger? What, for Berry, is the larger context that gives our lives meaning?

Berry seems reluctant to endorse the conventional response, to contend that our lives are meaningful to the extent they serve some transcendent value like God, Truth, Justice, or Beauty. He consistently rejects appeals to transcendent values, characterizing them as an intrinsic part of the moral vocabulary of the industrial regime, the vocabulary of freedom and power. Looking to Heaven, he insists, is just another way to avoid grappling with the earth, the actual material conditions of our existence. But Berry's assault on conventional spirituality is aimed primarily at the Christian tradition, and must be understood in that somewhat complicated context. His rejection of spirituality, like his rejection of autonomy, is less radical than it appears.

Berry is hardly unique among environmentalists in his suspicion of Christianity. As argued in chapter 2, a major theme in the preservationist tradition is the rejection of conventional Protestantism in favor of a more nature-centered spirituality. This early ambivalence toward Christianity, I suggested, was driven by a desire for spiritual autonomy—a desire with which Berry would not have much sympathy. But since the 1960s, new grounds for environmentalists to criticize Christianity have emerged, principally in the form

of Lynn White's controversial 1967 essay, "The Historical Roots of Our Ecological Crisis." White argued that medieval Christianity provided the ideological foundations for modern technological inventiveness, justified
exploitation of nature by giving humans dominion over the earth, and
destroyed the pagan religions that might have fostered a more respectful attitude toward nature.[53] The essay touched off a heated debate over the relationship between Christianity and our environmental practices, and has led
some environmentalists to look to pagan and Eastern religions for varieties
of spirituality more conducive to ecological sensitivity.[54]

Not everyone finds White persuasive, however. Robin Attfield, for example, argues that Christian teachings on nature have been quite complex,
encompassing a range of views from the dominion to the stewardship perspective.[55] This complexity has in fact allowed many American churches to
embrace a greener theology, enthusiastically joining the environmental cause
in what Roderick Nash calls the "greening of religion." Still, many Christians
remain wary, seeing in the environmental movement a dangerous turn toward
paganism and a vapid, New Age spirituality.[56] Complicating this ideological
picture for Berry is the fact that Christian churches, and especially Catholics,
are important allies for family farmers. The Catholic Church has been a strong
advocate for rural communities since the Dust Bowl era; since the late 1970s
it has taken a particular interest in the plight of small farmers.[57]

The prominence of Christian leaders in farm politics may account for
the evolution of Berry's views on Christianity from outright hostility to somewhat wary accommodation. His earliest critique of Christianity appears in
The Long-Legged House, published shortly after White's article. Berry's
focus was not on the Bible's dominion mandate, however, but on the cultural
effects of Christianity's heroic ethics. The ideals of Christianity, he argued,
"place an extraordinary moral burden on the individual.... The follower of
these beliefs finds himself in anxiety and trouble. If he loves his neighbor as
himself, he has no reason to expect that he will not be hated in return." We
react to this anxiety and trouble "by tak[ing] refuge in institutional formulas
and regulations, to substitute reverential lip service and dues paying for the
labor implied by the demands of the ideal upon the real."[58] Heroic ethics lead
to heroic institutions, such as the church and large-scale government bureaucracies. And heroic institutions relieve us of a sense of personal responsibility, fostering hypocrisy—as well as disrupting local communities with their
well-intentioned attempts to serve our grandiose ideals.

This complaint about the hypocrisy of spiritual authorities illustrates
Berry's strong and persistent anticlericalism. He invariably portrays minis-

ters and priests as pretenders to a spurious moral authority, outsiders with no real understanding of the people they are supposed to minister to. Priests "wait in their blackness to earn joy / by dying. They trust that nothing holy is free, / and so their lives are paid. Money slots / in the altar rails make a jukebox of the world."[59] Complains one of his characters of a minister attempting to comfort a grieving father, "Here in a way he'd come to say the last words over Tom. And what claim did he have to do it? He never done a day's work with us in his life, nor could have." The problem, in a nutshell, is that the preacher "has what I reckon you would call a knack for the Hereafter. He's not much mixed with this world."[60] Confining spiritual expertise to churches is no better than confining art and science to universities; such knowledge, if it is to remain useful, must arise out of the work and cares of everyday life.

Berry's hostility to organized religion is gradually accompanied, however, by a more accommodating attitude toward Christian theology. In *The Gift of Good Land,* for example, Berry "attempt[s] a Biblical argument for ecological and agricultural responsibility."[61] This essay, explicitly directed against Lynn White, endorses the stewardship interpretation of Genesis. The earth, Berry concludes, is given to us as a gift, but given "only for a time, and only for so long as it is properly used."[62] Thus the Bible in fact supports a view of humanity as tenants not owners, subject always to God's authority. But Berry's endorsement of the Bible is qualified; the essay also reiterates his concern about Christianity's heroic ethics and alleged inattention to the value of "life-long devotion and perseverance in unheroic tasks," of "good workmanship or 'right livelihood.' "[63] He develops this stance of qualified approval in his 1993 collection, *Sex, Economy, Freedom, and Community,* arguing that while the Bible supports a stewardship ethic, it also tends to foster a radical duality between body and soul that leads us to devalue the material world.[64] This worry about Christian dualism, which is in line with the usual interpretation of White's thesis, reappears in the 1995 collection *Another Turn of the Crank:* "I do not doubt the reality of the experience and knowledge we call 'spiritual' any more than I doubt the reality of so-called physical experience and knowledge," he explains. "But I strongly doubt the advantage, and even the possibility, of separating these two realities. What I'm arguing against here is not complexity or mystery but dualism."[65]

In sum, Berry criticizes Christianity for its heroic ethics, which lead to the institutionalization of spirituality as well as hypocrisy and the devaluation of ordinary life. He objects also to the use of the Bible to reinforce an exploitative stance toward nature, and to the dualism in Christian thought that leads us to devalue the material world. But for all this he refuses to abandon the faith—by turning to Buddhism, for example, like his fellow traveler Gary Snyder.[66] "I owe a considerable debt myself to Buddhism and Buddhists," he acknowledges. "But there are an enormous number of people—and I am one of them—whose native religion, for better or worse, is Christianity." He can no more abandon Christianity than he can abandon the Western philosophical tradition: "We were born to it; we began to learn about it before we became conscious; it is . . . an intimate belonging of our being; it informs our consciousness, our language, our dreams."[67] Ultimately his belief in our dependence on tradition overrides his reservations about this particular tradition: "We can turn away from it or against it, but that will only bind us tightly to a reduced version of it." Better that Christianity "should survive and renew itself so that it may become as largely and truly instructive as we need it to be."[68]

Rather than dismissing our spiritual traditions and practices, then, Berry would like to see them reformulated in a way more consistent with his ecological sensibility. In particular, he would like to make our spiritual practices more *earthy,* less concerned with relating our lives to some transcendent ideal.[69] Any appeal to otherworldly ideals turns our attention away from *this* world: "Where there is no accurate sense of the real world, idealism evaporates in the rhetoric of self-righteousness and self-justification."[70] Thus we need to find meaning in a way that keeps our attention focused here, in the material world.

One obvious source of meaning for Berry is the cycle of life itself: "It is impossible to contemplate the life of the soil for very long without seeing it as analogous to the life of the spirit. No less than the faithful of religion is the good farmer mindful of the persistence of life through death, the passage of energy through changing forms." This cycle, he suggests, is our only true contact with the infinite. If religion is, as Berry suggests, "what binds us back to the source of life," and the source of life is the soil, then farming serves as a kind of natural religion, binding us to the material basis of our lives.[71]

Under this view, we achieve immortality by fertilizing the soil with our decayed remains—not a particularly uplifting account of what makes our lives meaningful. But Berry also suggests that we might find spiritual meaning in our ability to contribute to the community. In the absence of Heaven, the life of the community can provide the larger context for making sense of our individual lives. This solution poses certain spiritual dangers, however. We must avoid putting ourselves in the role of the classical hero, whose life becomes exemplary because his great virtues allow him to benefit the community. Heroes under the classical view are more than mortal; they achieve a kind of immortality by virtue of their extraordinary qualities. This desire for a more-than-human goodness is precisely what Berry dislikes about ecocentrism and Christianity both: they are (he claims) rooted in a misanthropic hostility to ordinary human life and activity. Heroic ethics are merely another attempt to transcend the human condition.

What seems to make communal life meaningful for Berry is that the community helps to define one's place, one's proper role. It is not that we are assigned a role arbitrarily by birth; as discussed in chapter 6, choosing to enter a community and finding a place in it is part of the transition to adulthood. Once that choice is made, however, our lives are meaningful to the extent we fulfill those roles—to the extent we are "acting our parts among other creatures all made of the same dust and breath as ourselves."[72] A meaningful life, under this view, is a life not of heroism but of propriety: a life appropriate to one's place and time, centered on good, necessary work. "All of us," he suggests, "are makers, within mortal terms and limits, of our lives, of one another's lives, of things we need and use."[73] For Berry, this making takes on spiritual meaning: "To live, we must daily break the body and shed the blood of Creation. When we do this knowingly, lovingly, skillfully, reverently, it is a sacrament."[74] In other words, we are not Odysseus. We are Eumaios, Telemakhos, Penelope: the ones who faithfully performed their daily labors, maintaining the kingdom until he returned.

If this humble view of the significance of our lives isn't enough to satisfy our spiritual hunger, we may still find comfort in Berry's understanding of grace. The concept of grace suggests that our lives are made meaningful, at least in part, by the intrinsic pleasure and value of doing something well. Recall MacIntyre's definition of a practice: the point of a practice is to achieve the goods internal to it—not external rewards like Heaven or immortality. The point of living is living well. To the extent we achieve grace in our daily lives—not the otherworldly grace of the Christian saint, but the secular grace of a dancer—our lives become a work of art. Perhaps that is all the meaning to which we mere mortals can, or should, aspire.

In the utopian vision of Port William with which I opened chapter 5, "the houses are clean and white, and great trees stand among them and spread over them."

The fields lie around the town, divided by rows of such trees as stand in the town and in the woods, each field more beautiful than all the rest. . . . And in the fields and the town, walking, standing, or sitting under the trees, resting and talking together in the peace of a sabbath profound and bright, are people of such beauty that he weeps to see them.[75]

It is a graceful world, both peaceful and orderly. But given the central role of labor in Berry's moral theory, it's striking that in this utopia, *no one is working*. Berry chooses to depict his ideal community on the sabbath, on a day of rest. This suggests that spiritual and aesthetic values are in fact important to his vision of the good life—but not as those values are conventionally understood.

Consider Berry's description of a church service in the not-quite-utopian Port William: "The service has begun; the congregation is singing 'Amazing Grace, how sweet the sound,' the song pouring out the open doors and windows of the old church, mingling, beyond its intent, into the wild fecundity of the day." Jack Beechum enters the church and is swept up in the "rich mixture of smells: The staleness of the old building . . . ; the smell of the ground and of new growth from outside, the odors of soap and clean clothes." He isn't listening to the sermon; "the sermon is merely there, an agreeable presence, a distant drone among the humming and singing that the air is already full of."[76]

Religion here is imagined as a wholly sensual experience: earthy, sociable, distinctly nontranscendent. Berry's kind of spirituality doesn't try to transcend the gross material world; rather, he wants to find meaning in the world, to dance with it. He doesn't look to Heaven with Jefferson's yeoman farmer; his moral horizon ends at the boundaries of the place, the community. *This* world is where we realize the good life; this is where our labor and our art serve to attach us to the land and the community. Through labor we engage the physical world, including other people; we learn to adapt to its hard, unyielding materiality. Through art we learn affection, the "love that enforces care." The highest ideal achievable within this limited moral horizon is common grace: common in the sense that one can realize it in the ordinary activities of everyday life, but also in the sense that it can be realized and held in common by the community. Ultimately, it is not God or the hope of Heaven but this common grace—a secular grace—that keeps the world and preserves us in it.

The concept of grace completes Berry's moral theory; it does not, however, complete his ecological agrarianism. His moral virtues are active virtues; they are achieved through and expressed in active involvement in the world. So far, however, we have considered only private, or communal, productive activity: farming, painting, writing poetry. But Berry is clearly interested in wide-ranging social reform—the kind of reform one would expect to call for political activism. Accordingly, the final chapter considers how, in Berry's view, politics fits into a graceful life.

Chapter Eight

Tending Our Gardens

Wendell Berry walked into a George Wallace rally in October of 1968 with some trepidation. He was expecting that as a "rural Kentuckian with some conservative impulses" he might find his better judgment buffeted by a raw political enthusiasm, like a skeptic "swinging a little with a good primitive evangelist." Instead, he was bored by the posturing and inflated rhetoric. The Wallace supporters confronted a group of long-haired, bearded hecklers who had crashed the party with chants of "Sieg! Heil! Sieg! Heil!" Berry, bemused, found himself siding with the hippies—not so much for their ideas, whatever those might have been, as for their "gusto and style."[1]

If this is politics, I suppose we can only hope for less of it in our ideal republic. But what would take its place? Can Berry envision an alternative to this meaningless posturing and empty rhetoric? It's tempting to assume that because he has little good to say about politics he is apolitical, discouraging public action in favor of a solipsistic retreat into private domesticity. That assumption is incorrect, however. His political teachings may be more opaque than those of earlier agrarians, but he does give sustained attention to politics and government, offering a sociological critique that focuses on the meaning of political action for individual citizens. This critique echoes both Thoreau and the Populists, but Berry develops it in his own idiosyncratic way. Although he may not have a fully developed political theory, he does generate theoretical insights that can serve as a starting point for reinventing agrarian politics—from the ground up, so to speak.

Berry's critical perspective on politics continues a long tradition of hostility toward politicians and government in democratic agrarianism. John Taylor

179

of Caroline made these concerns central to his agrarian philosophy, arguing that corrupt legislation—namely, protective tariffs that favored manufactures over agriculture—accounted for the troubles of American farmers. "Why," he asked, "have so many employments, expensive, useless or pernicious, flourished wonderfully in the United States, whilst the fertility of the soil has been wonderfully diminishing?" It must be because laws that "bestow upon particular interests wealth and power" create "a system of partiality to be exercised by power without limitation, and capable of demolishing every barrier against usurpation and tyranny."[2] The revenue generated by such tariffs, he charged, would be used by corrupt governments "to increase their power, by accumulating money at the cost of nations, to be wasted in extravagance or employed still more perniciously, in extending patronage, or spreading corruption."[3]

Taylor saw government itself as the chief villain in this story. Just as monarchs handed out titles to create an aristocracy that would support the regime, ambitious politicians used legal privileges to create factions—bankers, capitalists, stockbrokers—whose interest lay in supporting the administration.[4] The result of this "political swindle" was that the "idle classes" had disproportionate wealth and power: The system delivers the majority, "shackled by protecting duties, bounties and prohibitions, into the hands of an inconsiderable monied aristocracy, or combinations of capitalists."[5]

Taylor's solution to this state of affairs was to increase the political power of farmers and laborers. The Constitution, he believed, was basically sound; the problem was the farmers' own political incompetence. "We farmers and mechanics have been political slaves in all countries, because we are political fools." Farmers have been taught that "politics are without our province, and in us a ridiculous affectation." Taylor would have agricultural societies "begin with efforts to elect into the general and state legislature, a genuine agricultural interest, uncorrupted by stock-jobbing, by a view of office, or by odious personal vices." Better representation of farming interests, he concluded, "constitute[s] the only chance for abrogating a policy, which is the ruin of agricultural prosperity."[6]

These themes of corruption, the disproportionate political power of monied interests, and the need for true representation of farming interests were inherited and elaborated by the Populists. "Politics," declared one critic, "stripped of all its glittering generalities, simply means the manipulation of public affairs in such a manner so that those who make politics their profession can direct the channels of trade—the distribution of wealth—to their special benefit." He continued, "Politics can cause this country to bloom and blossom like the rose; . . . or it can stagnate every kind of enterprise, reduce the masses to want and misery and cause our people to become restless, desperate and blood-thirsty."[7]

The parties, according to most Populist critics, were "guided and controlled by those who have created and profited by the monopolies now oppressing the people."[8] The Omaha Platform of 1892 declared that "the controlling influences dominating both . . . parties have permitted the existing dreadful conditions to develop without serious effort to prevent or restrain them." The reason for this failure was that the parties had become devices to serve the interests and ambitions of politicians; they were locked in a struggle not over ideology, but for "power and plunder."[9] As James Baird Weaver explained, "Every sensible person knows that a man may be an eminent and devoted Democrat or Republican, be entirely loyal to his party, and yet the world be profoundly ignorant concerning his views upon the most important questions of public concern." The parties have no ideological test of membership, so a man "may be the most pliant tool of monopoly and still be an acceptable and an unusually influential member of either of said parties."[10]

Populists worried that this lack of real ideological conflict infected politics generally. Milford Howard complained that politics had become "a matter of business." The wealthy "support political parties for the return they expect to get in dollars and cents. They care not whether the Democratic or Republican party wins, so long as both parties favor the money power." Nobody, in fact, "really cares anything about politics, except the politicians who are seeking the boodle."[11] The only people taken in by these sham partisan conflicts are the voters. The parties get "the loud-mouthed campaign orators to go out to harangue the people . . . and when the people are all worked up, almost to a frenzy, the wily old plutocrats get together and determine which candidates must be elected, and at once go to manipulating and wire-pulling."[12] The lack of true ideological conflict degrades political discourse; the political bosses influence voters not by appealing to their interests or values, but through rhetorical tricks. Echoing John Taylor, Jonathan Periam complained that farmers have been "all too much inclined to be led away by what has been vulgarly called the gift of gab."[13]

These defects in the electoral process lead to the corruption of government by corporate power. Such corruption, declared the Omaha Platform, "dominates the ballot-box, the legislatures, the Congress, and touches even the ermine of the bench." According to James Baird Weaver, Taylor's worst fears had been borne out: "The corporations and special interests of every class created during the past twenty-five years by various species of class legislation and favoritism, have grown rich and powerful." Corporations created by law have become so powerful that they can "bend to its uses the forms and powers of the law."[14] As Periam complained, the railway corporations "control, or have controlled, the legislation of several States, and have tampered with executive and even judicial officers."[15]

Despite this bleak view of politics, however, the Populists like John Taylor remained fundamentally optimistic about the possibilities of political action. Norman Pollack summed up the Populists' stance toward politics as essentially reformist; they wanted to create a social order that "not only ensures widespread suffrage and a fair count but makes participation in the political process meaningful through directly confronting major social problems."[16] They saw the need for extensive reforms of the political process—Populists at various times advocated direct election of Senators, rule changes in the House, and initiatives and referenda—but they generally envisioned government as a positive force for progress. " 'Government—national, state and municipal—is the key to the future of the human race,' " declared the Archangel Gabriel in Ignatius Donnelly's polemical novel, *Caesar's Column*. Henry Demarest Lloyd insisted to his Populist allies that institutional reform would redeem the nation: " 'Regenerate the individual' is a half-truth; the reorganization of the society which he makes and which makes him is the other half." Institutions are no more than "applied beliefs." "The love of liberty became liberty in America by clothing itself in the complicated group of structures known as the government of the United States."[17]

Moreover, the path to reform, according to most Populists, was democratic politics. Like Taylor, the Populists argued that the way to achieve the needed reforms was to elect people who would truly represent the interests of the majority. Periam thought that farmers could neutralize the baneful effects of partisan politics by voting "for such men, and such men only, as they know to be identified with their interests and those of the *whole* people." They must not be misled by empty political rhetoric, he warned; "we must cease lending willing ears to glib-tongued adventurers of every sort, and begin to think for ourselves."[18] Voters should focus on the candidates' character, and choose "men whose sturdy integrity and intelligence shall make them proof against the sophistry and blandishments of the insinuating lobbyist."[19]

Thus despite their concern over corruption of the political process and government, democratic agrarians have typically expressed an underlying conviction that a reformed democratic politics and government are critical to social progress. Berry, in contrast, is considerably less optimistic about the potential of politics and government to solve our problems. In his view the problem is not that our government is not representative enough, but that it represents all too well the distorted and unhealthy values of the populace. Therefore, although he draws on many of the Populists' themes, he uses them to support an approach to politics that has more in common with Thoreau's attempt to reform the moral character of the citizenry.

Thoreau represents a different tradition of political protest—so different, in fact, that many commentators insist he had little of value to say about politics at all.[20] Both Berry and Thoreau seem to advocate withdrawal from a political system that has become hopelessly corrupt, a stance that might be read as a rejection of politics and government altogether. But, as Bob Pepperman Taylor has pointed out, there are different ways to be apolitical. One might simply be entirely self-absorbed and therefore lack any interest in public affairs; alternatively, one might take the anarchist's position that government is an altogether misguided project. According to Taylor, however, Thoreau fits neither of these descriptions. He is instead "a critic whose primary concerns are the health of the democratic community . . . and the integrity of the citizenry upon which any decent democratic community must be built." Thoreau's political role is to be a prophet, a critic who "force[s] us to confront the gulf between our ideals and our practices."[21]

There are obvious parallels between Berry's retreat to his Kentucky farm and Thoreau's retreat to Walden; both separate themselves from the values of the larger society in order to adopt the critical stance of an outsider. But Berry might object to certain features of this role that Thoreau embraced. Taylor characterizes Thoreau as America's "bachelor uncle" whose aim is not to care for his contemporaries as much as it is to care for the values and institutions that would nurture future generations.[22] The metaphor captures Thoreau's attempt to distance himself from the commitments and concerns of ordinary social life, in order to create a "moral space" from which to examine the defects of American society. Berry, in contrast, views himself as a husband to the world, one who is deeply involved in the cares and commitments of social life. He contends that it is the rest of us who are occupying Thoreau's moral space of disengagement; Berry's complaint is precisely that we are *too disconnected* from our daily lives. In short, Berry may distance himself from contemporary American society in order to criticize it, but he does so through a deeper and more meaningful engagement in "ordinary" social life.[23]

Thus Berry like Thoreau criticizes the moral foundations of our political communities, but on somewhat different grounds. In *Walden* and *On Civil Disobedience,* Thoreau suggests that our lack of individual autonomy, our inability to break the chains of conventionality, results in unthinking and irresponsible complicity in such moral outrages as slavery and the Mexican War. Berry, too, is concerned about our unthinking acceptance of convention, but he worries that it leads to a thoughtless individualism and consumerism that undermines our commitment to our common life and to the earth we depend on. Although he doesn't highlight the connection between his moral theory and democratic politics as clearly as Thoreau does, it isn't difficult to decipher: Without a deeper connection to the land and each other, our politics will lack sophrosyne and grace. We will continue to overreach, to seek solutions that merely create more problems.

Despite their differences, however, Berry's political ethic is essentially Thoreauvian. He wants to encourage Americans to live more deliberately, and to adopt Thoreau's generous realism, his willingness to embrace the world in spite of its flaws. Although not perhaps as optimistic as the author of *Walden,* Berry is nevertheless similarly intent on exploring and expanding America's possibilities.[24] What sets him apart from Thoreau is his deeper and more extensive interest in politics itself. Drawing on and reworking certain Populist themes, Berry develops a critique of politics as a social practice that goes well beyond Thoreau's unsystematic criticisms. At the center of Berry's argument, however, lies a quintessentially Thoreauvian concern: what political action means to the individual. Berry asks, in essence, what sort of people our political system requires us to be.

He begins his critique in a Populist vein: Despite his family's long association with the Democratic party, Berry rejects conventional partisan politics. He believes in good farming, and "manifestly, good farming cannot be fostered or maintained under the rule of the presently dominant economic and cultural assumptions of our political parties."[25] As the Populists did before him, he concludes that neither party represents his interests or addresses the real issues. But while parties and partisanship were a major theme for the Populists, it is a minor part of Berry's broader analysis of modern politics. Berry is centrally concerned with preserving the possibility of meaningful political action, but unlike the Populists, he fears that the political process by its very nature is not conducive to meaningful action.

Berry objects most strongly to the way politics degrades language. "The speech of politicians, political rhetoric, grows out of the pretense that the politician is not a man, but is somehow infallible. This sort of speech . . . is preparing the world to fight—to the last man—the final war."[26] Politicians speak in moral absolutes, which not only leads them to oversimplify complex problems but also infuses their speech with an unhealthy self-righteousness.[27] "They have taken almost exclusively to the use of the rhetoric of ad-writers: catch phrases, slogans, clichés, euphemisms, flatteries, falsehoods, and various forms of cheap wit." Meaningful speech becomes impossible as slogans replace thoughtful, considered arguments. Worse yet, because such rhetoric can't lead to the resolution of conflict, it leads "to the use of power and the use of violence against each other."[28]

Furthermore, Berry contends that the degradation of speech results in the loss of accountability. When the audience can't interpret your words, they can't hold you to them. Politicians' actions are therefore divorced from their words; the proper relationship between words, objects, and persons breaks down.[29] The result is illustrated in his description of the Wallace rally: Instead of being engaged by ideas or moved by the emotions animating both sides, he was merely bored. The rally was virtually empty of meaning. Politics, he observes, is formed out of "the collision of 'interests,' slogans, oversimplified points of view." And no matter how righteous the cause, he continues, "it seems to me that a man is reduced by walking before the public with an oversimplification fastened to him."[30]

What, then, would meaningful political speech sound like? Berry's novels do contain a few speeches that contrast favorably with the meaningless babble of electoral politics. One is from his story "Pray Without Ceasing." Thad Coulter has killed Mat Feltner's father, and a lynch mob has gathered at Mat's house, looking for an excuse to storm the jail where Thad is being held. Mat comes out to address the crowd, giving "the only public speech of his life": " 'No, gentlemen. I appreciate it. We all do. But I ask you not to do it. . . . If you want to, come and be with us. We have food, and you all are welcome.' "[31] Considerably more effective than anything said at the Wallace rally, this simple speech made the crowd disperse and prevented the threatened violence.

The second example, from *A Place on Earth,* takes place in the imagination of Old Jack Beechum. It is a conversation about World War II between Wheeler Catlett, Old Jack, and Franklin Delano Roosevelt:

"Mr. President," Wheeler says, "how much longer do you think it'll last?"

"I don't know." The President looks straight at Wheeler. "It's a hard proposition. We'll have to fight them until they quit."

That's a responsible answer, Jack thinks. He has to say so. "That's right," he says. "Go to it. By God, we're for you, sir."

"Thank you, my friend," the President says.[32]

Again, the speech offers a stark contrast to the Wallace rally. Like Mat's address to the mob, it is simple, direct, and responsible. In each, the speaker states his position in terms that allow the audience to hold him to it. But despite the brevity of the speeches, we sense that the speakers appreciate the moral depth of the situation; these are not sound bites or campaign slogans. Both speeches reveal the speaker's reluctance to fight, the heavy sense of responsibility borne by those who have to lead in times of conflict. And, importantly, neither was a typical political speech. Mat Feltner is not a professional politician (he gave only this one public speech in his entire life) and he was speaking to people who knew him. Roosevelt's speech, although concerned with public matters, was an intimate, private conversation. The speakers were therefore able to reveal themselves more fully and honestly than George Wallace could in his campaign rally. They could speak as though they would be held accountable for their words. It is because most political speech doesn't take place under these conditions that politicians are seldom held accountable.

The loss of accountability is also due to a related feature of modern politics: specialization. Among the ghettos our society has produced, Berry argues, are the ghettos of politicians and bureaucrats. "These ghettos are not necessarily made up of groups living in the same place, but the people in them have the same assumptions, the same sort of knowledge, the same mentality, often much the same experience. They communicate mostly, or exclusively, with each other."[33] Politicians have become specialists: "Those equipped by wealth or by power to bear great responsibilities have gathered into communities of themselves, insulated specifically against the claims of responsibility." Not only does specialization impair accountability and representation, it narrows the mind, in politics as in other professions. Specialists are "answerable only to the requirements of their specialty."[34] That is, politicians are judged—or judge themselves, at least—on their skills as politicians: unifying the party, getting elected, winning partisan battles over legislation. The tribe of politicians, insulated from the rest of the community, comes to value these technical proficiencies more than they value qualities of judgment and character.

Political activists, too, are vulnerable to specialization. "Such specialists," Berry worries, "are the enemies of their causes. Too many are now expending themselves utterly in the service of political abstractions." The problem here is not so much that the activist is absorbed in the technical aspects of being a good activist; rather, he is trying to expiate "his growing sense of guilt." The result, however, is the same: "The political activist *sacrifices* himself to politics; though he has a cause, he has no life; he has become the driest of experts."[35] Both the professional politician and the activist have "narrow[ed] and desiccat[ed]" their lives. Their ideals follow: "Unsubstantiated in his own living, his motives grow hollow, puffed out with the blatant air of oratory."[36] Specialization and the degradation of language are therefore two sides of the same coin. Because the politician must narrow his life and focus on politics alone, he loses the broader perspective and richer experiences that would sustain his ideals. As his idealism erodes, he must rely on empty rhetoric to motivate followers. His increasing distance from the community he represents allows his rhetoric, and thus his accountability, to degenerate further. In the end, rather than serving his ideals or his community, he serves only the professional standards of the tribe of politicians.

Even if one could remain true to one's ideals, however, politics poses a more serious ethical danger. As Berry sees it, the most well-intentioned of politicians, the reformers and revolutionaries, are driven by the most problematic of motives: a heroic ambition to save the world. Their ambition, he contends, is just another manifestation of the desire for control and mastery that drives industrial capitalism. The professional reformers and revolutionaries "want to organize the people into a human machine."[37] That hubris worries him; it is simply the same drive for fame, self-importance, and power that he considers responsible for our ecological and cultural decay. Predictably, Berry points out the emptiness of such goals. "Political activity of any kind is doomed to the superficiality and temporariness of politics, able only to produce generalizations that will hold conflicting interests uneasily together for a time." What matters, what is truly meaningful, is "the life that attaches itself to the earth, that fulfills itself in the earth's meanings and demands."[38] Under this view, conventional politics, as practiced by ambitious, career-minded specialists, is inherently a difficult if not impossible way to bring meaning to one's life.

For all this, however, Berry is not politically passive and does not recommend withdrawal from politics. He instead adopts what Max Weber called an ethic of ultimate ends, rather than an ethic of responsibility. An ethic of responsibility, according to Weber, counsels one to choose means that will achieve, and are justified by, the end in view. In contrast, an ethic of ultimate ends counsels one to choose means that are justified without regard to whether they will achieve the end in view—to choose nonviolence, for example, because it is consistent with Christian ethics, even if a nonviolent approach is less effective at ending injustice.[39] While Weber considered such an ethic problematic for politics, Berry has his own doubts about the means/ends reasoning of the ethic of responsibility.[40] Given the uncertainty and difficulty of accomplishing even moderately ambitious ends, won't we find ourselves resorting to ever more powerful and violent means? (If politics is the "strong and slow boring of hard boards," as Weber puts it, won't we be tempted to use an electric drill?)[41] The cure, Berry worries, will be worse than the disease—or, more properly, the cure *is* the disease.

On this point Berry parts company with Thoreau. While both Berry and Thoreau advocate dissociation from and protest of corrupt political systems, Berry probably would not share Thoreau's admiration for John Brown's doomed raid on Harper's Ferry.[42] Such heroic escapades, even in the best of causes, grow out of the same problematic desire for control that Berry has identified as the root of America's problems. If we are to avoid the hubris— and violence—inherent in political action, he contends, we must abandon our concern with achieving particular goals, with winning. "If protest depended on success," he points out, "there would be little protest of any durability or significance."[43]

The question, then, is "why do something that you suspect, with reason, will do no good?" His answer (an answer Thoreau would undoubtedly approve of) is out of the hope, not of success, but of "preserving qualities in one's own heart and spirit that would be destroyed by acquiescence."[44] In defense of Edward Abbey, for example, Berry writes that Abbey's aim was not so much to save the planet as to "conserve himself as a human being." If that seems solipsistic, we must bear in mind that "to defend and conserve oneself as a human being in the fullest, truest sense, one must defend and conserve many others and much else."[45] Protest, then, is worthwhile if it is an expression of one's commitments and beliefs. As one of his characters wrestling with the futility of political debate concluded, the truth of his argument would preserve it, and him, in the face of overwhelming opposition. "He would stand up on it here. . . . That it was losing did not mean it was beaten."[46]

Protest, however, is not enough. Protests are incomplete because they only identify the problem. A more "complete" kind of action is a solution. It is "an action which one takes on one's own behalf, which is particular and complex, real not symbolic, which one can both accomplish on one's own and take full responsibility for."[47] For example, a consumer worried about the abuses of corporate power should not simply join an organization of consumers to lobby for consumer protection legislation. Rather, he should "begin to think and act in consideration of his responsibilities"—to be a critical and moderate consumer, buying less and reducing his dependence on corporations. Such a strategy would "vastly increase his capacities as a person" and would be effective in a smaller but more important way than a consumer protection law.[48] Berry calls this "living in protest": "to remove oneself as far as possible from complicity in the evils one is protesting, and to discover alternative possibilities."[49] Under this view, the simple act of gardening (organically, of course) is a form of political protest: As a method of food production, it decreases one's dependence on agribusiness and petroleum; as a method of entertainment it decreases one's dependence on mass media.[50] It also cultivates communal solidarity and attachment to the home and neighborhood. Thus gardening expresses a set of values completely opposed to those supporting industrial capitalism.

Most importantly, however, gardening and other ways of "living in protest" effectively—gracefully, in fact—address the root cause of our problems. One of the reasons Berry doesn't expect political action to make much difference is that "we don't live in the government or in institutions or in our public utterances and acts, and the environmental crisis has its roots in our *lives*." Unlike the Populists, who described ordinary Americans as reasonably virtuous and only politicians and capitalists as corrupt, Berry sees corruption everywhere. "Our country is not being destroyed by bad politics; it is being destroyed by a bad way of life." If we want to save the planet, "tinkering with the institutional machinery" won't be sufficient. We will have to make "fundamental changes in the way we are living."[51]

This is not to suggest that a virtuous citizen should not pursue a career in politics, however. At least one of Berry's most admirable characters, Wheeler Catlett, is actively involved in politics, having served as county chairman for Roosevelt's 1936 presidential campaign and helping to found a marketing cooperative (much like Berry's own father).[52] Berry defies long-standing narrative convention by making the lawyer a paragon of good citizenship. Despite Wheeler's education at an "eastern law school," his sophistication and his involvement with the political affairs of the community, Wheeler has remained uncorrupted. He is "a mainly practical man who sees the good that has been possible in this world and, beyond that, the good that is desirable in it," serving his people "as their defender against the law itself, before which they were a cipher."[53] Although he has seen enough of their "greed, arrogance, mean-ness, cowardice, and sometimes their inviolable stupidity," he believes in their "generosity, goodness, courage, and intelligence."[54]

> He has pled and reasoned, cajoled, bullied, and preached, pushing events always toward a better end than he knew he should expect, resisting always the disappointment that he knew he should expect, and when the disappointment has come, as it too often has, never settling for it in his own heart or looking upon it as a conclusion.[55]

Wheeler Catlett may have been modeled on Berry's father, the country lawyer who "in addition to, and in spite of, all else that he had become, . . . *remained* a farmer," or his brother, the Kentucky state senator.[56] The char-acter also calls to mind another state senator, Harry Caudill, who spoke, as Berry remembers him, "with the eloquence of resolute intelligence and with the moral passion of a lawyer who understood and venerated the traditions of justice."[57] What kept Caudill unjaded, he believes, is that "the land and people for whom he has spoken are his own." Like Wheeler and Berry's father and brother, Caudill "got his law degree and went home with it."[58]

A good politician, we can conclude, is one whose profession is an ex-pression of his devotion to his home and his connection to the local com-munity. Undoubtedly this connection helps him to represent his constituents better. But beyond that, Berry implies that being immersed in the local cul-ture helps to insulate these lawyers and politicians from the values of the tribe of professional politicians that congregate at the seats of power. Caudill may have fallen into that trap to some extent in embracing the TVA and other New Deal programs. No doubt Berry's ideal politician would have been more skeptical. But Caudill at least consistently kept his mind on the actual problems of his community: "The passion of his intelligence has been to know what he is talking about."[59]

For Berry, then, the most effective and important form of political activ-ity is, in the spirit of Thoreau rather than Voltaire, tending our own gardens. The goal is to reform the moral character of citizens—but that reform *must* begin at home. For Berry, political action should be an expression of one's values, a bid for personal integrity rather than an attempt to remake the world. Politics is meaningful only to the extent it is a natural outgrowth of one's daily domestic activity. Importantly, this ethic necessarily moderates any reformist program. While Berry would like to see dramatic changes in our economy and society, he consistently rejects ambitious programs of social engineering. If we are to remake the world, we must do it the hard way: by changing our own lives, and then building on and defending the positive aspects of our communities.

In sum, while the Populists wanted to reform politics by encouraging political action by farmers and workers, Berry wants to reform farmers and workers by asking them to disengage, at least temporarily, from conventional politics. He questions the values and assumptions underlying such politics: that we should ask the government and its "experts" to solve problems arising out of our own individual choices, that our public actions are more important and meaningful than our private actions, that the ends justify the means. These, he suggests, are the same distorted values that underlie industrial capitalism generally. Pursuing our goals by these means will therefore only perpetuate those problematic values. Under this view, rectifying the means will go a long way toward achieving his ends.

If Berry is able to give a certain kind of politics a legitimate place in his agrarian republic, he has a harder time explaining the role of government. His lack of faith in government is of course implicit in his critique of conventional politics. After all, if the government could through legislation and enforcement accomplish our ends, then perhaps we would be better served by embracing conventional politics—which is conventional precisely because it's effective at influencing policy. Berry can reject conventional politics only because he suspects government can do little to solve our problems. But this is not to say that Berry is an anarchist, any more than Thoreau is. Rather, he echoes Thoreau's point that because governments are always vulnerable to corruption, we would do better to focus on solutions that lie in the power of individuals and their immediate communities.[60]

But Berry goes further, drawing attention not simply to the corruption of American government but to the corrupting influence of that government on the character of citizens. The difference is illustrated by their contrasting views of corporations: Thoreau claims that "a corporation has no conscience; but a corporation of conscientious men is a corporation *with* a conscience."[61] Berry disagrees; as argued in chapter 4, he contends that the institutional structure of corporations prevents individual consciences from influencing decisions. Not only does a corporation not have a conscience, it discourages individuals from using their own consciences. And so, he fears, does government.

Berry's case against government is multifaceted. Not surprisingly, his early attacks on the coal companies echo Populist complaints that government has been corrupted by wealthy corporations. "The great enemy of freedom," he warns, "is the alignment of political power with wealth."[62] The mining companies have been "abetted by the mischief and greed of local officials."[63] But Berry spends little time on this theme compared with the Populists (or modern critics like Ralph Nader). Berry is relatively uninterested in legislative processes; that is not, in his opinion, where the problem lies. More central to his argument against government are his general critique of institutions and his more specific critique of federal (as opposed to local) government. We've already encountered his anti-institutionalism in his attack on Christianity; the same criticisms apply to the institutionalization of our charitable impulses in government programs. Institutional solutions, he argues, require us to treat people not as individuals but as members of some class about which we can generalize. Therein lies the problem; "generalizing may itself be inhumane," he suggests. "It is not just or merciful or decent to treat people as abstractions."[64] This tendency to act on generalizations is made worse by the fact that the people in charge of government institutions seldom consider themselves members of the community they are supposed to serve. "They are itinerant, in fact or in spirit, as their careers require them to be."[65] Moreover, even if the institutions could do their job well, "the usurpation of private duties by the institutions" relieves citizens of "a *concern* that is one of the necessary disciplines of citizenship."[66]

These familiar conservative complaints about the welfare state could be directed at state government as easily as federal government. But Berry has more specific concerns about big central government. First, like many green theorists he is skeptical that any large-scale organization can effectively manage the environment.[67] Environmental stewardship, he contends, requires intimate knowledge of and cultural adaptation to the particular place, and "the particular knowledge of particular places is beyond the competence of any centralized power or authority."[68] We should not expect employees of the national government to be any more responsible or careful than employees of large corporations; although they shouldn't be subject to market pressures, their decisions will nonetheless be unconstrained by ties of affection or interest. As I have pointed out, this freedom from local ties is also one of the advantages of government agencies—they can act in the public interest without regard to the local power structure. But Berry's critique expresses a concern (more often heard from conservatives than from greens) that government agents' understanding of "the public interest" will be too much influenced by the alien values and concerns of professional policy makers. They will be unresponsive to and unrepresentative of the communities in which they act.

Thus Berry's case for decentralization is based in part on the standard green argument against large-scale institutions and in part on a more traditionally conservative concern for protecting local communities from disruptive outside influences. In addition, however, Berry's resistance to federal activism reflects his distrust of nationalism: the belief that national interests are of paramount importance and national loyalties should outweigh local attachments. "The patriotism . . . that grows out of the concern for a particular place in which one expects to live one's life is a more exacting concern than that which grows out of concern for a nation," he claims.[69] Nationalism is "patriotism in the abstract," and it is "most apt to be fanatic or brutal or arrogant." Loyalty to abstract ideas, he asserts, fosters violence more than loyalty to particular people and things; the damage our violence inflicts on our ideals isn't tangible and obvious, as is the damage we inflict on concrete things. Thus "if one is going to destroy a creature, the job is made easier if the creature is first reduced to an idea and a price. Reduction, that is, facilitates manipulation or use without affection, and use without affection is abuse."[70] In other words, violence comes easier to us when we reduce our fellow citizens and the land they depend on to an abstraction called "the nation."

Of course, localism can also fuel violence, as anyone who lived through the civil rights movement is well aware. Berry is quite willing to acknowledge the violence endemic in the intense localism of southern political culture. But I believe he would attribute that violence to the fact that southerners have been too often attached to their local communities as abstractions, as ideas rather than places. Their patriotism typically does not reflect the intimate understanding of the land and community that animates his own localism. Berry contends that racial hierarchies insulated the white elites from such an understanding, which in turn made it easier for them to countenance violence against the people on whose labor they depended.[71]

Under Berry's reasoning, then, loyalty to ideas rather than places is a problematic basis for citizenship. Sounding a theme increasingly common among green theorists, Berry contends that true citizenship means being a citizen of a community and place; it begins at home.[72] Citizenship is "the unceasing labor of keeping responsibly conscious" of where one is. Accordingly, he tells us, "my devotion thins as it widens. I care more for my household than for the town of Port Royal, more for the town of Port Royal than for the County of Henry," and so on. But "I *do not* care more for the United States of America than for the world."[73] He must "attempt to care as much for the world" as for his household, because his household depends on the world—but by "world" he means not the international community (an oxymoron, in Berry's view) but the land itself.[74] The national government, he believes, is relatively unimportant to the community that actually has meaning for him.

In fact, in Berry's view, there is, properly speaking, no such thing as a national community. There is only a national "public," which Berry defines as "simply all the people, apart from any personal responsibility or belonging."[75] Publics are valuable in their own way, he acknowledges, granting that "a public government, with public laws and a public system of justice, founded on democratic suffrage, is in principle a good thing." He goes on to cite the usual justifications for central government: "Ideally, it makes possible a just and peaceable settlement of contentions arising between communities. It also makes it possible for a mistreated member of a community to appeal for justice outside the community." But a public functioning properly, as a "political body intent on justice," should focus on the individual; the community, in contrast, "is centered on the household—the family place and economy."[76] Living as a member of a public—which is what he thinks giving priority to national citizenship means—offers only "self-realization, self-aggrandizement, self-interest, self-fulfillment, self-enrichment, self-promotion, and so on." In contrast, living as a member of community (giving priority to local citizenship) allows a person "to understand his or her life in terms of membership and service."[77]

Much of Berry's hostility to national government, then, derives from the same concerns about preserving the possibility of meaningful action that animate his critique of politics. To influence national government, one must become a "public person": to enter the public arena and communicate with people who don't know you and to whom you have no deep sense of responsibility. National citizenship is at best attachment to an abstract set of ideas or principles, not to concrete people and places. Participation in national politics thus threatens to erode one's local commitments—commitments to living people, complex relationships, and tangible, vulnerable things—without replacing them with anything equally meaningful or exacting.

Nevertheless, Berry recognizes that national government does have a legitimate role to play in local affairs. It is conceivable, he grudgingly allows, "that our people in Washington might make decisions tending toward sustainability and self-sufficiency in local economies. The federal government could do much to help, if it would."[78] But his view of government is shaped by his libertarian conception of freedom; freedom, he asserts, means being free from government action, rather than participating in exercising the will of the community through government action. Thus he concludes that "the most appropriate government powers" are those that "protect the small and weak from the great and powerful."[79]

What that means in practice is hard to say; Berry has said very little about specific policy proposals, and what he has proposed is unexceptional. In *The Unsettling of America,* for example, he suggests that federal government should tax the wealthy corporations more heavily in order to reduce their economic power.[80] He also advocates low-interest loans to help those who want to buy small farms and a system of production and price controls to help buffer small farmers from the vagaries of commodity markets. (The federal government has operated such a system since the New Deal, although the 1996 Freedom to Farm Act attempted to dismantle it—a policy he has criticized.)[81] In addition, he advocates "a program" to promote local self-sufficiency in food; he implies that this program would include promoting growers' and consumers' cooperatives.[82] Finally, he suggests that every town and city "be required to operate an organic waste depot where sewage, garbage, waste paper, and the like would be composted and given or sold at cost to farmers."[83]

In short, despite his concerns about nationalism and "big government," Berry doesn't offer a particularly original conception of the respective roles of federal and local government. In his version of federalism, national government would be responsible for creating a protected space for local community to flourish. It would prevent the concentration of wealth, provide impartial justice to individuals, and support efforts to maintain local culture and traditions. It would also presumably coordinate efforts among communities to deal with environmental (and other social) problems that transcend political boundaries. However, many of the Great Society social programs would be abandoned; the War on Poverty (and crime, and drugs, and most of our other social ills) would be fought, if at all, at the local level.

At this point it appears that Berry's radical attack on industrial capitalism has remarkably conservative political implications. But before we conclude that he is in fact a conservative at heart, we should recall his more progressive-sounding attacks on such right-wing shibboleths as property rights, economic growth, and free markets. Like the Jeffersonian agrarianism he often invokes, Berry's political theory is neither straightforwardly liberal nor unproblematically conservative.

Berry himself would agree that his political commitments defy easy categorization.[84] The job is made more difficult by the fact that, for all his attention to the practice of politics, he has little to say about the policy issues by which we usually distinguish liberals from conservatives. Nevertheless, Berry does take a stand on the proper ends of government, usually a good litmus test of one's ideological commitments. His claim that government cannot create a community but can only provide a protected space for it to develop would seem to put him in the conservative camp. As always, however, Berry's views must be carefully qualified.

There are of course strains of progressive thought that emphasize local community over national government as the best place to exercise citizenship and realize social progress. Jane Addams, for example, justified her settlement houses on these grounds, stressing the importance of direct action and intimate knowledge of a particular community.[85] This progressive theme is usually aimed at encouraging grassroots democratic action, a goal shared by most green theorists. But liberal progressives like Addams have a much more positive view of government than Berry does. State and national legislation were always on Addams's agenda; she wanted social progress to *begin* at the local level, not end there. Thus it is correct to conclude that Berry's localism has more in common with the strain of American conservatism that defends local community, usually against federal civil rights enforcement, welfare programs, and other Great Society initiatives.[86]

Unlike most conservative briefs for community, however, Berry's is place-based rather than identity-based; that is, he is concerned with protecting the way of life that evolves in a particular place, rather than with preserving the racial, religious, and ethnic identities that many conservatives consider to be the foundation of community.[87] For Berry, community is based on our dependence on one another's productive (and reproductive) labor. If we find a sustainable way to work together, presumably we will develop the common traditions and understandings that conservatives mistakenly consider as the foundation (rather than the result) of community. Thus our genealogical roots in Europe, Africa, Israel, or elsewhere are irrelevant; the history that matters is the history of the place where we live *now*.

In contrast to the advocates of states' rights, then, Berry is not concerned with protecting racial, religious, or ethnic homogeneity. He even grants federal government a role in defending civil rights, acknowledging that one legitimate function of national government is to provide justice for individuals when the local community doesn't offer it. Nevertheless, like most conservatives he clearly disapproves of progressive policies that end up drastically altering the structure and dynamics of local communities; he suggests that those policies too often end up destroying the community in order to save it. He is less concerned with empowering state or even local governments, however, than with limiting government generally. Government, in his view, can do little to help and much to hurt both community life and individual liberty.

This libertarian impulse also explains Berry's theory of citizenship. He favors republican over liberal understandings of citizenship, emphasizing civic duties over rights, but his goal is to reduce the need for government regulation of individual behavior. Such republican conceptions of citizenship are common to many green theorists, who hope that a strong sense of civic duty will motivate ecologically responsible behavior. But again, Berry's theory of citizenship also echoes conservative arguments that meaningful political commitment becomes more attenuated as it travels farther from one's local community. Like states' rights advocates, Berry uses this idea to undermine the legitimacy of federal regulation. Again, however, his primary concern is with defending the home and local community against *any* government intrusion.

Clearly much of Berry's political theory is aimed at limiting the scope of government action—but not because of the usual conservative doubts about the legitimacy of government power. Rather, Berry is concerned with preserving the possibility of meaningful political action. Just as his thinking about politics begins with his diagnosis of the emptiness and meaninglessness of conventional politics, his case against big central government is based in large part on his understanding of citizenship—which in turn derives from his concern over what meaningful political activity actually consists of. This is what leads him to conclude that we need more small-scale, intimate, face-to-face democracy. The problem with national politics is that it requires you to leave your community and enter an arena where people don't know you and can't hold you accountable for your words and actions. The more time you spend in that arena, the more your values will be shaped by the rootless tribe of professional politicians. This dynamic accounts for the corrupting influence of conventional politics, and points toward the need for an approach to political activism rooted in one's sense of responsibility to a particular place.

In sum, despite the conservative tone of his political critique, Berry does not fit easily into either the modern conservative or the modern liberal mold. He is too critical of capitalism for most conservatives, too concerned about strengthening local communities for most liberals. Instead, his political theory borrows freely from both of these traditions (as well as the older Jeffersonian republican tradition), building on Thoreau's political ethic to construct at least a rough outline of the proper role of government and the scope and meaning of political action. But has he achieved the right mix of ideas? Is his ecological agrarianism well designed to achieve his political and ecological goals?

Certainly Berry's anticorporate, neo-Populist ideology would seem to have some potential for unifying many disparate groups unhappy with the overall direction of American society. Attributing rural social and environmental decay to the pernicious influence of corporate power resonates with suspicions of corporations that date back to the Jacksonian era. Small farmers, environmentalists, consumers, and even unions can rally behind an attack on agribusiness. But the strategy has drawbacks as well. The neo-Populist impulse is typically associated with extremes in American politics. Berry's ideas may appeal to politically disparate groups on the fringes, but they are probably too far from the mainstream to win broad support.[88]

Of course, Berry's goal isn't to win elections. Nevertheless, his appeal to fringe elements in American society could be worrisome. For example, his defense of farmers against corporate power could fuel extremists on the far right, given the disturbing tendency of neo-Populism among farmers to drift toward racism and anti-Semitism. In the late 1970s, radical farm groups such as the American Agriculture Movement (AAM) drew on anti-Semitic rhetoric about international capitalist conspiracies, blaming the Trilateral Commission, David Rockefeller, and Jewish financiers for corrupting American values.[89] Similarly, the antiurbanism of most agrarian rhetoric often takes on racist overtones, playing on racial stereotypes to denigrate urban dwellers as lacking civic virtue.

To be fair, Berry doesn't encourage this sort of racial politics. He is not strongly antiurban; on the contrary, he acknowledges that great civilizations need great cities, and contends that the virtues of stewardship are as necessary for city dwellers as for rural folk.[90] And his critique of corporate power is free of anti-Semitic paranoia. The only conspiracy he hints at is between American policy makers and agribusinessmen. As Berry himself points out, political rhetoric tends to divide the world into "us" and "them"—but he does his best to fight that tendency. He consistently traces the power of corporations back to the decisions of ordinary consumers; corporations are exactly what we have allowed them to become. Thus the problem, he insists, is not with any "them," but with us—*all* of us.

Still, we may worry that Berry's emphasis on strengthening families and communities could result in illiberal social policies. Many green theorists have been criticized for embracing a problematic vision of homogeneous local communities and failing to explain how such communities would maintain an equitable distribution of power.[91] Berry is hardly silent on the issues of power and difference, of course. As I've argued, his endorsement of community is qualified by a number of liberal themes: his desire to limit government regulation of individual behavior, his recognition of the limits of humans' ability to impose order on the world, his critique of social hierarchy. Given his assumption of human fallibility, the exercise of power is always for Berry a dangerous enterprise that should be approached reluctantly, with great care and limited expectations. Still, liberal critics might want him to give more attention to the notion that it is not only ecological necessity but also individual rights that limit the legitimate exercise of power by the community. Similarly, they might wish he would qualify his anti-institutionalism with the recognition that we need political institutions that will ensure citizens are given equal voice in such exercises of power.

Despite these reservations, though, we should recognize that Berry's emphasis on community is also one of his strengths, allowing him to correct the overemphasis on individualism that has always troubled democratic agrarianism.[92] Berry's critique of autonomy and recognition that interdependence is a normal and desirable condition gives legitimacy to cooperative endeavors (such as politics) and makes it easier to justify government action generally (such as regulation aimed at protecting the environment). Moreover, his insistence that meaningful political activity must be rooted in devotion to a place supports political organizations and activities that operate at the local level. In these respects, like the progressives before him, he supports a broader, more participatory democracy.

Berry's localism may in fact be more problematic for liberals than his well-qualified communitarianism. His insistence that loyalty to place should be the basis of citizenship challenges the cosmopolitanism typical of many versions of liberalism. While Berry argues that nationalism fosters violence and injustice, many liberals have the same concerns about parochialism. Parochialism, after all, prevents us from recognizing duties to people who aren't members of our communities, as well as insulating communities from the critical perspectives that outsiders can offer.[93] But Berry points out that loosening local ties has costs as well: It diminishes incentives to take care of the earth and the community. This necessary and labor-intensive work, he contends, is best done by people with long-term commitments to a particular place, just as raising children is best done by people motivated by love and willing to establish a long-term relationship with them. Liberal cosmopolites seeking self-realization may be admirably principled and tolerant, but they probably won't be very reliable stewards. So we have to make a real and troublesome trade-off: to maintain vital communities and ecological health, we need to encourage strong ties to place among many people, which in turn tends to foster parochialism.

To complicate matters, localism may not serve ecological health as well as Berry anticipates. While many environmentalists share Berry's interest in revitalizing and empowering local communities, the fact remains that the environmental problems provide the paradigmatic case for national and even international regulation. Many of our most serious environmental problems—global warming, air and water pollution, conservation of resources, biodiversity—demand coordination among many geographically dispersed groups; decentralization only makes such coordination more difficult. As Robyn Eckersley points out, "In view of the urgency and ubiquity of the ecological crisis, ultimately only a supraregional perspective and multilateral action by nation states can bring about the kind of dramatic changes necessary to save the 'global commons' in the short and medium term."[94] Berry would worry about those "dramatic changes," of course; he argues for a more gradual change that would be less disruptive of communities. But protecting the earth does seem to require some sort of national and international action. Eckersley makes a reasonable case that the environment would be best served by "a political decision making framework that can represent, address, and resolve . . . social and cultural differences both within and across communities and regions."[95] Vital local communities are not enough; we need a strong, effective national government to facilitate coordination among local communities and among nations.[96]

Berry's overemphasis on local community is driven in large part by his suspicion of government generally, and it is this, I think, that most seriously compromises his political theory. Berry's conservative and libertarian impulses have led him to underestimate the importance of government in constituting community. For Berry, community develops largely independently of political institutions. It is "a locally understood interdependence of local people, local culture, local economy, and local nature."[97] This definition overlooks the vital role that laws and political institutions (like parties) play

in shaping the local culture and economy and influencing how people interact with one another. Berry seems committed to the view that government
does nothing to generate or structure community; it can at most protect the
preexisting community from outside disruptions. Ironically, though, that
understanding of the relationship between government and community is
contradicted by Berry's own analysis of the role of human institutions in
community life. In defending marriage as a necessary convention, Berry
argues that natural energies and forces must be constrained and ordered by
human institutions; while those institutions are necessarily imperfect and
can only partially regulate nature, they are nonetheless essential. We are not
animals; we cannot rely on natural instinct to regulate our common life.[98]
Surely if we need marriage to order sexual relations, we also need government and politics to order other kinds of relations.

Of course, marriage for Berry is more than a legal institution; it is a fundamental relationship, "the basic and central community tie" that "begins
and stands for the relation we have to family and other human associations."[99] Presumably, then, marriage would exist without government and
laws. Nevertheless, some sort of authority must lie behind such basic and
critical institutions. Custom and tradition may serve this role to some extent,
but (as I argued in chapter 4) custom and tradition seldom work alone; laws
can give them crucial support. And, more importantly, a rationalized, democratic government has many advantages over custom and tradition—not
the least of which is that, like the institution of marriage, it provides a means
for citizens to consciously ratify their decision to live together. Thus instead
of viewing government simply as an alien intrusion into the community, we
should recognize that it can be a means to exercise collective stewardship
over the community's customs, traditions, and way of life. Government, in
short, is not only an umbrella over the community; it is part of the scaf-
folding. Political institutions and laws help to create community, providing
the necessary structure for ordering our relationships with one another.

Of course, none of this vitiates Berry's concern that an overly bureaucratic government can impair the life of the community. This worry should
lead us to consider ways to humanize government agencies—by changing
the itinerant nature of government careers, for example, making it possible
for government employees to become more fully part of the community.
Instead of relieving us of a sense of responsibility for the community, government agencies should provide a means for exercising that responsibility.
Under this view, government bureaucrats should see themselves not as the

enlightened saviors of the community but as potential members of it, offering their labor and commitment (and government resources) to the common enterprise.

Humanizing public administration is not enough to answer all Berry's concerns, however. We would also have to ensure that policy making at the national level serves to support rather than undermine community, and that national politics itself remains meaningful. On the first point, the Populists were surely correct that representation is the key to more humane government policies. Berry would qualify that point, though: effective representation of *interests* is not sufficient. If representatives view their constituents as a collection of independent, individual interests, our policies will continue to favor life plans that aim at individual autonomy and self-realization over those aimed at community-centered stewardship. Under Berry's view, what we need instead are representatives who speak for particular *places*—who seek policies that recognize and are protective of the complex interdependencies that constitute community life. Such representatives should approach politics as, essentially, an extension of gardening—a kind of domestic stewardship that aims at helping communities realize their best possibilities.

Admittedly, this conception of representation creates a serious danger of parochialism. Berry's worries notwithstanding, it is essential to counter this attachment to local community with a sense of higher-order memberships— an attachment to the region, state, nation, and world as a whole. The purpose of such attachments is not to distract us from our responsibility for caring for the local community, but to give us greater appreciation for interconnections among communities and the supralocal forces affecting our local community. Ties to particular communities in turn should help us make better judgments about the trade-offs inherent in seeking broad social change. In particular, it should make us more sensitive to the disruption of community life such changes usually entail.

A good representative, then, must be a citizen not only of her local community but of the larger political communities in which the local community is embedded. But how can such representatives avoid the demoralizing effects of national politics? Berry may be right that politics begins to lose its meaning when the participants no longer see themselves as members of the same community, sharing a common responsibility to the same things and people. On the other hand, he may be too pessimistic about the possibility of achieving this sense of community at the national level. The danger, of course, is that we will grasp "the nation" merely as an abstract idea that we will then defend without regard to its true nature and necessities—a sure formula, he warns, for the kind of mentality that seeks to destroy a village in order to save it. Berry's concept of citizenship would require us to understand the country—even the world—as a real, physical *place:* to learn its physical features, its natural and social history, the character of the people who live here with us, the patterns of our interactions with nature and each other. Although we can't recreate the intimacy of local politics at the national level, perhaps we can foster a sense of responsibility and community rooted in this understanding of our common membership in the national household.[100] This sense of membership may be attenuated at the national level, of course (even more so at the international level). But our sense of national community needn't disintegrate altogether; the nation *is* a place as real and palpable as the town, the neighborhood, even the household—and we are just as much responsible for maintaining it.

In sum, even Berry implicitly acknowledges that we can't effectively care for the earth and each other without an effective national government. Unfortunately, his conservative and libertarian impulses prevent him from formulating an adequate theory of federalism. What he needs is more of the progressive impulse—in particular, a stronger faith in the possibility of humanizing government and achieving national community. Such a faith could be grounded in his understanding of the role of institutions in constituting community. If marriage is necessary to order human communities, so too is government. And if a sense of membership and responsibility to place is necessary to make politics meaningful, then that ethic is what must govern national-level politics.

The implication of Berry's agrarianism, then, is that we must learn to look at the country as a whole as our common home and to understand ourselves as members of a national community. Vital local communities are of course essential to fostering the disposition and values that will make us reliable stewards at the local and national levels. And no doubt there will be tensions between national and local loyalties; I don't mean to disregard the complications that this approach to citizenship would entail. But Berry's own attachment to American political traditions suggests that local and national citizenship can be mutually supportive, and that revitalizing local community is not merely an end in itself but a means to a more meaningful and humane national politics.

CONCLUSION

What is perhaps most striking about Wendell Berry's thought is how *traditional* it is. In contrast to those who present their environmental philosophies as radical revisions or rejections of Western ideas, Berry is self-consciously attempting to renew those ideas, to make them "newly applicable to contemporary needs and occasions."[1] The result is a philosophy that challenges some of the fundamental values of democratic agrarianism—individualism, autonomy, the virtues of the market—even while affirming its central claim that small farmers are vital to the republic. But the untraditional results of his traditionalism should not surprise us. In Berry's view, to inherit a tradition is to engage it creatively and critically, to develop its best possibilities. Tradition properly used should evolve with each generation. Agrarianism certainly has done so, demonstrating a remarkable vitality and flexibility over the centuries. Berry's ability to adapt it to twenty-first-century problems suggests that it will continue to play an important role in the way Americans think about politics, nature, and community.

Still, purists might argue that Berry's agrarianism is less an extension than a rejection of Jeffersonian agrarianism, that it represents the abandonment of an ideology that has, finally, outlived its usefulness. Under this view, Berry made a decisive break with the Populists by defending small farmers not on the grounds of economic and social justice, as earlier agrarians did, but in the interests of protecting the environment. In making that argument he has undoubtedly subordinated the Populists' interest in preserving the conditions for economic and political autonomy. Berry's goal is not autonomy but grace; he wants to preserve the conditions necessary to live in harmony with the natural and social world. His moral theory is therefore radically different from that of his agrarian predecessors. In place of the American ideal of rugged individualism, he reaches back to revive the classical agrarian

205

virtues—particularly the humility and pragmatism summed up in the concept of sophrosyne.

Nor is this the only respect in which he differs from earlier agrarians. An important implication of Berry's ecological agrarianism is that public support for farmers should *depend* on their environmental stewardship. Populists and other agrarians typically argued that farmers were inherently, by virtue of their labor, more virtuous than other citizens. Berry cannot take that for granted; at issue for him is the nature of agricultural labor itself. To the extent that farmers rely on machines driven by fossil fuels, they will not only fail to develop the proper agrarian virtues but will contribute to the cultural and ecological decay infecting rural America. Thus Berry's claim is the more limited one that small family farmers are merely more *likely* to make better stewards than corporations—or, more precisely, that a community of small farmers is more likely to develop a culture of stewardship than a community dominated by and dependent on large corporations. He contrasts family farming and corporate agriculture not simply to criticize corporations but to illuminate the social conditions necessary to create and maintain this culture of stewardship. In Berry's view, policies designed to encourage family farming are justified only if they actually support such a culture.

It appears, then, that Berry ultimately places protection of the environment above protection of the farmer. Nevertheless, his Populist sympathies are never entirely eclipsed by his love for the land. His case against corporations and absentee ownership brings into environmentalism the host of social and economic justice concerns of the Populists. Specifically, in his analysis of the environmental consequences of corporate power and irresponsibility, he identifies a key connection between the unequal distribution of political power and the degradation of the environment: To the extent political and economic power is concentrated in entities that are not integrated into the community, he argues, stewardship of both the community and the land will suffer. This principle is the most critical—and the most vulnerable—element of his ecological agrarianism. Berry's case for family farming rests on the proposition that even an enlightened corporate agriculture will not take care of the land adequately, a proposition that progressives may find overly pessimistic. But his argument deserves serious consideration. Stewardship, he insists, is not just a matter of following the right rules and procedures—which corporations perhaps can be made to do—but of cultivating "a complex set of attitudes, a certain culturally evolved stance, in the face of the unexpected and the unknown." Corporations may do many things well, but we have little reason to believe that they would maintain the social conditions, the *cul-

ture of stewardship, that Berry believes is essential to creating responsible farmers.

Even if we reject Berry's defense of family farming, though, there is still much in his agrarianism that remains relevant to contemporary social and agricultural issues. In particular, he offers a challenging critique of dominant American values, a rich and complex understanding of what constitutes good farming, and an alternative conception of the good life and virtues needed to live it. Berry's fictional Port William farmers offer a powerful standard of community and environmental stewardship against which to judge corporate agriculture and American society generally. In this respect, his agrarianism does keep alive the Jeffersonian/Populist tradition: Like his predecessors, he draws on an ideal vision of rural America to call into question the moral, social, and political consequences of economic concentration and corporate hegemony.

If Berry remains a good Populist, however, his green credentials may be more suspect. In fact, some environmentalists might contend that Berry's ideology is not very green at all, that he rejects the basic ideological commitments of the green movement. Evaluating that claim is a little tricky because there's considerable debate over what those commitments are. Since the 1960s, when Berry began writing, the preservationist/conservationist dichotomy in environmentalism has evolved into a continuum of environmental philosophies. At one end we find reform environmentalists (sometimes called "light greens"), who seek green objectives within the framework of liberal, democratic politics. They may challenge some of the conclusions but not the basic premises of neoclassical economics, modern science, and liberal political theory. Reform environmentalists contend that scientific reasoning properly applied, technological progress properly understood, and liberal values properly extended and realized ought to result in a sustainable society. At the other end of the spectrum lie the "deep greens," who offer a more radical challenge to the philosophical commitments of industrial capitalism. Their arguments derive from a complex of ideas and values that looks like a genuinely new ideology, commonly referred to as "ecologism," distinctive from and on par with other grand ideological traditions such as liberalism, socialism, and feminism.[2] Berry's position on this spectrum is hard to specify. Certainly he is more critical of science, technology, and liberalism than most reform environmentalists—but to what extent does he embrace ecologism?

Much depends, of course, on how we define ecologism. According to Andrew Dobson, ecologism "holds that a sustainable and fulfilling existence presupposes radical changes in our relationship with the non-human world, and in our mode of social and political life."[3] Dobson contends that the core value of ecologism is ecocentrism, a radical transformation of our human-centered value system.[4] Ecocentric theorists, as explained in chapter 3, argue that our environmental problems stem in large part from our anthropocentric worldview; they would have us transcend anthropocentrism by understanding ourselves as equal members of the biotic community and learning to value nature for its own sake. Berry, as I pointed out in that chapter, is deeply suspicious of ecocentrism, at least in its more extreme formulations. His agrarianism derives from a pragmatic, anthropocentric concern for preserving the conditions for human survival, rather than preserving nature for nature's sake. Moreover, to the extent his moral philosophy centers on the value of *labor,* our actual physical interaction with nature, it is not very accommodating to ecocentric perspectives that encourage us to respect other creatures' intrinsic value and relationship to the environment. On the other hand, like many ecocentrics, Berry puts a great deal of importance on humility as a guide to ecologically sensitive behavior. It is important to recall that sophrosyne governs not only land use but land nonuse; it is supposed to restrain the urge to develop every inch of the planet, to teach us how to leave some things alone. Clearly Berry has absorbed at least some of the lessons of ecocentrism.

Nevertheless, there is a deep tension between ecocentrism and the practical work of farming; farmers *must* think of nature primarily in terms of its value to humans. Thus if ecocentrism is the hallmark of ecologism, then we must reach the (surely counterintuitive) conclusion that Berry's agrarianism isn't very green after all. But perhaps we can define ecologism more broadly. Robyn Eckersley, for example, suggests that ecocentrism could represent the most radical wing of green political thought without serving as its defining feature.[5] She does warn that this more ecumenical approach "threatens the unique identity of green political thought, reducing it to a broad arena of environmental debate around recurrent themes, issues, values, and strategies."[6] But I would contend that liberalism, socialism, feminism, and other ideologies can also best be understood as broad arenas of debate around recurrent themes and issues—or, even better, as evolving traditions linked by a common history of ideas and practices. As I suggested in the introduction, it would be difficult to identify a set of principles shared by all liberals, from John Locke to Jeremy Bentham to Martin Luther King Jr. We identify liberals, as we identify greens, not by a philosophical litmus test but by their genealogy and family resemblance.

Berry, by virtue of both intellectual genealogy and family resemblance, surely belongs among the greens. As argued in chapters 1 and 2, Berry's agrarianism clearly derives from the early permanent agriculturalists as well as the ideas of back-to-the-land advocates, such as the Twelve Southerners and the Nearings. Moreover, it resembles in key respects the ecologism of other New Left figures such as Barry Commoner, Murray Bookchin, and E. F. Schumacher. Granted, Commoner, Bookchin, and Schumacher are considerably farther to the left than Berry. Although like Berry they see environmental degradation as stemming from the social relations of production, they draw on socialist critiques of capitalism to explain that connection. So for Bookchin, the environmental crisis is essentially a problem of social organization to which the leftist tradition has the solutions. Commoner agrees, arguing that capitalism, because it depends on economic growth, is fundamentally inconsistent with environmental stewardship.[7] Schumacher, although more skeptical of socialism, nevertheless approves of its potential to create the conditions for transcending capitalism.[8]

Berry's kinship with these theorists may seem unlikely, given the lack of direct socialist influences on his thought. But Populism was an important precursor and contributor to American socialism, some versions of which (such as the Nearings') have a strong back-to-the-land component. And, of course, the seminal critique of corporate agriculture, McWilliams's *Factories in the Field,* came out of the leftist tradition. So it isn't surprising that Berry shares some intellectual common ground with those more directly influenced by socialism. Although he ultimately endorses liberal political institutions and some version of capitalism, many of Berry's basic principles are consistent with (if not derived from) socialist thought. In particular, he shares with leftist theorists a strong concern for the welfare of the producer and endorses much of their critique of corporate power and market-driven behavior. In addition, his belief in social equality, his critique of individualism, his interest in how physical labor shapes our character and consciousness, and his materialism (or, as he would put it, his rejection of body/spirit dualism) all resonate with leftist ideology.

But whatever his shade of green or red, we can at least conclude that Berry has formulated an intelligent, thoughtful agrarianism that encompasses a broad range of values—ecological, aesthetic, spiritual, economic, political, and cultural. To those of us interested in the evolution of ideas, that alone is a significant achievement. But of course this is not merely an intellectual exercise for Berry. His goal is not to design an elegant philosophical system but to create a new, politically useful language with which to press the claims of small farmers and the rural community. To what extent has he accomplished this practical project?

Berry's actual influence on farm politics and agriculture policy is necessarily hard to gauge. Berry is perhaps best seen as summarizing and synthesizing ideas that have been circulating for some time among agriculturalists and environmentalists. Although he is one of the most widely read—and I would argue one of the best—expositors of these ideas, it is difficult to distinguish his specific influence from that of the Rodales, Wes Jackson, Marty Strange, and the many other voices in the sustainable agriculture movement. Nevertheless, we can draw some conclusions about the influence of Berry's way of thinking and talking.

There is certainly reason to expect that Berry's agrarianism, like that of Liberty Hyde Bailey and the Twelve Southerners, would remain peripheral to mainstream environmental politics. As evidence for this view, consider former vice president and presidential candidate Al Gore's environmental manifesto, *Earth in the Balance*. Gore ought to be sympathetic to Berry's agrarianism; after all, both grew up on farms in the tobacco-growing region of the Appalachians, both have strong family ties to the Democratic party, and both consider themselves environmentalists deeply concerned with the problems of rural America.[9] And Gore does indeed sound very much like Berry in his analysis of the spiritual craving behind the culture of consumption. Like Berry, Gore attributes "the froth and frenzy of industrial civilization" to "our deep loneliness for that communion with the world that can lift our spirits and fill our senses with the richness and immediacy of life itself." This spiritual void, he argues, drives us to "lose ourselves in the forms of culture, society, technology, the media, and the rituals of production and consumption."[10] Gore's discussion of agriculture, however, does not draw on Berry at all. While he and Berry identify many of the same environmental problems posed by modern agriculture, Gore's solutions are limited to "changing our agricultural methods" (which he apparently considers a fairly straightforward project) and ending subsidies that don't promote sustainability.[11] Noticeably absent from his discussion are proposals aimed at creating a culture of stewardship, which (according to Berry) would cure both our agricultural and our spiritual problems.

If Gore is resistant to Berry's ideas on agriculture, other policy makers may be even more so. Even Gore's modest proposals for reform seem out of place in the insular world of agricultural policy, which has traditionally been impervious to most of the radical impulses that circulate on its fringes. Agriculture policy tends to be dominated by an exclusive clique consisting of farm-state legislators and representatives of a few conservative interest groups like the American Farm Bureau.[12] In fact, some policy experts question whether ideology plays *any* significant role in agricultural policy.[13] But the insularity of agricultural policy has been under attack for some time; in recent years it has opened up to a more diverse array of voices, including environmentalists and advocates for rural community development.[14] In this new context ideology may matter a great deal—Berry's agrarianism could prove useful not only to family farm advocates attempting to form alliances with environmentalists, but to policy makers attempting to negotiate an increasingly pluralistic political arena.[15] His conception of an ecologically sound agriculture, based on the principles of stewardship and farming as a public profession, provides a common ground for the array of interests seeking to reform rural America. Moreover, it provides policy makers and the general public a holistic way to think about the competing values—economic, social, environmental, and cultural—that our agriculture must serve, and a way to conceptualize farming that honors those values. At the same time, his insistence that we understand and appreciate the way of life of the traditional farming community—that we see its potential, not simply its defects—brings a Populist sensibility to agroecological policy debates, counteracting the elitism that typically infects environmentalism. The values of stewardship, he suggests, are not going to be discovered and cultivated among progressive urban and suburban intellectuals (the mainstay of the environmental movement). A lifelong commitment to the hard and often unrewarding work of stewardship requires the qualities of character—the discipline, persistence, and humility—that we are most likely to find, or resurrect, among the lingering remnants of rural America.

Such predictions are necessarily speculative, but there is evidence that Berry's ideas are starting to infiltrate agricultural policy debate. It's hardly surprising, of course, that groups like ACRES USA, the National Family Farm Coalition, and the Center for Rural Affairs have echoed Berry in proclaiming environmental stewardship as a central value of agriculture policy.[16] But more mainstream voices have also begun to adopt this sort of language. Dan Glickman, secretary of agriculture under President Clinton, stated in an interview in December 2000 that he expects conservation rather than crop production issues to become "the driving intellectual force" behind farm programs: "I suspect that you are going to see more and more farm policy based on how farmers treat their land."[17] His suspicion was confirmed the following spring, when Senator Harkin introduced the Conservation Security Act. The bill proposed to extend earlier conservation efforts by paying farmers directly for their stewardship—an idea endorsed by Berry in 1996.[18] In introducing the bill, Harkin characterized farmers and ranchers as not only producers but also stewards "of our nation's natural resources." Since all Americans benefit from their stewardship, he reasoned, "it is only right that we contribute to conserving private lands."[19]

The Conservation Security Act was drafted by a coalition of environmentalists and farm-state lawmakers—an alliance that would have seemed unlikely if not impossible thirty years earlier. But such alliances will undoubtedly become more common as farmers increasingly rely on their stewardship role to justify public support for family farming. Of course, cooperation between farmers and environmentalists remains problematic; there's a good deal of tension over specific policy proposals that pit environmental protection against the economic interests of farmers.[20] And many farm advocates still prefer to rely on Populist-inspired calls for economic justice to combat corporate agriculture. But, as pointed out in chapter 2, that strategy looks more like narrow interest group politics—just one special interest battling another—than a broad-based Populism aimed at democratic reform. The larger and more significant debates over American agriculture are those centered on values other than the independence of the entrepreneurial farmer: the values of stewardship and community. That such values are finding a place in contemporary agriculture policy—that we can talk about them at all without sounding nostalgic or wishful or absurd—is due in large part to the efforts of Berry and his allies in the sustainable agriculture movement.

Nevertheless, if Berry's ideas are to continue to inform public debate about the future of agriculture, they need further elaboration. Clearly, many dimensions of his social and moral theories call for further exploration. I will mention only two: his leisure ethic and his political theory. Developing a stronger leisure ethic, I would argue, is essential for both philosophical and political reasons. Philosophically, Berry's vision of the good life remains incomplete without a persuasive account of the value of leisure. He contends that both labor and leisure are important components of a graceful life, but his emphasis on the role of labor in teaching us our proper relationship to the natural world leaves us without a good reason (other than sheer exhaustion) to stop working. It also leaves us without guidance on how to spend our leisure hours. It may be, for example, that the problem with the tourists he complains of who spend their weekends racing along the river in motorboats is not that they don't value labor but that they don't know what to do with themselves when they're not working. Berry recognizes that we will all be unable to work from time to time; that point is central to his critique of autonomy. The lack of a leisure ethic ensures that those periods of retirement will be plagued by a sense of futility and uselessness, which in turn could (and probably does) lead to the frenzied consumerism that the Twelve Southerners complained of.

The lack of a well-developed leisure ethic also exacerbates the ideological conflict between Berry and the deep greens. Emphasizing labor privileges our instrumental relationship to the natural world, threatening to obscure its intrinsic and aesthetic value. I have argued that the most promising way to correct this imbalance is to explore Berry's suggestion that leisure activities, such as contemplation of natural beauty, are a way to develop a deeper love for the material world—"the love that enforces care." As ecocentric theorists argue, cultivating a noninstrumental relationship to nature may motivate us to use the world more carefully. Importantly, the same principle applies to our social world: leisure activities that help us to develop and maintain noninstrumental relationships with one another—that teach us to respect one another's intrinsic value—should help us to strike the right balance between preserving individual autonomy and maintaining the bonds of community.

Berry of course worries that a strong leisure ethic leads us to devalue work and helps to justify a leisure class, a class exempted from the daily discipline of common labor. But a leisure ethic can also have more democratic implications: If leisure is necessary to the good life, then it ought to be available to everyone. We may be called to earn our bread through labor, but surely we are also called, at appropriate times, to a life of leisure—a life devoted simply to enjoyment and the art of living.

Berry's agrarianism could also benefit from a more developed political theory. Like most greens, he favors decentralized political institutions, but he never fully explores their drawbacks for effective environmental management. Moreover, his libertarian impulses lead him to question the legitimacy, or at least desirability, of government in general. This is hardly a promising beginning to a political theory—but it must be recognized that the American founders started with similar dispositions. Rather than going back to Thoreau and Pinchot, as Bob Pepperman Taylor suggests, we might do better to develop the political dimension of Berry's agrarianism by recovering the original understandings of federalism, civic virtue, and consent held by the founding generation. This is not the place to elaborate those understandings; suffice to say that the founders' vision of a highly decentralized federation based on consent *at every level* would seem to be compatible with Berry's call for a more meaningful and responsible civic life.

And to counter Berry's libertarianism, we could build on his insight that institutions are necessary to order human affairs. Accepting the necessity of government institutions would, for example, allow us to consider more effectively how such institutions can help us to cope with the informational demands of environmental management—another missing piece of his agrarian puzzle. It would also open the door to thinking about how to humanize government bureaucracy and integrate it more fully into the life of the community. On these points Berry's Populist predecessors were considerably more inventive than later agrarians have been. Like them, we should view government less as an intruder that necessarily disrupts community and more as an expression of and a means for collective stewardship of our common life.

No doubt further scholarly exploration of Berry's thought will uncover additional questions and complexities—and, I hope, generate in the academic community a richer and more robust discussion concerning the philosophy and practice of agriculture. The academic community, however, is not Berry's primary audience. He is writing to a broader public, to everyone who is or should be concerned with achieving a healthy and sustainable relationship to the living world. His message to that public is worth reiterating: Our goal is not simply to preserve the planet; it is to preserve *ourselves as humans* on the planet. To be sure, preserving ourselves requires preserving "many others and much else" as well. But he cautions that heroic schemes aimed at dramatic transformations, whether technological, social, or moral, threaten to destroy the very social and natural resources that are necessary to maintaining a sustaining and sustainable human community. In short, we do not need to be animals or buddhas. We simply need to be more *human*—to replace our quest for godlike power and freedom with the more modest but more rewarding pursuit of sophrosyne, propriety, and common grace.

NOTES

Introduction

1. Jane Smiley, *A Thousand Acres* (New York: Ballentine Books, 1991), p. 119.

2. Patrick Mooney and Theo Majka, *Farmers' and Farm Workers' Movements* (New York: Twayne Publishing, 1995), pp. 98, 101. See also Samuel Hays, *Beauty, Health, and Permanence* (Cambridge: Cambridge University Press, 1987), pp. 300–301 (on the cooperation between environmentalists and farm workers on pesticide regulation in the 1970s); William P. Browne, *Private Interests, Public Policy, and American Agriculture* (Lawrence: University Press of Kansas, 1988), pp. 132–33 (on the increasing conciliation between public interest and farm groups); Randal S. Beeman and James Pritchard, *A Green and Permanent Land* (Lawrence: University Press of Kansas, 2001), pp. 131–40.

3. These aspects of his work are explored to some extent in *Wendell Berry,* ed. Paul Merchant (Lewiston, Idaho: Confluence Press, 1991). See also Allan Carlson, *The New Agrarian Mind* (New Brunswick, N.J.: Transaction Publishing, 2000), pp. 177–201; Andrew Angyal, *Wendell Berry* (New York: Twayne Publishing, 1995); Daniel Cornell, "The Country of Marriage: Wendell Berry's Personal Political Vision," *Southern Literary Journal* 16 (fall 1983): 59–70; Eric Freyfogle, "The Dilemma of Wendell Berry," *University of Illinois Law Review* 1994 (2): 363–85; James A. Montmarquet, "American Agrarianism: The Living Tradition," in *Agrarian Roots of Pragmatism,* ed. Paul B. Thompson and Thomas C. Hilde (Nashville: Vanderbilt University Press, 2000); D. A. Hamlin, "Moral Husbandry: The Nashville Agrarians, Wendell Berry, and the Hidden Wound of Race," *Journal of the American Studies Association of Texas* 28 (1997): 55–78. Angyal's is the only book-length study of Berry's thought; it provides primarily a summary rather than a critical analysis of Berry's body of work.

4. Richard Hofstadter, *Age of Reform* (New York: Alfred A. Knopf, 1955), pp. 23–24; A. Whitney Griswold, *Farming and Democracy* (New York: Harcourt,

Brace, 1948), p. 5; Grant McConnell, *The Decline of Agrarian Democracy* (Berkeley: University of California Press, 1953); Luther Tweeten, "Sector as Personality," *Agriculture and Human Values* (winter 1987): 66–74; Carlson, *New Agrarian Mind,* pp. 203–14; Paul Thompson, "Agrarianism as Philosophy," in Thompson and Hilde, *Agrarian Roots of Pragmatism,* p. 49.

5. James A. Montmarquet, "Agrarianism, Wealth, and Economics," *Agriculture and Human Values* 4 (spring–summer 1987): 47–52; James A. Montmarquet, "American Agrarianism," in Thompson and Hilde, *Agrarian Roots of Pragmatism,* pp. 51–76; Thompson, "Agrarianism as Philosophy," in Thompson and Hilde, *Agrarian Roots of Pragmatism,* pp. 25–50; Elizabeth Sanders, *Roots of Reform* (Chicago: University of Chicago Press, 1999), pp. 387–419.

6. Angyal, *Wendell Berry,* p. x; Patrick Murphy, "Two Different Paths in the Quest for Place: Gary Snyder and Wendell Berry," *American Poetry* 2 (1): 66 (1984).

7. Angyal, *Wendell Berry,* pp. xvii–xx.

8. Angyal's bibliography offers a partial list of this literature. See *Wendell Berry,* pp. 167–73. See also the essays collected in Merchant, *Wendell Berry;* Robert Collins, "A More Mingled Music: Wendell Berry's Ambivalent View of Language," *Modern Poetry Studies* 11 (1/2, 1982): 35–56; Richard Pevear, "On the Prose of Wendell Berry," *The Hudson Review* 35 (summer 1982): 341–47; Speer Morgan, "Wendell Berry: A Fatal Singing," *The Southern Review* 10 (October 1974): 865–77; Jeffery Alan Triggs, "Moving the Dark to Wholeness: The Elegies of Wendell Berry," *Literary Review* 31 (spring 1988): 279–92; Lionel Basney, "Wendell Berry: The Grace That Keeps the World," *The Other Side* 23 (January/February 1987): 46–48; Steven Weiland, "Wendell Berry: Culture and Fidelity," *Iowa Review* 10 (winter 1979): 99–104.

9. *Life Is a Miracle* (Washington, D.C.: Counterpoint Press, 2000), p. 113.

10. A better source for the development of Berry's thought is Angyal, *Wendell Berry,* which examines each of his works in chronological order.

11. See William Harbour, *The Foundations of Conservative Thought* (Notre Dame: University of Notre Dame Press, 1982), pp. 138, 143–48, 176.

12. *Life Is a Miracle* (Washington, D.C.: Counterpoint Press, 2000), pp. 50, 3.

13. David Danbom, "Romantic Agrarianism in Twentieth-Century America," *Agricultural History* 65 (fall 1991): 9; Douglas Anderson, "Wild Farming," in Thompson and Hilde, *Agrarian Roots of Pragmatism,* pp. 153–63.

14. Cf. David Orden, Robert Paarlberg, and Terry Roe, *Policy Reform in American Agriculture* (Chicago: University of Chicago Press, 1999), p. 227 (claiming that ideology is unimportant to agricultural policy).

15. This section draws on the arguments developed by Quentin Skinner, in *Foundations of Modern Political Thought,* 2 vols. (Cambridge: Cambridge University Press, 1978), 1: x–xiv.

Chapter One: Agrarian Visions

1. Carol Polsgrove and Scott Sanders, "Wendell Berry," *The Progressive* (May 1970): 36.

2. Ibid.

3. Angyal, *Wendell Berry,* pp. 1–4; "John Berry Jr.: Independent Thinker," *Louisville Courier-Journal,* March 26, 1979.

4. Thomas D. Clark, "Agriculture," in *The Kentucky Encyclopedia,* ed. John Kleber (Lexington: University Press of Kentucky, 1992), p. 9; Bruce K. Johnson, "Economy," in ibid., p. 281. Berry discusses the impact of this transformation on his own home town in *What Are People For?* (San Francisco: North Point Press, 1990), pp. 199–200, and *Sex, Economy, Freedom, and Community* (New York: Pantheon Books, 1992), pp. 6–8.

5. *The Long-Legged House* (New York: Harcourt, Brace & World, 1969), pp. 171–72.

6. Angyal, *Wendell Berry,* pp. 13, 15, 16–17. This seminar, interestingly, included Ken Kesey and Larry McMurtry.

7. *Long-Legged House,* pp. 173–74.

8. Ibid., pp. 173; 175–76. The "village virus" comment is a reference to Sinclair Lewis's *Main Street.*

9. Ibid., p. 176.

10. Ibid.

11. Ibid., pp. 176, 177.

12. See "The Whole Horse," *The Land Report* 64 (summer 1999): 3–7.

13. See James A. Montmarquet, *The Idea of Agrarianism* (Moscow, Idaho: University of Idaho Press, 1989).

14. Carl C. Taylor, *The Farmers' Movement, 1620–1920* (New York: American Book Company, 1953), p. 2; James A. Montmarquet, "Agrarianism, Wealth, and Economics," *Agriculture and Human Values* 4 (spring/summer 1987): 47; Christopher Duncan, *Fugitive Theory* (Lanham: Lexington Books, 2000), pp. 12–13; Thomas Paine, "Agrarian Justice," in *The Complete Writings of Thomas Paine,* ed. Philip Foner, 2 vols. (New York: Citadel Press, 1945), 1: 611. See also Thomas Govan, "Agrarian and Agrarianism: A Study in the Use and Abuse of Words," *Journal of Southern History* 30 (February–November 1964): 35–47.

15. "Farewell Order to the Armies of the United States" [1783], in *Basic Writings of George Washington,* ed. Saxe Commins (New York: Random House, 1948), pp. 499–503; "Farewell Address" [1796], in ibid., pp. 627–29.

16. See, e.g., Ely Bates, *Rural Philosophy: Or Reflections on Knowledge, Virtue, and Happiness, Chiefly in Reference to a Life of Retirement in the Country* (Philadelphia: B. B. Hopkins, 1807), pp. x–xi.

17. Victor Davis Hanson, *Fields without Dreams* (New York: The Free Press, 1996), p. ix.

18. Leo Marx, *The Machine in the Garden* (Oxford: Oxford University Press, 1964) (on the pastoral ideal in American literature); Hanson, *Fields without Dreams,* p. x.

19. Hanson, *Fields without Dreams,* p. x.

20. J. Hector St. John de Crèvecoeur, *Letters from an American Farmer* [1782] (New York: Penguin Classics, 1963).

21. Thomas Jefferson, "Notes on Virginia" [1784], in *The Life and Selected Writings of Thomas Jefferson,* ed. Adrienne Koch and William Peden (New York: Random House, 1993), p. 259.

22. Jefferson to John Adams, Monticello, October 28, 1813, in Koch and Peden, *Life and Selected Writings,* p. 579; Jefferson to Peter Carr, Monticello, September 7, 1814, ibid., p. 589.

23. Jean Yarbrough, *American Virtues* (Lawrence: University Press of Kansas, 1998), p. 64.

24. Ibid., pp. 60, 125–26, 140–42; Jefferson to de Creve-Coeur, January 15, 1787, in Koch and Peden, *Life and Selected Writings,* p. 380.

25. Leo Marx makes a similar point, suggesting that Jefferson's tendency to attribute to yeomen farmers the cultivation of gentlemen planters, a common trope in early agrarian rhetoric, allows him to avoid grappling with class differences. Marx, *Machine in the Garden,* pp. 127–28.

26. Yarbrough, *American Virtues,* pp. 79–80; Drew McCoy, *The Elusive Republic* (Chapel Hill: University North Carolina Press, 1980), p. 132.

27. John Taylor, *Arator* [1818] (Indianapolis: Liberty Fund, 1977), pp. 115, 123.

28. George Fitzhugh, "Sociology for the South" [1854], in *Antebellum Writings of George Fitzhugh and Hinton Rowan Helper on Slavery,* ed. Harvey Wish (New York: Capricorn Books, 1960), p. 93.

29. Ibid., p. 94. Of course, this is just a small part of Fitzhugh's defense of slavery.

30. Dorse Hagler, "The Agrarian Theme in Southern History to 1860" (Ph.D. diss., University of Missouri, 1968), pp. 63–64, 105–14, 202. Hagler's analysis of southern antebellum farm journals concludes that most southern agrarians rejected Fitzhugh's contention that agricultural labor is degrading, but nevertheless worried that farmers neglected education and self-improvement. See pp. 187–88, 190. His study suggests that the democratic agrarian tradition was the dominant agricultural ideology even in the South, except among those explicitly attempting to defend slavery. See pp. 202–3.

31. Ibid., pp. 85–86, 112–14.

32. Ibid., p. 108 (Ruffin's endorsement of this position).

33. Ibid., pp. 85–86, 110.

34. The French Physiocrats were the usual authorities for this proposition. They argued that agriculture's ability to provide surplus value stemmed from the inherent generativity of nature itself; in contrast, the products of manufacturers usually don't exceed the value of the labor and material used in making them. See Montmarquet, "Agrarianism, Wealth, and Economics," pp. 49–51; Elizabeth Fox-

Genovese, *The Origins of Physiocracy* (Ithaca: Cornell University Press, 1976), pp. 301–2.

35. J. G. A. Pocock recounts how land came to figure prominently in Anglo-American republicanism. *The Machiavellian Moment* (Princeton: Princeton University Press, 1975), pp. 376, 386–91, 446–61, 506–52.

36. James Harrington, *Oceana* [1656], in *The Political Works of James Harrington*, ed. J. G. A. Pocock (Cambridge: Cambridge University Press, 1977), pp. 158, 257–58.

37. See Yarbrough, *American Virtues,* pp. 56–60, 64–65, for a good discussion of agrarian virtues.

38. "Common Sense," in *The Complete Writings of Thomas Paine,* 1:18; Yarbrough, *American Virtues,* pp. 74, 76; McCoy, *Elusive Republic,* pp. 142, 177. McCoy points out that for eighteenth-century writers, manufacturing usually referred primarily to the production of luxury items. Ibid., pp. 108–9.

39. Taylor, *Arator,* p. 53.

40. This is not to suggest that the Populists or their successors were uninterested in agricultural education, however. Many southern antebellum farm journals shared Taylor's interest in soil conservation and in improving farming practices. Hagler, "The Agrarian Theme," p. 182. But the Populists focused more on keeping education practical and accessible to farmers. See Sanders, *Roots of Reform,* pp. 317–39. In general, the Populists' interest in education was subordinate to their broader social and political goals. For example, the Grange, the progenitor of the farmers' organizations that would coalesce into the Populist movement, began as an organization dedicated to improving farming techniques, but it wasn't able to sustain that focus. Pressure from members forced the leadership to take up the political and economic issues that came to dominate its agenda. Taylor, *The Farmers' Movement,* p. 114.

41. In this chapter, I will use the term "Populism" to refer to the political movement that arose in the 1870s and declined after 1896. In subsequent chapters I will use "Populist" more broadly to refer to the political tradition that had its origins in this movement.

42. On Populist ideology and programs generally, see Lawrence Goodwyn, *The Populist Moment* (Oxford: Oxford University Press, 1978); Bruce Palmer, *Man Over Money* (Chapel Hill: University of North Carolina Press, 1980); Gretchen Ritter, *Goldbugs and Greenbacks* (Cambridge: Cambridge University Press, 1997); Norman Pollock, ed., *The Populist Mind* (Indianapolis: Bobbs-Merrill, 1967); Sanders, *Roots of Reform.*

43. Jonathan Periam, *The Groundswell* (Cincinnati: E. Hannaford, 1874), pp. 39, 461–62.

44. Palmer, *Man Over Money,* p. 11.

45. W. Scott Morgan, "History of the Wheel and Alliance, and the Impending Revolution" [1889], in Pollock, *The Populist Mind,* p. 32.

46. Periam, *The Groundswell,* p. 40 (emphasis added).

47. Jefferson to Colonel Smith, Paris, November 13, 1787, in Koch and Peden, *Life and Selected Writings*, p. 403.

48. See Palmer, *Man Over Money*, p. 46.

49. James Weaver, "A Call to Action" [1892], in *A Populist Reader*, ed. George B. Tindall (Gloucester, Mass.: Peter Smith, 1976), pp. 64, 73.

50. Washington's agrarian philosophy is developed in *Up from Slavery* [1901] (New York: Airmont Publishing, 1967). For an example of DuBois's agrarianism, see "On the Wings of Atalanta," in W. E. B. DuBois, *The Souls of Black Folks* [1903] (New York: Penguin Books, 1989), pp. 63–73.

51. See, e.g., *Standing by Words* (San Francisco: North Point Press, 1983), pp. 47, 134–36.

52. Charles Otken, "The Credit System" [1894], in Tindall, *A Populist Reader*, p. 47.

53. Weaver, "A Call to Action," in Tindall, *A Populist Reader*, pp. 69–70.

54. Editorial, "Farmers' Alliance (Lincoln)," February 28, 1891, in Pollock, *The Populist Mind*, p. 19.

55. Periam, *The Groundswell*, p. 403.

56. Ibid., p. 402.

57. James H. Davis, "A Political Revelation" [1894], in Pollock, *The Populist Mind*, p. 28.

58. Lorenzo D. Lewelling, speech of July 28, 1904, in Pollock, *The Populist Mind*, pp. 5, 6.

59. Jacob Coxey, "Address of Protest" [1894], in Tindall, *A Populist Reader*, p. 162.

60. Editorial, "Farmers' Alliance (Lincoln)," February 28, 1891, in Pollock, *The Populist Mind*, p. 19.

61. Nelson Dunning, "The Farmers' Alliance History and Agricultural Digest" [1891], in Tindall, *A Populist Reader*, p. 101; Ignatius Donnelly, "Caesar's Column" [1891], in ibid., p. 114.

62. On the survival of these and related republican themes in contemporary farm politics, see Jon Lauck, *American Agriculture and the Problem of Monopoly* (Lincoln: University of Nebraska Press, 2000), pp. ix–xii.

63. "Gabriel's Utopia," in Tindall, *A Populist Reader*, p. 111.

64. William Bowers, *The Country Life Movement in America, 1900–1920* (Port Washington, N.Y: Kennikat Press, 1974), pp. 9–12; Willard Cochrane, *The Development of American Agriculture* (Minneapolis: University of Minnesota Press, 1979), pp. 99–100.

65. Bowers, *The Country Life Movement*, pp. 13, 14.

66. On the European movement, see Anna Bramwell, *Ecology in the Twentieth Century: A History* (New Haven: Yale University Press, 1989), pp. 64–91. On the American movement, see Bowers, *The Country Life Movement*, pp. 15–29; David Shi, *The Simple Life* (New York: Oxford University Press, 1985), pp. 176–218.

67. *What Are People For?* pp. 103–8; *A Continuous Harmony* (San Diego: Harcourt Brace, 1972), pp. 120–21.

68. Twelve Southerners, *I'll Take My Stand* [1930] (Baton Rouge: Louisiana State University Press, 1977).

69. Louise Cowan, *The Fugitive Group: A Literary History* (Baton Rouge: Louisiana State University Press, 1959), p. 240; John L. Stewart, *The Burden of Time* (Princeton: Princeton University Press, 1965), p. 110; Hamlin, "Moral Husbandry," 55–78, at 55.

70. The Agrarians continue to draw critical attention. See Duncan, *Fugitive Theory,* Mark Malvasi, *The Unregenerate South* (Baton Rouge: Louisiana State University Press, 1997); William Havard and Walter Sullivan, eds., *A Band of Prophets* (Baton Rouge: Louisiana State University Press, 1982); Paul Conkin, *The Southern Agrarians* (Knoxville: University of Tennessee Press, 1988); Louis D. Rubin, *The Wary Fugitives* (Baton Rouge: Louisiana State University Press, 1978).

71. Duncan would dispute the following analysis, arguing that the Fugitives should not be read as a defense of antebellum southern society or of aristocracy. *Fugitive Theory,* pp. 141–42, 145. His reading, however, does not give sufficient attention to the arguments for social hierarchy that pervade the book, nor to the close parallels between the Agrarians' and earlier aristocratic agrarians' portrait of antebellum southern society.

72. *I'll Take My Stand,* p. xliv.

73. Ibid., p. 3.

74. Ibid., p. 5.

75. Ibid.

76. Ibid., pp. 5–6, 8, 10.

77. Ibid., p. 10.

78. Ibid.

79. Rubin, *The Wary Fugitives,* p. 196.

80. Ralph Borsodi, *This Ugly Civilization* (New York: Simon & Schuster, 1929), pp. 5, 209.

81. Ibid., pp. 216–17.

82. Helen Nearing, *The Good Life* [1954] (New York: Schocken Books, 1989), pp. 5–6, 20.

83. Ibid., p. 3.

84. *Harlan Hubbard* (Lexington: University Press of Kentucky, 1990), p. 1.

85. Harlan Hubbard, *Shantyboat: A River Way of Life* [1953] (Lexington: University Press of Kentucky, 1977), p. 3.

86. *Harlan Hubbard,* p. 5.

87. Ibid., p. 88.

88. Ibid., p. 89.

89. Taylor, *The Farmers' Movement,* p. 347. See Lowell Harrison and James Klotter, *A New History of Kentucky* (Lexington: University Press of Kentucky, 1997), pp. 266–67, 295, on the influence of Populism in Kentucky in the nineteenth century.

90. Christopher Waldrep, *Night Riders* (Durham: Duke University Press, 1993), pp. 24–34.

91. Senate Committee on Agriculture and Forestry, *Hearings on the Agricultural Act of 1948,* 80th Cong., 2d sess., 1948, p. 397. "Parity" was coined as early as 1903, and came to mean that the prices of agricultural commodities should be maintained at the level they reached in the five years before World War I.

92. Compare the more bitter and more radical rhetoric of an earlier generation. Charles Fort, president of the Dark Tobacco District Planters' Protective Association in 1904, had complained to the United States Senate that "tobacco is the most slavish crop . . . we have to work fifteen months in a year on a crop of tobacco." But all Fort asked for was relief from a tax on tobacco, to help "the poor people and the negroes who are dependent." Suzanne Marshall, *Violence in the Black Patch of Kentucky and Tennessee* (Columbia: University of Missouri Press, 1994), pp. 105–6.

93. *Night Comes to the Cumberland* (Boston: Little, Brown, 1962); Thomas Kiffmeyer, "From Self-Help to Sedition: The Appalachian Volunteers in Eastern Kentucky, 1964–1970," *Journal of Southern History* 64 (February 1998): 77.

94. *Night Comes to the Cumberland,* p. x.

95. Ibid., pp. 305, 307.

96. *What Are People For?* pp. 30–31.

97. Ibid., p. 31 (quoting Caudill).

98. Ibid., p. 31. See Kiffmeyer, "From Self-Help to Sedition," on the Kentucky legislature's suspicions of communist sympathies among opponents to strip mining.

99. *Night Comes to the Cumberland,* p. 367.

Chapter Two: The Greening of Agrarianism

1. Terry Tempest Williams, "A Full Moon in May," in Merchant, *Wendell Berry,* p. 63.

2. Ibid., pp. 61–62.

3. Ibid., p. 63.

4. Bramwell, *Ecology in the Twentieth Century,* pp. 5–6; Bramwell, *The Fading of the Greens* (New Haven: Yale University Press, 1994), pp. 32, 37. Bramwell's thesis has been criticized on numerous grounds. See Dale Jamieson, "Ecology Then and Now," *Science, Technology, and Human Values* 17 (winter 1992): 129–31; Donald Worster, review of *Ecology in the Twentieth Century,* by Anna Bramwell, *Isis* 81 (4): 799–800 (1990). But her point about the interest of European environmentalists in agriculture and rural community is well supported.

5. See Beeman and Pritchard, *A Green and Permanent Land,* on the influence of ecologism in the United States.

6. Robert Gottlieb has criticized this version of the history of environmentalism for neglecting movements aimed at improving urban environments. *Forcing the Spring: The Transformation of the American Environmental Movement* (Washing-

ton, D.C.: Island Press, 1993), p. 6. His point is well taken, but for our limited purposes we can focus on those movements directly concerned with rural areas.

7. Henry David Thoreau, *Walden and Civil Disobedience* [1854] (New York: Penguin Books, 1983), pp. 260, 244, 263–64.

8. See "Nature" [1836], in *The Selected Writings of Ralph Waldo Emerson*, ed. Brooks Atkinson (New York: The Modern Library, 1940), pp. 3–42.

9. Thoreau, *Walden*, pp. 164–65.

10. Ibid., pp. 165, 161–62.

11. Ibid., pp. 200, 202, 207.

12. Ibid., p. 211.

13. Ibid., p. 212.

14. Ibid., p. 47.

15. Roderick Nash, *Wilderness and the American Mind*, 3d ed. (New Haven: Yale University Press, 1982), pp. 84–95.

16. Thoreau, "Maine Woods," quoted in Nash, *Wilderness and the American Mind*, p. 91.

17. Nash, *Wilderness and the American Mind*, p. 94.

18. Thoreau, *Walden*, pp. 88, 83.

19. Ibid., p. 114.

20. John Muir, "A Thousand Mile Walk to the Gulf" [1916], in *The Wilderness Journeys* (Edinburgh: Canongate Classic, 1996), p. 1.

21. Muir, "My First Summer in the Sierra" [1911], in *The Wilderness Journeys*, p. 44.

22. "Story of My Boyhood and Youth" [1913], in *The Wilderness Journeys*, p. 36.

23. "A Thousand Mile Walk to the Gulf," in *The Wilderness Journeys*, p. 34.

24. "Story of My Boyhood and Youth," in *The Wilderness Journeys*, p. 84.

25. "My First Summer in the Sierra," in *The Wilderness Journeys*, pp. 11–12.

26. Ibid., pp. 12–13.

27. See chapter 6.

28. Edward Abbey, *Desert Solitaire* (New York: Ballantine Books, 1968), p. 177.

29. Ibid.

30. Ibid., p. 208.

31. Leo Marx and Bob Pepperman Taylor have similarly identified concerns over the negative aspects of the emerging industrial order as the primary force behind what they call the "pastoral tradition" represented by Thoreau. Marx, *Machine in the Garden;* Taylor, *Our Limits Transgressed* (Lawrence: University Press of Kansas, 1992), p. 4; see also Henry Nash Smith, *Virgin Land* (Cambridge: Harvard University Press, 1950), pp. 52–80. In contrast, the idea that nature should be valued for itself, independently of its importance to social life, appeared relatively late in American environmentalism and has never been a dominant theme. Taylor, *Our Limits Transgressed,* pp. 53–57 (on emergence of biocentric ethics after 1940). Cf. Roderick Nash, *Rights of Nature* (Madison: University of Wisconsin Press, 1989) (arguing that

intrinsic value arguments appear as early as the eighteenth century, but acknowledging that such arguments didn't become prominent until the twentieth century).

32. Samuel Hays, *Conservation and the Gospel of Efficiency* (Cambridge: Harvard University Press, 1959), pp. 1–2. On conservationism generally, see Hays, ibid.; Richard Andrews, *Managing the Environment, Managing Ourselves* (New Haven: Yale University Press, 1999), pp. 94–108, 136–53.

33. Gifford Pinchot, *The Fight for Conservation* (New York: Doubleday, Page, 1911), pp. 12–13.

34. See, for example, the 1907 rider to Forest Service annual appropriation, requiring congressional approval for future forest reserves in the West. Andrews, *Managing the Environment,* p. 146. Andrews points out that conservationism remained troubled by "the ambiguous relationship between environmental and populist values." Ibid., p. 148.

35. Pinchot, *Fight for Conservation,* p. 77.

36. Ibid.

37. Worster, *Nature's Economy,* 2d ed. (Cambridge: Cambridge University Press, 1994), p. 269; see also Hays, *Beauty, Health, and Permanence,* pp. 13–14.

38. Worster, *Nature's Economy,* pp. 230–32.

39. Liberty Hyde Bailey, *The Country-Life Movement in the United States* (New York: MacMillan, 1911), pp. 15, 19.

40. *Report of the Commission on Country Life* (New York: Sturgis & Walton, 1911).

41. Liberty Hyde Bailey, *The Holy Earth* (New York: Charles Scribner's Sons, 1915), pp. 1, 3, 15.

42. Ibid., p. 16.

43. Ibid., pp. 25, 22, 28.

44. Ibid., p. 30.

45. *What Are People For?* pp. 103–8.

46. Beeman and Pritchard, *A Green and Permanent Land,* pp. 9–34; Worster, *Nature's Economy,* pp. 221–53.

47. The American movement was in fact part of the larger ecology movement centered in England, Germany, and the United States. For a more detailed study of its themes, see Beeman and Pritchard, *A Green and Permanent Land,* pp. 35–63; Worster, *Nature's Economy,* pp. 221–53.

48. Hugh Bennett, *Soil Conservation* (New York: McGraw-Hill, 1939), p. vii. See also Morris Llewellyn Cooke, "Is the United States a Permanent Country?" *Forum/Century* 99 (4): 236–40 (1938); Rexford Tugwell, "Farm Relief and a Permanent Agriculture," *Annals of the American Academy of Political and Social Science* (March 1929): 275, 280–81.

49. Beeman and Pritchard, *A Green and Permanent Land,* p. 31.

50. Sanders, *Roots of Reform,* pp. 387–89; Orville Kile, *The Farm Bureau through Three Decades* (Baltimore: Waverly Press, 1948), p. 336.

51. Bennett, *Soil Conservation,* pp. v, 8.

52. Ibid., pp. 3, 13.

53. Paul Sears, *Deserts on the March* (Norman: University of Oklahoma Press, 1935), pp. 45–46.

54. Edward Faulkner, *Plowmans' Folly and A Second Look* (Washington, D.C.: Island Press, 1943, 1947).

55. Sears, *Deserts on the March,* pp. 50, 73–74.

56. Bramwell, *Ecology in the Twentieth Century,* pp. 66–71.

57. Hagler, "The Agrarian Theme," pp. 8, 193; Beeman and Pritchard, *A Green and Permanent Land,* pp. 43–44 (Sears's reliance on Kropotkin).

58. Paul Sears, "Science and the New Landscape," *Harper's Magazine,* July 1939, p. 210.

59. I do not mean to suggest that New Deal agriculture policy in general was unconcerned with small farmers; they were in fact the main clients of the Resettlement Administration. But programs designed to help small farmers were typically justified by social justice rather than ecological arguments. See A. Whitney Griswold, *Farming and Democracy* (New York: Harcourt, Brace, 1948), pp. 163–67.

60. Tugwell, "Farm Relief and a Permanent Agriculture," p. 275.

61. Beeman and Pritchard, *A Green and Permanent Land,* pp. 24–25.

62. House Committee on Agriculture, *Hearings on Long-Range Agricultural Policy,* 80th Cong., 1st sess., pt. 1, 1947, p. 146.

63. Louis Bromfield, "The High Cost of Poor Farming," [1945–46] in *From the Land,* ed. Nancy Pittman (Washington, D.C.: Island Press, 1988), p. 76. See also Bromfield, *A Few Brass Tacks* (New York, London: Harper & Bros., 1946), pp. 171–72.

64. Bromfield, *A Few Brass Tacks,* p. 176.

65. James Patton, *The Case for Farmers* (Washington, D.C.: Public Affairs Press, 1959), pp. 6, 40.

66. Ibid., p. 43.

67. Ibid., pp. 1–2.

68. Borsodi, "The Case Against Farming as a Big Business," quoted in Beeman and Pritchard, *A Green and Permanent Land,* p. 19.

69. Carey McWilliams, *Factories in the Field* (Boston: Little, Brown, 1939), p. 48.

70. Ibid., pp. 9, 303–4, 324–25. See also P. Alston Waring and Walter M. Teller, *Roots in the Earth* (New York: Harper & Bros., 1943), pp. 102–3 (concerned about factory farming taking over in Florida).

71. Paul Lasley, "The Crisis in Iowa," in *Is There a Moral Obligation to Save the Family Farm?* ed. Gary Comstock (Ames: Iowa State University Press, 1987), pp. 98–100. See also Mooney and Majka, *Farmers' and Farm Workers' Movements,* p. 90 (the number of farms decreased from 5.4 million in 1950 to 2.1 million in 1987); John Shover, *First Majority—Last Minority* (De Kalb: Northern Illinois University Press), p. 4 (between 1929 and 1965, more than 30 million people moved away from farms).

72. Cochrane, *The Development of American Agriculture,* p. 197.

73. Ibid., p. 202.

74. Ibid., pp. 203–5, 229.

75. Ibid., pp. 230–31.

76. McWilliams, *Factories in the Field,* pp. 48–49.

77. Ibid., p. 324.

78. Ibid., p. 325.

79. Walter Goldschmidt, *As You Sow* (Montclair, N.J.: Allanheld, Osmun, 1947).

80. Ibid., pp. 187, 203.

81. Ibid., pp. 415, 416.

82. Ibid., p. viii. For example, James Patton cited the Goldschmidt study in his testimony for the House Agriculture Committee in 1947. House Committee, *Long-Range Agricultural Policy,* p. 146. On the debate over monopolistic practices, see Lauck, *American Agriculture,* pp. 19–38.

83. Waring and Teller, *Roots in the Earth,* pp. 36–37. The permanent agriculture school had also complained of absentee ownership, but generally directed their criticisms at independent farmers rather than corporate agriculture. See Sears, *Deserts on the March,* pp. 28–29; Bromfield, *A Few Brass Tacks,* p. 176.

84. Waring and Teller, *Roots in the Earth,* pp. 102–18. Interestingly, however, the authors' discussion of farm *size* (as opposed to farm tenure) does not draw on this argument; they make no connection between large farms and soil erosion or poor stewardship. Rather, they defend small farms in standard Populist terms, arguing that owners of large farms have an unfair advantage, influencing legislation and manipulating the markets to squeeze out small farms.

85. Aldo Leopold, *A Sand County Almanac* [1949] (New York: Ballantine Books, 1966), p. 199.

86. Ibid., p. 6.

87. Rachel Carson, *Silent Spring* [1962] (Boston: Houghton Mifflin, 1994), p. 10.

88. Ibid., pp. 64, 72, 99.

89. Ibid., pp. 16, 258–59.

90. Al Gore, introduction to *Silent Spring,* by Carson, p. xv; I. L. Baldwin, "Chemicals and Pests," *Science* 137 (28 September 1962): 1,042–43; Book review, *Time,* September 28, 1962, pp. 45–48.

91. See Beeman and Pritchard, *A Green and Permanent Land,* pp. 101–30, for a detailed discussion of the sustainable agriculture movement.

92. Ibid., p. 133.

93. Ibid., pp. 16–17.

94. Caudill's analysis can be found in *Night Comes to the Cumberland,* pp. 305–24.

95. *Long-Legged House,* p. 18.

96. Ibid., pp. 20, 22.

97. "Response to a War," *The Nation,* April 24, 1967, p. 527; Wendell Berry and Ralph Meatyard, *The Unforeseen Wilderness* [1971] (San Francisco: North Point Press, 1991); Angyal, *Wendell Berry,* p. 67.

98. *A Continuous Harmony,* p. 175.

99. Ibid., p. 176.

100. Kiffmeyer, "From Self-Help to Sedition," p. 83.

101. *Long-Legged House,* p. 90.

102. *A Continuous Harmony*, p. 171. See also *The Unsettling of America* (San Francisco: Sierra Club Books, 1986), p. 22.

103. *A Continuous Harmony,* p. 169. He also objects to the word "environment," implying as it does that it surrounds us rather than includes us. See *Life Is a Miracle,* p. 8. The point is well taken, but I will nevertheless use the word throughout this study for lack of a better alternative.

104. *Long-Legged House,* p. 15. See also *Life Is a Miracle,* pp. 8, 45.

105. For further discussion of this point, see chapter 7; on Berry's view of language, see Collins, "A More Mingled Music," pp. 35–56.

106. *Sex, Economy, Freedom, and Community,* pp. 33–34.

107. "Response to a War," p. 528.

108. See, e.g., Easterbrook, "Making Sense of Agriculture" in Comstock, *Is There a Moral Obligation to Save the Family Farm?* pp. 3–30. Easterbrook argues that failing farms are evidence that the invisible hand of capitalism is working properly, making food production more efficient. Farms go out of business because we have "too many farmers" (or at least "too much farming"). Ibid., p. 11.

109. Jim Hightower, *Hard Tomatoes, Hard Times* [1973] (Cambridge, Mass: Schenkman Publishing, 1978); Russell Parker and John Connor, "Consumer Loss Due to Monopoly in Food Manufacturing," in Comstock, *Is There a Moral Obligation to Save the Family Farm?* pp. 233–37; Shover, *First Majority—Last Minority*, p. 167; Lauck, *American Agriculture,* pp. 163–76.

110. Luther Tweeten, "Food for People and Profit," in Comstock, *Is There a Moral Obligation to Save the Family Farm?* pp. 246–63.

111. Victor Davis Hansen, for example, mourns the disappearance of the yeoman farmer as "a cultural type" that provided a critical countervoice to a material and uniform culture. *Fields without Dreams,* p. xvi.

Chapter Three: The Fragile Planet

1. *Home Economics* (New York: North Point Press, 1987), pp.104–5.

2. This was a standard argument for restricting the franchise to property owners. Paul Thompson, "Agrarianism and the American Philosophical Tradition," *Agriculture and Human Values* 7 (winter 1990): 4. Thompson points out that this proposition was conventional to the point of triteness among the physiocrats. See Fox-Genovese, *The Origins of Physiocracy,* p. 131.

3. *Another Turn of the Crank* (Washington, D.C.: Counterpoint Press, 1995), p. 52.

4. Ibid., p. 52. This idea is not original; Berry echoes Patton, *The Case for Farmers,* p. 39.

5. *The Unsettling of America,* p. 10.

6. *The Gift of Good Land* (San Francisco: North Point Press, 1981), pp. 131–33; *The Unsettling of America*, pp. 171–72, 179.

7. *The Unsettling of America*, 84; *A Continuous Harmony*, p. 167. Such concerns were important in galvanizing the postwar environmental movement. See Hays, *Beauty, Health, and Permanence*, pp. 174, 177–82; Gottlieb, *Forcing the Spring*, pp. 93–94.

8. Thomas Robert Malthus, "An Essay on the Principle of Population" [1798], in *The Works of T. R. Malthus*, 8 vols., ed. E. A. Wrigley and David Souden (London: William Pickering, 1986), 1: 12–13.

9. Malthus, "An Essay on the Principle of Population" [1826], in Wrigley and Souden, *Works of T. R. Malthus*, 2: 16.

10. Cf. Robert Goodin, *Green Political Theory* (Cambridge, U.K.: Polity Press, 1992), p. 1 (comparing Malthus's and modern limits to growth arguments). "Neo-Malthusian" arguments can be found in William Ophuls and Stephen Boyan Jr., *Ecology and the Politics of Scarcity Revisited* (New York: W. H. Freeman, 1992), p. 3 (also misinterpreting Malthus); Donella Meadows, Dennis Meadows, Jorgen Randers, and Williams Behrens III, *The Limits to Growth* (New York: Universe Books, 1972), pp. 45–87; Robert Heilbroner, *An Inquiry into the Human Prospect* [1974] (New York: W. W. Norton, 1980), pp. 31–58; Paul R. Ehrlich, *The Population Bomb* (New York: Ballantine Books, 1968), pp. 36–67; Garret Hardin, "The Tragedy of the Commons," *Science* 162 (December 13, 1968): 1,243–48.

11. Worster, *Nature's Economy*, p. 152.

12. George Perkins Marsh, *Man and Nature* [1864] (Cambridge: Belknap Press, 1965), p. 3.

13. Marx, *Machine in the Garden*, pp. 42–43; Nash, *Wilderness and the American Mind*, p. 9.

14. Marsh, *Man and Nature*, p. 36.

15. Ibid., p. 35.

16. On Marsh's influence, see Arthur A. Ekirch, *Man and Nature in America* (New York: Columbia University Press, 1963), pp. 77–80; Stewart Udall, *The Quiet Crisis* (New York: Holt, Rinehart & Winston, 1963), p. 76.

17. Hagler, "The Agrarian Theme," pp. 103–5, 182–85; Udall, *The Quiet Crisis*, p. 70.

18. Marsh, *Man and Nature*, p. 186–87.

19. Cf. Hays, *Conservation and Gospel of Efficiency;* Gottlieb, *Forcing the Spring;* Taylor, *Our Limits Transgressed;* Victor Scheffer, *The Shaping of Environmentalism in America* (Seattle: University of Washington Press, 1991). But see Philip Shabecoff, *A Fierce Green Fire* (New York: Hill & Wang, 1993), pp. 44–47; Udall, *Quiet Crisis,* pp. 70–71 (discussing early concerns about soil conservation).

20. See, e.g., Andrew Dobson, *Green Political Thought*, 2d ed. (London: Routledge, 1990), pp. 34–35. Dobson argues that while the roots of environmental thought lie in the nineteenth century, what he calls the ecological *ideology* is really

a post–World War II phenomenon, having evolved in response to the environmental devastation of twentieth-century industrialism.

21. Berry would object to the machine metaphor, but would endorse the notion that it is alien and possibly incomprehensible. See *Life Is a Miracle,* pp. 46–47.

22. *A Continuous Harmony,* p. 164.

23. Murray Bookchin, *The Philosophy of Social Ecology* (Montreal: Black Rose Books, 1990), pp. 159–60; Steven Chuse, ed., *Defending the Earth: A Dialogue between Murray Bookchin and Dave Foreman* (Boston: South End Press, 1991), pp. 20, 125; Taylor, *Our Limits Transgressed,* pp. 27–40; Brian Doherty and Marius de Geus, *Democracy and Green Political Thought* (London: Routledge, 1996), pp. 1–3; Robyn Eckersley, *Environmentalism and Political Theory* (Albany: State University of New York Press, 1992), pp. 12–16.

24. *Home Economics,* p. 106; *Another Turn of the Crank,* pp. 48–49.

25. Hardin, "The Tragedy of the Commons," p. 1,247.

26. Ibid., p. 1,247; Ophuls and Boyan, *Ecology and the Politics of Scarcity Revisited,* pp. 285–86.

27. Ophuls and Boyan, *Ecology and the Politics of Scarcity Revisited,* p. 282. Ophuls does insist that liberal democracy as we know it cannot survive under conditions of scarcity, but he gives us little reason to believe a strong but democratic state couldn't manage our environmental problems.

28. See, e.g., Doherty and de Geus, introduction to *Democracy and Green Political Thought,* p. 1.

29. Ironically, Ophuls accuses Hardin of proposing a Hobbesian state. Ophuls and Boyan, *Ecology and the Politics of Scarcity Revisited,* p. 196. Unlike Ophuls and Hardin, Heilbroner does envision the rise of "iron" governments capable of controlling population growth. *An Inquiry into the Human Prospect,* pp. 38–39. Other theorists, however, recognize that a democratic, liberal state can be active and strong. See, e.g., de Geus, "The Ecological Restructuring of the State," in Doherty and de Geus, *Democracy and Green Political Thought,* p. 193.

30. For the green critique of liberals' focus on rights, see Eckersley, *Environmentalism and Political Theory,* pp. 17, 23; Ophuls and Boyan, *Ecology and the Politics of Scarcity Revisited,* pp. 199–200. On restrictions on property rights in American law, see Lawrence Friedman, *A History of American Law,* 2d ed. (New York: Simon & Schuster, 1985), pp. 183–84; Morton Horwitz, *The Transformation of American Law* (Oxford: Oxford University Press, 1992), pp. 27–30; Richard Andrews, *Managing the Environment,* p. 37.

31. The classic formulation of this argument is Jürgen Habermas, *Structural Transformation of the Public Sphere* [1969] (Cambridge: MIT Press, 1992).

32. *The Unsettling of America,* p. 8.

33. Ibid., p. 222.

34. See, e.g., Alasdair MacIntyre, *After Virtue,* 2d ed. (Notre Dame: University of Notre Dame Press, 1984), pp. 6–22. I don't necessarily agree that moral relativism

causes these problems, although it may be a symptom of them. More common, I think, is what Richard Rorty calls an ironic stance toward our beliefs: we know they're contingent, but that doesn't undermine their authority for us. They're still *our* beliefs—and, as Berry points out, there's widespread consensus on many of them. Rorty, *Contingency, Irony, and Solidarity* (Cambridge: Cambridge University Press, 1989), pp. 73–95.

35. *The Unsettling of America*, p. 222.

36. Bramwell, *The Fading of the Greens*, p. 29; Ophuls and Boyan, *Ecology and the Politics of Scarcity Revisited*, pp. 13–14.

37. *A Continuous Harmony*, p. 168.

38. Leopold, *A Sand County Almanac;* Bill Devall and George Sessions, *Deep Ecology* (Salt Lake City: Gibbs M. Smith, 1985); Warwick Fox, *Toward a Transpersonal Ecology* (Boston: Shambhala, 1990); Arnold Naess, "A Defence of the Deep Ecology Movement," *Environmental Ethics* 6 (fall 1984): 265–70.

39. See Sonya Salamon, *Prairie Patrimony* (Chapel Hill: University of North Carolina Press, 1992). Salamon describes two dominant value systems among American farmers, a deeply conservative "yeoman" ideology and a more progressive "entrepreneurial" outlook. Neither is particularly conducive to ecocentric values.

40. Devall and Sessions, *Deep Ecology,* pp. 9, 36; Bramwell, *Fading of the Greens,* p. 17; Dobson, *Green Political Thought,* p. 5.

41. Dobson, *Green Political Thought,* pp. 21, 48. See also Fox, *Toward a Transpersonal Ecology,* pp. 185–86 (calling this strategy "intellectual cowardice").

42. Fox, *Toward a Transpersonal Ecology,* p. 217.

43. Robyn Eckersley is one of the few theorists who acknowledges these issues, but she does so only in the context of criticizing Murray Bookchin for his failure to address such questions in his (nonecocentric) social theory. She conspicuously fails to ask the same questions of the ecocentric theorists she endorses. *Environmentalism and Political Theory,* pp. 152–54.

44. See Fox, *Toward a Transpersonal Ecology,* p. 16; Bookchin, *The Philosophy of Social Ecology,* pp. 58–60 (blaming the Socratic tradition); Lynn White, "The Historical Roots of Our Ecological Crisis," *Science* 155 (March 10, 1967): 1,203–7 (blaming Christianity); David Ehrenfeld, *The Arrogance of Humanism* (New York: Oxford University Press, 1978) (blaming Renaissance humanism); Eckersley, *Environmentalism and Political Theory,* p. 23 (blaming Locke); Ophuls and Boyan, *Ecology and the Politics of Scarcity Revisited,* p. 191 (blaming Adam Smith and Karl Marx); Greta Gaard, "Living Interconnections with Animals and Nature," in *Ecofeminism,* ed. Greta Gaard (Philadelphia: Temple University Press, 1993), p. 1 (blaming patriarchy). These arguments should be distinguished from those of Barry Commoner and E. F. Schumacher, who focus on the genesis of environmentally destructive *practices* in post–World War II productive technology. Barry Commoner, *The Closing Circle* (New York: Alfred A. Knopf, 1975), pp. 8, 12; E. F. Schumacher, *Small Is Beautiful* [1973] (New York: Harper Perennial, 1989), pp. 18–19.

45. John Passmore, *Man's Responsibility for Nature* (New York: Charles Scribner's Sons, 1974), pp. 28–40; Robin Attfield, *The Ethics of Environmental Concern* (New York: Columbia University Press, 1983), pp. 20–50; Shi, *The Simple Life.*

46. This argument is developed in *The Unsettling of America.*

47. *Another Turn of the Crank,* p. 73; see also *Sex, Economy, Freedom, and Community,* p. 96.

48. *Standing by Words* (San Francisco: North Point Press, 1983), pp. 203, 210.

49. *Home Economics,* p. 148 (emphasis added).

50. Eckersley, *Environmentalism and Political Theory,* pp. 56, 83.

51. Ibid., pp. 61–62; Fox, *Toward a Transpersonal Ecology,* pp. 225–29, 233–41 (quoting a range of deep ecologists who use such language).

52. *Home Economics,* p. 148.

53. Murray Bookchin has the same complaint. *The Philosophy of Social Ecology,* pp. 157–60.

54. *Another Turn of the Crank,* p. 71.

55. Ibid., pp. 72–73.

56. See Dobson, *Green Political Thought,* pp. 90–91 (rightly criticizing ecocentrics on this score). See also Eckersley, *Environmentalism and Political Theory,* p. 126.

57. Gary Snyder, *Earth House Hold* (New York: New Directions, 1957), p. 36.

58. *Home Economics,* p. 149; see also *Another Turn of the Crank,* pp. 71–75. While this may seem a politically dangerous tactic, it might make Berry's philosophy more palatable to an American audience. Ecocentrism is viewed with great suspicion by many American churches who see it as part of a dangerously anti-Christian, New Age philosophy. The support of the Christian establishment, at least in the United States, may well be worth the risk of alienating some of the green leadership. I'll discuss Berry's relationship to Christianity in chapter 6.

59. *Home Economics,* pp. 141–42.

60. See, e.g., *The Unforeseen Wilderness; Collected Poems, 1957–1982* (New York: North Point Press, 1995), p. 69; Angyal, *Wendell Berry,* p. 46 (discussing Berry's successful twenty-year effort to save the Red River Gorge). But see Murphy, "Two Different Paths," pp. 60–68 (exploring the different views of wilderness offered by Gary Snyder and Wendell Berry); Devall and Sessions, *Deep Ecology,* p. 122 (criticizing Berry for failing to see the necessity of "big wilderness" and defending only small pockets of wilderness). Devall and Sessions argue that Berry lacks "deep ecological consciousness," but they may underestimate his support for wilderness preservation, as I will discuss in chapter 5.

61. *What Are People For?* pp. 148, 151; see also *What Are People For?* p. 116; *Collected Poems,* p. 16.

62. "Farming with Horses," *Organic Gardening and Farming* 21 (March 1974): 72–73. See also "Profit in Work's Pleasure," *Harper's,* February 1988, p. 21 (on a sheep breeder's pleasure in pleasing his sheep); *The Gift of Good Land,* p. 191. I

should point out that some automotive enthusiasts would question Berry's assertion that one can't achieve fellow feeling with a machine.

63. Fox, *Toward a Transpersonal Ecology*, p. 262.

64. Council on Environmental Quality and U.S. Department of State, *Global 2000 Report to the President*, 3 vols. (Washington, D.C.: U.S. Government Printing Office, 1980); Worldwatch Institute, *State of the World 2000* (New York: W. W. Norton, 2000); World Resources Institute, *World Resources, 2000–2001* (New York: Basic Books, 2000).

65. Julian Simon and Herman Kahn, eds., *The Resourceful Earth* (Oxford: Basil Blackwell, 1984); Ronald Bailey, *Eco-Scam* (New York: St. Martin's Press, 1993); Aaron Wildavsky, *But Is It True?* (Cambridge: Harvard University Press, 1995).

66. See William Ruckelshaus, "Risk, Science, and Democracy," *Issues in Science and Technology* 1 (spring 1985): 19–38, at 23–24; Hays, *Beauty, Health, and Permanence*, pp. 330–62.

67. Hays, *Beauty, Health, Permanence*, pp. 329–59.

68. *Life Is a Miracle*, p. 17.

69. *The Gift of Good Land*, pp. 47–48; 89–97; *The Unsettling of America*, pp. 172–73.

70. *The Gift of Good Land*, p. 92.

71. Ibid., pp. 124–25.

72. Jackson, "Challenges Facing Kansans: Environmental, Economic, and Political." Available on the Land Institute website, http://www.landinstitute.org/texis/scrip...paper/+/ART/2000/07/01.

73. Jackson, "The Need of Being Versed in Country Things," *The Land Report* 67 (summer 2000).

74. Jackon, "Challenges Facing Kansans."

75. *Life Is a Miracle*, p. 126.

76. Berry's critique of scientism is developed most fully in *Life Is a Miracle*, his response to E. O. Wilson's *Consilience* (New York: Alfred A. Knopf, 1998). Wilson's work is a typical if somewhat jejune example of scientism; Berry's critique is notable less for its originality than for the skill with which he demolishes Wilson's argument.

77. Bramwell, *Ecology in the Twentieth Century*, pp. 39–63; Worster, *Nature's Economy*, pp. 16–25.

78. *Life Is a Miracle*, p. 19.

79. Ibid., p. 28.

80. See generally *Life Is a Miracle*.

81. *The Unsettling of America*, pp. 172–73. This critique of the land-grant universities is developed even more forcefully by Jim Hightower in *Hard Tomatoes, Hard Times*.

82. *Home Economics*, p. 78.

83. Ibid.

84. Ibid.

85. See chapter 8.

Chapter Four: Settling America

1. *Another Turn of the Crank,* pp. 49–50 (emphasis added).

2. Bramwell, *Ecology in the Twentieth Century,* pp. 66–71.

3. *A Continous Harmony,* p. 79.

4. *Long-Legged House,* pp. 15–18.

5. See Beeman and Pritchard, *A Green and Permanent Land,* pp. 14–15, on cross-cultural comparisons by permanent agriculture advocates. A favorite source was F. H. King's study of Asian agriculture, *Farmers of Forty Centuries* (Madison, Wis.: Mrs. F. H. King, 1911).

6. *The Gift of Good Land,* pp. 3–76; 258–61 (Amish agriculture). See also *Home Economics,* pp. 21–48 (Irish agriculture); *Another Turn of the Crank,* pp. 41–44 (Menominee forestry).

7. *Gift of Good Land,* p. 8.

8. Ibid., pp. 8, 18–19.

9. Ibid., p. 51.

10. Ibid., p. 59.

11. See Martin Lewis, *Green Delusions* (Durham: Duke University Press, 1992), pp. 43–81, for an insightful critique of this argument.

12. *Gift of Good Land,* pp. 9–14.

13. Ibid., pp. 51–52.

14. "A Defense of the Family Farm," in Comstock, *Is There a Moral Obligation to Save the Family Farm?* pp. 352–56.

15. *The Unsettling of America,* pp. 40–41. This theme was popular among defenders of small farms during the Vietnam era. See Lauck, *American Agriculture,* pp. 30–31.

16. *Unsettling of America,* pp. 17, 18.

17. Bureau of the Census, *1992 Census of Agriculture,* Geographic Area Series, vol. 1, pt. 51, *United States: Summary and State Data,* p. 4. Berry might point out, however, that this figure does not reflect the influence of large corporations on American agriculture, since such corporations dominate the input and processing sectors of the agricultural economy, and can exert further control over production methods through contract farming.

18. *Unsettling of America,* p. 3.

19. Ibid., p. 4.

20. Frederick Jackson Turner, *The Frontier in American History* [1920] (Malabar, Fla.: Robert E. Krieger Publishing, 1985), p. 30. Turner in fact argued that the unsettled state of American society helped us to adapt to the land by freeing us of European habits and dispositions. See pp. 205–6.

21. *Unsettling of America,* pp. 18–23.

22. Peter Berg and Raymon Dasmann, "Reinhabiting California," in *Reinhabiting a Separate Country,* ed. Peter Berg (San Francisco: Planet Drum Foundation, 1978), pp. 217–20; Kirkpatrick Sale, *Dwellers in the Land* (Philadelphia: New Society Publishers, 1991), pp. 41–43; Schumacher, *Small Is Beautiful,* pp. 67–80; Devall

and Sessions, *Deep Ecology*, pp. 21–24, 112; Gary Paul Nabhan, *Cultures of Habitat* (Washington, D.C.: Counterpoint, 1997), pp. 2–3, 318–19. On Bailey, see chapter 2.

23. Turner, *The Frontier in American History*, p. 264.

24. *Unsettling of America*, pp. 171–73.

25. *Home Economics*, p. 106.

26. See, e.g., *Sex, Economy, Freedom, and Community*, p. 3.

27. *Another Turn of the Crank*, pp. 48–49.

28. Ibid., pp. 54–55.

29. See Clay Fulcher, "Vertical Integration in the Poultry Industry: The Contractual Relationship," *Agricultural Law Update* (January 1992): 4–6; Neil Hamilton, "Why Own the Farm if You Can Own the Farmer (and the Crop)?" *Nebraska Law Review* 73 (1994): 48–102; Lauck, *American Agriculture*, pp. 28–29, on early criticism of and resistance to vertical integration in poultry production.

30. Of course, given farmers' lack of bargaining power relative to large corporations, this notion of franchise farming may not be as attractive to farmers as, for example, attempting vertical integration "from the bottom up" with agricultural cooperatives. Such an approach could capture some of the economic benefits enjoyed by large corporations without the risk of exploitation by powerful corporate interests.

31. *Gift of Good Land*, p. xi.

32. *Home Economics*, pp. 164, 165.

33. *What Are People For?* p. 8; *Home Economics*, p. 15.

34. *A Continuous Harmony*, p. 135.

35. *Life Is a Miracle*, pp. 10–11.

36. *A Continuous Harmony*, p. 98.

37. See, for example, R. Burnell Held and Marion Clawson, *Soil Conservation in Perspective* (Baltimore: Johns Hopkins Press, 1965), pp. 253–93, on the reasons small farmers may fail to practice soil conservation.

38. *Unsettling of America*, p. 32.

39. Ibid., pp. 40, 4–7, 39–42.

40. Ibid., p. 75.

41. *Gift of Good Land*, pp. 210, 216 (what makes farmers good is the quality of their products and fertility and order of their farms, not their profitability); *Unsettling of America*, p. 76 (objecting to the characterization of agriculture as a "field").

42. *Home Economics*, p. 107.

43. Michael Sandel, ed., *Liberalism and Its Critics* (New York: New York University Press, 1984); Richard Sennett, *The Fall of Public Man* (New York: W. W. Norton, 1974).

44. *Long-Legged House*, p. 77; *Fidelity* (New York: Pantheon Books, 1992), p. 9; *Sex, Economy, Freedom, and Community*, p. 128; *What Are People For?* p. 184.

45. Eckersley, *Environmentalism and Political Theory*, pp. 166–67.

46. *Another Turn of the Crank*, p. 3.

47. Eric Hobsbawm, "Introduction: Inventing Traditions," in *The Invention of Tradition,* ed. Eric Hobsbawm and Terence Ranger (Cambridge: Cambridge University Press, 1983), pp. 1–4.

48. *Standing by Words,* p. 207 (emphasis added).

49. Ibid., p. 210.

50. Michael Oakeshott, *Rationalism in Politics* [1962] (Indianapolis: Liberty Press, 1991), pp. 5–9.

51. Edmund Burke, *Reflections on the Revolution in France* [1790] (New York: Holt, Rinehart & Winston, 1959), pp. 94, 93.

52. Ibid., p. 92.

53. Ibid., p. 105.

54. *Seventh Reports,* Calvin's Case, quoted in J. G. A. Pocock, *The Ancient Constitution and The Feudal Law* (Cambridge: Cambridge University Press, 1957), p. 36. This section is informed generally by Pocock's cogent discussion of custom.

55. Hobsbawm draws our attention to a class of "invented" traditions that refer to the past but are in fact of recent origin. *Invention of Tradition,* passim. Obviously this wouldn't meet Berry's criteria of a true tradition.

56. *The Gift of Good Land,* p. 27.

57. Ibid., p. 28.

58. Ibid., p. 27.

59. Ronald Dworkin, *Law's Empire* (Cambridge, Mass.: The Belknap Press, 1986), pp. 228–38.

60. For example, in *Standing by Words,* pp. 211–12, he says critical evaluation of traditions should lead to renewal of old forms, but he also praises Walt Whitman's rejection of old poetic forms in order to invent a new one. The implication is that the goal is not merely fidelity to the past; there must also be some standard by which to judge the success of an innovation.

61. *The Hidden Wound* [1970] (San Francisco: North Point Press, 1989), pp. 22–47.

62. *Hidden Wound,* pp. 58–59. See also *Standing by Words,* pp. 209–10.

63. *Hidden Wound,* p. 78. Berry attributes this insight to Allen Tate. Ibid., p. 79.

64. In fact, ecocentric critiques range from hopelessly simplistic (Ehrenfeld, *The Arrogance of Humanism*) to sophisticated and insightful (Eckersley, *Environmentalism and Political Theory*).

65. See Neil Hamilton, "Agriculture Without Farmers? Is Industrialization Restructuring American Food Production and Threatening the Future of Sustainable Agriculture?" *Northern Illinois University Law Review* 14 (1994): 613–57.

66. *See Another Turn of the Crank,* pp. 5, 14. In spite of his general distrust of "big government," Berry acknowledges it has a legitimate function: to create and protect a condition in which personal effort is meaningful, to protect the political power of the poor, and to "protect, by strict forbiddings, the disruption of the integrity of a community or a local enterprise or an ecosystem by any sort of commercial or industrial enterprise." *Long-Legged House,* p. 10. See also *Hidden Wound,*

p. 136; *Another Turn of the Crank,* p. x ("A democratic government fails in failing to protect the integrity of ordinary lives and local communities.") See chapter 7 for a more extensive discussion of Berry's views of government.

67. Susan Okin, *Justice, Gender, and the Family* (New York: Basic Books, 1989), p. 72. I have explored Berry's relationship to feminism in more depth elsewhere. See "Wendell Berry's Feminist Agrarianism," *Women's Studies* 30 (2001): 623–46.

68. See Deborah Fink, *Agrarian Women* (Chapel Hill: University of North Carolina Press, 1992); "Making the 'Invisible Farmer' Visible," in *Women and Farming,* ed. Wava Haney and Jane Knowles (Boulder: Westview Press, 1988), p. 8; Sonya Salamon and Karen Davis-Brown, "Farm Continuity and Female Land Inheritance: A Family Dilemma," in Haney and Knowles, *Women and Farming,* pp. 195–210; Salamon, *Prairie Patrimony,* pp. 119–20; Carolyn Sachs, *The Invisible Farmers* (Totowa, N.J.: Rowman & Allanheld, 1983), pp. 1–44.

69. Fink, *Agrarian Women,* pp. 2–4; Carolyn Sachs, *Invisible Farmers,* pp. xii, 3, 18–20.

70. "Women and Farming," in Haney and Knowles, *Women and Farming,* pp. 261–62. See also Salamon, *Prairie Patrimony,* p. 54; Sachs, *Invisible Farmers,* pp. 88, 101, 110–11.

71. Salamon, *Prairie Patrimony,* pp. 54–55, 119–35.

72. The following stories are told in *The Memory of Old Jack* (New York: Harcourt, Brace, Jovanovich, 1974); *A Place on Earth,* rev. ed. (San Francisco: North Point Press, 1983); *The Wild Birds* (San Francisco: North Point Press, 1985).

73. *Sex, Economy, Freedom, and Community,* p. 120.

74. *Home Economics,* pp. 140–41.

75. See *The Unsettling of America,* pp. 171–223.

76. *Gift of Good Land,* p. 167; *Continuous Harmony,* p. 75.

Chapter Five: A Place on Earth?

1. *Remembering* (San Francisco: North Point Press, 1988), p. 123. Utopian visions are common in Berry's writing. See, e.g., *Jayber Crow* (Washington, D.C.: Counterpoint Press, 2000), p. 352; *Harlan Hubbard,* pp. 47–48; *A Place on Earth,* p. 69.

2. *The Unsettling of America,* p. 94.

3. Geoffrey B. Frasz, "Environmental Virtue Ethics: A New Direction for Environmental Ethics," *Environmental Ethics* 15 (fall 1993): 259–74; Thomas Hill, "Ideals of Human Excellence and Preserving Natural Environments," *Environmental Ethics* 5 (fall 1983): 211–24; Louke van Wensveen, *Dirty Virtues* (Amherst, N.Y.: Humanity Books, 2000).

4. G. E. M. Anscombe, "Modern Moral Philosophy," in *Virtue Ethics,* ed. Roger Crisp and Michael Slote (Oxford: Oxford University Press, 1997), pp. 26–44. The article originally appeared in *Philosophy* 3 (1958): 1–19.

5. Daniel Statman, introduction to *Virtue Ethics,* ed. Daniel Statman (Washington, D.C.: Georgetown University Press, 1997), pp. 10, 13.

6. Ibid., p. 15, quoting John Cottingham, "Religion, Virtue, and Ethical Culture," *Philosophy* 69 (1994): 291–316. This is not to suggest that all virtue ethicists are relativists. For some, the right pathways of emotion and action must conform to human nature—although they must still be learned through participation in a civic culture.

7. Gregory Velazco y Trianosky, "What Is Virtue Ethics All About?" in Statman, *Virtue Ethics,* pp. 45, 67.

8. Statman, introduction to Statman, *Virtue Ethics,* p. 12; Michael Stocker, "The Schizophrenia of Modern Ethical Theories," in Crisp and Slote, *Virtue Ethics.* For a Kantian reply to this criticism, see Barbara Herman, *The Practice of Moral Judgment* (Cambridge: Harvard University Press, 1993), pp. 1–22.

9. Michael Slote, "Virtue Ethics and Democratic Values," *Journal Social Philosophy* 24 (fall 1993): 5. Van Wensveen points out that virtue ethics has also been criticized for contributing to the oppression of women. *Dirty Virtues,* pp. 115–25.

10. It should be noted that utilitarianism can be criticized on this score as well.

11. Statman, introduction to Statman, *Virtue Ethics,* p. 8.

12. Gary Watson, "On the Primacy of Character," in Statman, *Virtue Ethics,* p. 67.

13. *Home Economics,* p. 15; *The Unsettling of America,* p. 47.

14. Don Herzog, *Without Foundations* (Ithaca: Cornell University Press, 1985), p. 18.

15. Ibid., p. 20.

16. Ibid., p. 21.

17. Ibid., p. 24.

18. Ibid., p. 217.

19. Ibid., p. 25.

20. Ibid., p. 225.

21. Ibid., pp. 235, 225.

22. It's unnecessary, and probably unfruitful, to delve into the question of whether Berry would ascribe to a correspondence theory of truth, although I am inclined to think that a pragmatic conception of truth—some version of a coherence theory—would be more consistent with his general distrust of metaphysics.

23. *A Place on Earth,* p. 24.

24. *Watch with Me* (New York: Pantheon Books, 1994).

25. *Long-Legged House,* p. 175.

26. Julia Hornbostel, " 'This Country's Hard on Women and Oxen': A Study of the Images of Farm Women in American Fiction," in Haney and Knowles, *Women and Farming,* pp. 109–19.

27. Annette Kolodny, *The Land Before Her* (Chapel Hill: University of North Carolina Press, 1984), pp. 131–58; Hornbostel, 'This Country's Hard,' pp. 110–11.

28. But see "A Jonquil for Mary Penn," in *Fidelity.*

29. *Hidden Wound,* pp. 9–10.

30. Ibid., p. 12.

31. Note for example the parallels between the autobiographical material in *The Long-Legged House* and the plot of *Nathan Coulter* [1960], rev. ed. (San Francisco: North Point Press, 1985). Berry explores the difficulties of deriving truth from collective memory in some detail in *A Hidden Wound* and *A World Lost* (Washington, D.C.: Counterpoint Press, 1996).

32. *Long-Legged House*, p. 48.

33. *Remembering*, p. 124.

Chapter Six: Beyond Individualism

1. *Long-Legged House*, pp. 3–4.

2. See *Long-Legged House*, p. 7 (citing Caudill, *Night Comes to the Cumberland*); *What Are People For?* pp. 30–35.

3. *Night Comes to the Cumberland*, pp. 384–85.

4. *Long-Legged House*, p. 8.

5. Ibid., pp. 8–10.

6. Ibid., p. 9.

7. Ibid., p. 60.

8. *What Are People For?* pp. 70, 72–73.

9. Ibid., p. 75.

10. Ibid., pp. 75–76.

11. *A Continuous Harmony*, p. 153.

12. *The Unsettling of America*, p. 111.

13. Joel Feinberg, "Autonomy," in *The Inner Citadel*, ed. John Christman (New York: Oxford University Press, 1989), pp. 31–43; Gerald Dworkin, "The Concept of Autonomy," in ibid., p. 54.

14. *What Are People For?* pp. 64–66, 71–87 (Hemingway, Huck Finn). See Nash Smith, *Virgin Land*, pp. 81–89, on the mythic frontiersman in American literature.

15. *Memory of Old Jack*, p. 5.

16. Ibid., pp. 62, 80.

17. Ibid., pp. 161, 162.

18. *The Unsettling of America*, p. 94.

19. Ibid., p. 94.

20. Ibid., p. 94.

21. Ibid., pp. 83–84. Berry's ideas on energy are likely derived from Albert Howard, who in turn was influenced by the nineteenth-century energy economists. See Albert Howard, *An Agricultural Testament* (London: Oxford University Press, 1940); Bramwell, *Ecology in the Twentieth Century*, pp. 64–91.

22. The following discussion is based on Helen North, *Sophrosyne: Self-Knowledge and Self-Restraint in Greek Literature* (Ithaca: Cornell University Press, 1966).

23. *What Are People For?* pp. 5–6.

24. North, *Sophrosyne,* pp. 3–6.

25. *The Gift of Good Land,* p. 270. See also ibid., pp. 43, 269; *The Unsettling of America,* p. 31 (on good manners).

26. *Standing by Words,* p. 47; *The Unsettling of America,* p. 55; *Home Economics,* p. 15.

27. *Standing by Words,* pp. 134, 138.

28. *The Unsettling of America,* pp. 128–29; *Hidden Wound,* p. 88; *What Are People For?* p. 160. See chapter 8 for a more extensive discussion of Berry's attitudes toward politics.

29. *Hidden Wound,* p. 85.

30. Christine Di Stefano, "Autonomy in the Light of Difference," in *Revisioning the Political,* ed. Nancy Hirschmann and Christine Di Stefano (Boulder: Westview Press, 1996), p. 96; Wendy Donner, "Self and Community in Environmental Ethics," in *Ecofeminism,* ed. Karen Warren (Bloomington: Indiana University Press, 1997), pp. 375–89. See Smith, "Wendell Berry's Feminist Agrarianism," for further discussion of Berry's relationship with feminism.

31. Donner, "Self and Community in Environmental Ethics," in Warren, *Ecofeminism,* pp. 375–89 (defending autonomy); Di Stefano, "Autonomy in the Light of Difference," in Hirschmann and Di Stephano, *Revisioning the Political,* pp. 95–116 (summarizing the debate over autonomy within feminism).

32. Di Stefano, "Autonomy in the Light of Difference," p. 96.

33. *A Continuous Harmony,* p. 162.

34. Judith Plant, "Learning to Live with Differences," in Warren, *Ecofeminism,* pp. 121, 125. See also Petra Kelly, "Women and Power," in ibid., pp. 112–19; Greta Gaard, "Living Interconnections with Animals and Nature," in Gaard, *Ecofeminism,* pp. 1–2. Berry's critique of rugged individualism seems derived partly from Wallace Stegner's *Big Rock Candy Mountain* (New York: Hill & Wang, 1938). See "Wallace Stegner and the Great Community," in *What Are People For?* pp. 48–57; *Another Turn of the Crank,* pp. 67–69.

35. The thesis is elaborated in Nash, *Wilderness and the American Mind;* R. W. B. Lewis, *American Adam* (Chicago: University of Chicago Press, 1955); Catherine Zuckert, *Natural Right and the American Imagination* (Savage, Md.: Rowan & Littlefield, 1990).

36. Smith, *Virgin Land,* pp. 52–80, offers a good discussion of this conceptual framework.

37. Wallace Stegner, "Wilderness Letter" [1960], in *Marking the Sparrow's Fall* [1948]; ed. Page Stegner (New York: Henry Holt, 1998), p. 112. In works like *Big Rock Candy Mountain,* however, Stegner expresses reservations about the ideology of rugged individualism.

38. *Home Economics,* pp. 6, 7.

39. Ibid., p. 7.

40. See, e.g., Peter Berg and Raymon Dasmann, "Reinhabiting California," in Berg, *Reinhabiting a Separate Country,* pp. 217–20; Sale, *Dwellers in the Land,* pp. 41–43; Schumacher, *Small Is Beautiful,* pp. 67–80; Devall and Sessions, *Deep Ecology,* pp. 21–24, 112; Nabhan, *Cultures of Habitat,* pp. 2–3, 318–19.

41. *Long-Legged House,* p. 143.

42. *Memory of Old Jack,* p. 67.

43. Ibid., pp. 13–14, 81, 134.

44. Sale, *Dwellers in the Land,* p. 55 (a natural region is "any part of the earth's surface whose rough boundaries are determined by natural characteristics"; Devall and Sessions, *Deep Ecology,* pp. 21–24 (suggesting that bioregions must be defined by geological and biological features like climate zones, watershed, vegetation, fauna, or soils). Schumacher and Berg, however, give more attention to cultural factors in defining a place. *Small Is Beautiful,* pp. 186–88; *Reinhabiting a Separate Country,* p. 218 (a bioregion "refers both to geographical terrain and a terrain of consciousness").

45. *Memory of Old Jack,* p. 145.

46. *The Wild Birds* (San Francisco: North Point Press, 1985), p. 66.

47. *A Place on Earth,* pp. 54–55.

48. *Memory of Old Jack,* p. 67. On Berry's use of marriage imagery, see Jack Hicks, "Wendell Berry's Husband to the World," in Merchant, *Wendell Berry,* pp. 118–34; Herman Nibbelink, "Thoreau and Wendell Berry: Bachelor and Husband of Nature," in ibid., pp. 135–51.

49. *Memory of Old Jack,* p. 72.

50. *Long-Legged House,* p. 39.

51. Ibid., p. 39.

52. Ibid., p. 41.

53. Ibid., p. 143.

54. *Memory of Old Jack,* p. 38.

55. Ibid., p. 185.

56. Berry and Meatyard, *The Unforeseen Wilderness,* p. 61.

57. *The Unsettling of America,* p. 30.

58. *Home Economics,* p. 18.

59. *The Unforeseen Wilderness,* pp. 37, 36.

60. Ibid., pp. 35, 36, 38.

61. Ibid., p. 50.

62. Ibid., pp. 37–38.

63. *Home Economics,* p. 104.

64. Ibid., p. 115.

65. Ibid., p. 114.

66. Ibid., p. 116.

67. John Shover, *First Majority—Last Minority,* p. 123.

68. *Wild Birds,* p. 53.

69. Ibid., p. 65.

70. Ibid., pp. 66–67.

71. Ibid., pp. 67–68.

72. Ibid., pp. 72–73.

73. See *Remembering* and "Making It Home," in *Fidelity,* pp. 83–105, for a darker vision of autonomy as an unhealthy state of separation that has to be healed. On Berry's view of the moral implications of choice, see Hayden Carruth, "Human Authenticity in the Age of Massive, Multiplying Error," *Parnassus* (fall/winter 1986): 141–42.

74. *Remembering,* p. 60. Berry's recognition of the moral value of choice indicates that a basic level of moral autonomy remains an important element of his philosophy. The choice to acknowledge one's dependencies and responsibilities is praiseworthy precisely because the actor is free not to.

75. *What Are People For?* p. 160.

76. Ibid., p. 162.

77. In fact, Berry has spilled a lot of ink depicting this struggle. See *Nathan Coulter; Wild Birds,* pp. 27–43; *Long-Legged House,* pp. 121–66.

78. *What Are People For?* pp. 162–63. Berry explores this cycle of leaving and returning in *Remembering* and *Jayber Crow.* See also Mark Shadle, "Traveling at Home: Wandering and Return in Wendell Berry," in Merchant, *Wendell Berry,* pp. 103–17.

79. See Joan Tronto, "Care as a Political Concept," in Hirschmann and Di Stefano, *Revisioning the Political,* p. 150, on the need to introduce the concept of the life cycle into our understanding of autonomy.

80. Robert Young, "Autonomy and the 'Inner Self,'" in Christman, *The Inner Citadel,* p. 77. See also Dworkin, "The Concept of Autonomy," in ibid., p. 60.

81. Of course, most moral philosophers recognize that there are other moral values that might rank higher than autonomy. Under Berry's conception of the ideology of rugged individualism, however, autonomy does figure as an ultimate ideal.

82. This is hardly a new theme in American moral traditions; it was a favorite subject of nineteenth-century novels, for example. Modern moral philosophers, however, have spent a great deal more time on the moral significance of autonomy than on the moral significance of various kinds of dependencies.

83. *What Are People For?* p. 184; *Long-Legged House,* p. 41.

84. *What Are People For?* p. 164. On government as a problematic dependency, see *Long-Legged House,* p. 77; *Fidelity,* p. 91.

85. *What Are People For?* p. 165.

86. *The Gift of Good Land,* p. 155.

87. See Robert Devigne, *Recasting Conservatism* (New Haven: Yale University Press, 1994), pp. 137, 144–45, on American conservatives' economic theory. Berry points out a basic contradiction in American conservative thought between their endorsement of strong local communities and their support for an economy led by large, entrepreneurial private corporations.

88. *Sex, Economy, Freedom, and Community,* p. 128.

89. *What Are People For?* p. 184.

90. Berry offers a chilling picture of the usual alternative to messy, troublesome community life in *Jayber Crow,* pp. 29–45 (recounting Crow's childhood in an orphanage run by reasonably competent, well-intentioned administrators).

91. *Memory of Old Jack,* pp. 222–23.

Chapter Seven: A Secular Grace

1. *Nathan Coulter,* pp. 139–41. See also *Wild Birds,* pp. 35–38; "A Friend of Mine," in *Two More Stories of the Port William Membership* (Frankfort, Ky.: Gnomon Press, 1997), pp. 7–37. Feeding an unhealthy addiction by growing tobacco may seem inconsistent with Berry's ideals. He addresses that issue in *Another Turn of the Crank,* pp. 53–68, arguing that despite the dangers of tobacco consumption, the culture of growing tobacco has been on the whole good for the land and the farmers. However, he says he would support efforts to replace tobacco with other crops.

2. *The Unsettling of America,* p. 20.

3. *A Continuous Harmony,* p. 111.

4. Ibid., p. 117.

5. *The Unsettling of America,* p. 12.

6. *The Gift of Good Land,* p. 168.

7. *A Place on Earth,* pp. 31–34.

8. Ibid., pp. 166–71, 259–69.

9. *Jayber Crow.*

10. I don't mean to suggest that Berry was influenced by Arendt. She does not claim to invent this distinction; rather, she argues that it underlies our general cultural understandings about work. *The Human Condition* (Chicago: University of Chicago Press, 1958), p. 85. Arendt's work/labor distinction has of course been widely criticized as obscuring more than it illuminates. See Seyla Benhabib, *The Reluctant Modernism of Hannah Arendt* (Thousand Oaks, Calif.: Sage Publications, 1996), pp. 123–24. However, most of the criticisms are aimed at the use to which she puts these distinctions in her political philosophy; they do not undermine the general point that some such distinction—albeit rough and imprecise by philosophical standards—is often at work in Western thought about work. Thus for our purposes, these categories can serve as a useful heuristic.

11. Ibid., p. 88.

12. Ibid., pp. 93–94.

13. Ibid., p. 50.

14. Ibid., pp. 52, 93–94.

15. Ibid., p. 123. Another reason that nature itself cannot serve as the thing we hold in common is that nature, for Arendt, is not durable; it is dynamic, producing

and consuming its creations. Under this view, places created out of nature and maintained by human labor and action (such as gardens, towns, or even picnic sites) could perhaps constitute part of our common world, even if nature per se cannot. See Peter Cannavò, "The Familiar Chair and Table: Hannah Arendt and the Politics of Place" (paper presented at the Western Political Science Association Annual Meeting, Long Beach, Calif., March 22–24, 2002), p. 9.

16. *What Are People For?* p. 67.

17. *Memory of Old Jack,* pp. 153–54.

18. *A Place on Earth,* p. 33.

19. *The Unsettling of America,* p. 121.

20. MacIntyre, *After Virtue,* p. 187.

21. Ibid., p. 188.

22. Ibid., p. 191.

23. *A Continuous Harmony,* pp. 146–47.

24. Cf. MacIntyre, *After Virtue,* p. 191, arguing that it is characteristic of goods internal to practices that their achievement enriches the whole community.

25. *Memory of Old Jack,* p. 78.

26. *What Are People For?* p. 142.

27. *Another Turn of the Crank,* p. 42.

28. Ibid., p. 44.

29. *The Gift of Good Land,* p. 84.

30. *The Unsettling of America,* p. 62.

31. *The Gift of Good Land,* pp. 134–35.

32. *What Are People For?* p. 67.

33. *The Unsettling of America,* p. 18.

34. *Hidden Wound,* p. 85.

35. See chapter 8 for a more extensive discussion of Berry's view of politics.

36. Hamlin, "Moral Husbandry," pp. 55–78 (arguing that Berry's position is simply borrowed from the Vanderbilt Agrarians); Berry, "Still Standing," *Oxford American* 25 (January/February, 1999): 64–69.

37. *A Continuous Harmony,* pp. 120–21, quoting Twelve Southerners, *I'll Take My Stand* [1930] (Baton Rouge: Louisiana State University Press, 1977), pp. xli–xlii. The lacunae are Berry's.

38. *The Unsettling of America,* p. 114.

39. Ibid., pp. 114, 20; *A Continuous Harmony,* p. 111.

40. *Long-Legged House,* pp. 32–33; *A Continuous Harmony,* p. 111.

41. *What Are People For?* p. 139.

42. Ibid., p. 8.

43. Ironically, it was John Crowe Ransom, Robert Penn Warren, and Allen Tate, among others, who promoted this academic, specialized approach to poetry—a fact that is not lost on Berry. "Still Standing," p. 65.

44. *A Continuous Harmony,* pp. 56, 61.

45. The one intellectual in Berry's community is Jayber Crow, the barber, whose undemanding work leaves him time to read. *Jayber Crow,* pp. 33–35, 47; *A Place on Earth,* p. 63.

46. Angyal, *Wendell Berry,* p. xi.

47. *What Are People For?* p. 192.

48. Ibid., p. 192.

49. Ibid., pp. 88–89; *Standing by Words,* p. 20.

50. *Harlan Hubbard,* pp. 48–49 (emphasis added).

51. *A Continuous Harmony,* p. 17.

52. See Robert Collins, "A More Mingled Music," pp. 35–56.

53. White, "The Historical Roots of Our Ecological Crisis," pp. 1,203–7.

54. Nash, *Rights of Nature,* pp. 112–16.

55. Attfield, *Ethics of Environmental Concern,* pp. 20–50; Elspeth Whitney, "Lynn White, Ecotheology, and History," *Environmental Ethics* 15 (summer 1993): 151–69.

56. Nash, *Rights of Nature,* pp. 87–120.

57. Browne, *Private Interests, Public Policy,* pp. 65, 66; *Pastoral Letters of the United States Catholic Bishops,* 4 vols., ed. Hugh J. Nolan (National Conference of Catholic Bishops, U.S. Catholic Council, 1983), 3: 195–97, 465, 466–69; Nash, *Rights of Nature,* pp. 98, 111–12; Lauck, *American Agriculture,* pp. 26–27.

58. *Long-Legged House,* pp. 57, 58.

59. *Collected Poems, 1957–1982* (New York: North Point Press, 1995), p. 17 (from *The Broken Ground* [New York: Harcourt, Brace & World, 1964]).

60. *A Place on Earth,* p. 100.

61. *Gift of Good Land,* p. 267.

62. Ibid., pp. 270–71.

63. Ibid., p. 277.

64. *Sex, Economy, Freedom, and Community,* pp. 93–116.

65. *Another Turn of the Crank,* p. 90.

66. See, e.g., Snyder, *Earth House Hold.* Interestingly, the Eastern spiritual authority Berry cites most often is not Buddha or Lao Tzu but Confucius. See *Continuous Harmony,* p. 41; *Hidden Wound,* preface; *Unsettling of America,* p. 16.

67. For example, Jack Hicks discusses Berry's Christian view of man "as a distinctly flawed being fallen from natural wholeness." Jack Hicks, "Wendell Berry's Husband to the World: A Place on Earth," *American Literature* 51 (May 1979): 239–40. See also Basney, "The Grace That Keeps the World," p. 48.

68. *Sex, Economy, Freedom, and Community,* pp. 95–96; see also *Another Turn of the Crank,* p. 77 (endorsing religion over superstition).

69. For a good discussion of spiritual themes in Berry's poetry, see Triggs, "Moving the Dark to Wholeness," pp. 279–92.

70. *Long-Legged House,* p. 48.

71. *The Unsettling of America,* pp. 86, 81.

72. *Sex, Economy, Freedom, and Community,* p. 110.

73. Ibid.

74. *The Gift of Good Land,* p. 281.

75. *Remembering,* p. 123.

76. *Memory of Old Jack,* pp. 43–44.

Chapter Eight: Tending Our Gardens

1. Berry, "American Pox," *The Nation,* November 4, 1968, p. 457.

2. Taylor, *Arator,* pp. 54–55.

3. Ibid., p. 57.

4. Ibid. p. 74.

5. Ibid., pp. 77–78, 96.

6. Ibid., p. 107.

7. Editorial, *Platte County Argus* (Columbus, Nebraska), June 4, 1896, in Pollack, *The Populist Mind,* pp. 41–42.

8. Circular of the Los Angeles county committee of the People's Party, September 14, 1891, in Pollack, *The Populist Mind,* p. 54.

9. "Omaha Platform," in Pollack, *The Populist Mind,* p. 61; James B. Weaver, *A Call to Action* (Des Moines: Iowa Printing, 1892), pp. 356–57.

10. Weaver, *A Call to Action,* p. 62.

11. Ibid., p. 240.

12. Ibid., pp. 240–41.

13. Periam, *The Groundswell,* p. 73.

14. Ibid., p. 19.

15. Ibid., p. 403.

16. Pollack, introduction to *The Populist Mind,* p. xix.

17. Donnelly, "Caesar's Column," in Pollack, *The Populist Mind,* p. 482; Lloyd, "Wealth Against Commonwealth," in Pollack, *The Populist Mind,* p. 523.

18. Periam, *The Groundswell,* p. 469.

19. Ibid., pp. 82–83.

20. E.g., Vincent Buranelli, "The Case against Thoreau," *Ethics* 67 (1957): 257–68; George Hochfield, "Anti-Thoreau," *Sewanee Review* 96 (summer 1988): 433–43.

21. Bob Pepperman Taylor, *America's Bachelor Uncle* (Lawrence: University Press of Kansas, 1996), pp. 8, 13.

22. Ibid., p. 12.

23. On Thoreau and Berry, see Herman Nibbelink, "Thoreau and Wendell Berry: Bachelor and Husband of Nature," in Merchant, *Wendell Berry.*

24. Taylor, *America's Bachelor Uncle,* pp. 32, 33.

25. *Another Turn of the Crank,* pp. ix–x.

26. *A Continuous Harmony* (New York: Harcourt, Brace & Co., 1972), p. 61.

27. *The Gift of Good Land,* pp. 164–65.

28. *A Continuous Harmony,* p. 92.

29. *Standing by Words,* p. 25; *A Continuous Harmony,* p. 41.

30. *Long-Legged House,* p. 90.

31. *Fidelity,* p. 57.

32. *A Place on Earth,* p. 50.

33. *Long-Legged House,* p. 50.

34. Ibid., p. 50.

35. Ibid., p. 83.

36. Ibid., p. 83.

37. *A Continuous Harmony,* p. 41.

38. *Long-Legged House,* p. 91.

39. Max Weber, "Politics as a Vocation" [1920], in *From Max Weber,* ed. H. H. Gerth and C. Wright Mills (New York: Oxford University Press, 1946), p. 120.

40. *A Continuous Harmony,* pp. 91–92.

41. Weber, "Politics as a Vocation," in Gerth and Mills, *From Max Weber,* p. 128.

42. "A Plea for Captain John Brown," [1859] in *Henry David Thoreau: Collected Essays and Poems,* comp. Elizabeth Hall Witherell (New York: Library of America, 2001).

43. *What Are People For?* p. 62. For a critique of the idea that ends and means must be consistent, see Goodin, *Green Political Theory,* pp. 120–23.

44. *What Are People For?* p. 62.

45. Ibid., pp. 39–40.

46. *Remembering,* p. 87.

47. *The Gift of Good Land,* p. 167.

48. *The Unsettling of America,* pp. 23–24.

49. *Long-Legged House,* p. 87.

50. *The Gift of Good Land,* pp. 167–68.

51. *A Continuous Harmony,* pp. 75–76.

52. *Memory of Old Jack,* pp. 219, 213.

53. *Wild Birds,* pp. 3, 52, 115.

54. Ibid., p. 116.

55. Ibid.

56. *Hidden Wound,* p. 71.

57. *What Are People For?* p. 31.

58. Ibid., p. 33.

59. Ibid.

60. Thoreau, "Civil Disobedience," in *Walden and Civil Disobedience,* pp. 385–86. On Thoreau's alleged anarchism, see Nancy Rosenblum, "Thoreau's Militant Consciousness," *Political Theory* 9 (February 1981): 81–110; Taylor, *America's Bachelor Uncle,* pp. 99–118.

61. Thoreau, "Civil Disobedience," in *Walden and Civil Disobedience,* p. 387.

62. *Hidden Wound,* p. 127.

63. *Long-Legged House,* p. 20; *Sex, Economy, Freedom, and Community,* p. 10.

64. *Long-Legged House,* p. 55.

65. *Sex, Economy, Freedom, and Community,* p. 152.

66. *Long-Legged House,* p. 53.

67. The classic statement of this position is Schumacher, *Small Is Beautiful.* See also Doherty and de Geus, introduction to Doherty and de Geus, *Democracy and Green Political Thought,* pp. 1, 3.

68. *What Are People For?* p. 210.

69. *Long-Legged House,* p. 49.

70. *Harlan Hubbard,* p. 33.

71. See *Hidden Wound,* p. 78, and chapter 4, supra.

72. See, e.g., Doherty and de Geus, introduction to Doherty and de Geus, *Democracy and Green Political Thought,* p. 1; John Barry, "Sustainability, Political Judgement, and Citizenship," in ibid., pp. 125–26; Peter Christoff, "Ecological Citizens and Ecologically Guided Democracy," in ibid., pp. 151–69; Sale, *Dwellers in the Land,* p. 53; Goodin, *Green Political Theory,* pp. 147–150.

73. *A Continuous Harmony,* p. 56; *Long-Legged House,* p. 77.

74. *Long-Legged House,* p. 77; *Sex, Economy, Freedom, and Community,* p. 120.

75. *Sex, Economy, Freedom, and Community,* p. 147.

76. Ibid., p. 148.

77. Ibid., p. 149.

78. Ibid., p. 16.

79. *Unsettling of America,* p. 219; *Home Economics,* p. 174.

80. *Unsettling of America,* pp. 219–20.

81. *Sex, Economy, Freedom, and Community,* pp. 45–51.

82. *Unsettling of America,* pp. 220–21.

83. Ibid., p. 221.

84. See, e.g., Cornell, "The Country of Marriage," pp. 59–60, 69.

85. Jane Addams, *Twenty Years at Hull House* [1910] (New York: Signet Classic, 1961), pp. 75–85. See also John Dewey, *Reconstruction in Philosophy,* rev. ed. (Boston: Beacon Press, 1948), pp. 202–7, recognizing the importance of subnational groups in social life.

86. Devigne, *Recasting Conservatism,* pp. 66–67, 164–70, 199.

87. See Ted Honderich, *Conservatism* (Boulder: Westview Press, 1990), pp. 161–65; William Harbour, *The Foundations of Conservative Thought* (Notre Dame: University of Notre Dame Press, 1982), p. 148.

88. Ralph Nader's poor showing in the 2000 presidential election would seem to support that proposition, although as a third party candidate he had plenty of other handicaps. But see the conclusion, infra, on influence of Berry's ideas in farm politics.

89. Browne, *Private Interests, Public Policy,* p. 81. On racist themes in Populist thought, see Morris Schonbach, *Native American Fascism During the 1930s and 1940s* (New York: Garland Publishing, 1985), pp. 56–66.

90. *Sex, Economy, Freedom, and Community,* p. 21.

91. See, e.g., Michael Kenny, "Paradoxes of Community," in Doherty and de Geus, *Democracy and Green Political Thought,* pp. 19–35.

92. Lauck, *American Agriculture,* p. 164.

93. See, e.g, Jeremy Waldron, "Minority Cultures and the Cosmopolitan Alternative," in *The Rights of Minority Cultures,* ed. Will Kymlicka (Oxford: Oxford University Press, 1995), pp. 93–119.

94. Eckersley, *Environmentalism and Political Theory,* p. 174.

95. Ibid., p. 175.

96. Christoff, "Ecological Citizens and Ecologically Guided Democracy," in Doherty and de Geus, *Democracy and Green Political Thought,* pp. 195–96; Dobson, *Green Political Thought,* pp. 120–22, 178–79; Eckersley, *Environmentalism and Political Theory,* pp. 170–78.

97. *Sex, Economy, Freedom, and Community,* p. 120.

98. Ibid., p. 120.

99. *A Continuous Harmony,* p. 160. On the theme of marriage in Berry's work, see Hicks, "Wendell Berry's Husband to the World," pp. 238–54; Cornell, "The Country of Marriage," pp. 63–64.

100. Christoff, "Ecological Citizens and Ecologically Guided Democracy," in Doherty and de Geus, *Democracy and Green Political Thought,* p. 163 (arguing in favor of a notion of planetary citizenship).

Conclusion

1. *Life Is a Miracle,* p. 71.

2. Dobson, *Green Political Thought,* p. 5.

3. Ibid., p. 1.

4. Ibid., p. 5.

5. Robyn Eckersley, "Politics," in *A Companion to Environmental Philosophy,* ed. Dale Jamieson (Malden, Mass.: Blackwell Publishing, 2001), p. 325.

6. Ibid., p. 326.

7. Chuse, *Defending the Earth,* pp. 32, 57–59; Commoner, *The Closing Circle,* pp. 275–88.

8. Schumacher, *Small Is Beautiful,* p. 271.

9. Al Gore, *Earth in the Balance* (New York: Penguin Books, 1992), p. 2.

10. Ibid., pp. 220–21.

11. Ibid., pp. 128, 339–40.

12. Mark Hansen, *Gaining Access* (Chicago: University of Chicago Press, 1991), pp. 78–163; Browne, *Private Interests, Public Policy,* pp. 16–18.

13. David Orden, Robert Paarlberg, Terry Roe, *Policy Reform in American Agriculture* (Chicago: University of Chicago Press, 1999), p. 227.

14. Browne, *Private Interests, Public Policy,* pp. 64–88; William P. Browne, *Cultivating Congress* (Lawrence: University Press of Kansas, 1995), pp. 22–39.

15. Orden, Paarlberg, and Roe, *Policy Reform in American Agriculture,* p. 77. The authors credit the environmental lobby with helping farmers to win benefits under the 1983 farm bill and noting that the coalition had to overcome sharp ideological conflicts. They attribute the success of the alliance to logrolling, however, failing to note the importance of ideological innovation.

16. Browne, *Private Interests, Public Policy,* p. 65; National Family Farm Coalition home page, www.nffc.net; *Center for Rural Affairs* newsletter, January 2001, p. 4.

17. "What Farmers Face," *National Journal,* Dec. 9, 2000, p. 3,820.

18. See chapter 3, supra.

19. *Conservation Security Act,* 107th Cong., 1st sess., S. 932; *Congressional Record,* 107th Cong., 1st sess., 2001, pp. 5,461–62.

20. On the challenges facing the environmental lobby in influencing agriculture policy, see Browne, *Cultivating Congress,* pp. 193–197.

❦ BIBLIOGRAPHY

Works by Wendell Berry

"Abundant Reward of Reclaiming a 'Marginal' Farm." *Smithsonian* 11 (August 1980): 76–83.

"American Pox." *The Nation,* November 4, 1968, p. 457.

Another Turn of the Crank. Washington, D.C.: Counterpoint Press, 1995.

The Broken Ground. New York: Harcourt, Brace & World, 1964.

Collected Poems, 1957–1982. New York: North Point Press, 1995.

"Composting Privy." *Organic Gardening and Farming* 20 (December 1973): 88–97.

A Continuous Harmony. San Diego: Harcourt Brace, 1972.

"Farming with Horses." *Organic Gardening and Farming* 21 (March 1974): 72–77.

Fidelity. New York: Pantheon Books, 1992.

The Gift of Good Land. San Francisco: North Point Press, 1981.

Harlan Hubbard: Life and Work. Lexington: University Press of Kentucky, 1990.

The Hidden Wound [1970]. San Francisco: North Point Press, 1989.

"Hill Land Farming: How the 'Experts' View Its Future." *Organic Farming and Gardening* 24 (April 1977): 68–71.

Home Economics. San Francisco: North Point Press, 1987.

Jayber Crow. Washington, D.C.: Counterpoint Press, 2000.

Life Is a Miracle. Washington, D.C.: Counterpoint Press, 2000.

"Life On (and Off) Schedule." *Organic Farming and Gardening* 24 (August 1977): 44–51.

The Long-Legged House. New York: Harcourt, Brace & World, 1969.

Meeting the Expectations of the Land. Edited by Wes Jackson, Wendell Berry, Bruce Colman. San Francisco: North Point Press, 1984.

The Memory of Old Jack. New York: Harcourt, Brace, Jovanovich, 1974.

Nathan Coulter [1960]. Rev. ed. San Francisco: North Point Press, 1985.

November Twenty Six Nineteen Hundred Sixty Three. New York: George Braziller, 1963.

A Place on Earth. Rev. ed. San Francisco: North Point Press, 1983.

"Profit in Work's Pleasure." *Harper's,* February 1988, p. 21.

Remembering. San Francisco: North Point Press, 1988.

"Response to a War." *The Nation,* April 24, 1967, pp. 527–28.

Sayings and Doings. Frankfort, Ky.: Gnomon Press, 1975.

Sex, Economy, Freedom, and Community. New York: Pantheon Books, 1992.

"Some Difficulties to Think About Before Buying a Farm." *Organic Farming and Gardening* 24 (July 1977): 59–61.

Standing by Words. San Francisco: North Point Press, 1983.

"Still Standing." *Oxford American* 25 (January/February 1999): 64–69.

Two More Stories of the Port William Membership. Frankfort, Ky: Gnomon Press, 1997.

The Unforeseen Wilderness [with Ralph Meatyard] [1971]. Rev. ed. San Francisco: North Point Press, 1991.

The Unsettling of America. San Francisco: Sierra Club Books, 1986.

Watch with Me. New York: Pantheon Books, 1994.

What Are People For? San Francisco: North Point Press, 1990.

The Wild Birds. San Francisco: North Point Press, 1985.

A World Lost. Washington, D.C.: Counterpoint Press, 1996.

Secondary Sources

Abbey, Edward. *Desert Solitaire.* New York: Ballantine Books, 1968.

Addams, Jane. *Twenty Years at Hull House* [1910]. New York: Signet Classic, 1961.

Andrews, Richard. "Class Politics or Democratic Reform: Environmental and American Political Institutions." *Natural Resources Journal* 20 (April 1980): 221–41.

———. *Managing the Environment, Managing Ourselves.* New Haven: Yale University Press, 1999.

Angyal, Andrew. *Wendell Berry.* New York: Twayne Publishing, 1995.

Arendt, Hannah. *The Human Condition.* Chicago: University of Chicago Press, 1958.

Atkinson, Brooks, ed. *The Selected Writings of Ralph Waldo Emerson.* New York: The Modern Library, 1940.

Attfield, Robin. *The Ethics of Environmental Concern.* New York: Columbia University Press, 1983.

Bailey, Liberty Hyde. *The Country-Life Movement in the United States.* New York: MacMillan, 1911.

———. *The Holy Earth.* New York: Charles Scribner's Sons, 1915.

Bailey, Ronald. *Eco-Scam.* New York: St. Martin's Press, 1993.

Basney, Lionel. "Wendell Berry: The Grace That Keeps the World." *The Other Side* 23 (January/February 1987): 46–48.

Bates, Ely. *Rural Philosophy: Or Reflections on Knowledge, Virtue, and Happiness, Chiefly in Reference to a Life of Retirement in the Country.* Philadelphia: B. B. Hopkins, 1807.

Beeman, Randal S., and James A. Pritchard. *A Green and Permanent Land.* Lawrence: University Press of Kansas, 2001.

Benhabib, Seyla. *The Reluctant Modernism of Hannah Arendt.* Thousand Oaks, Calif.: Sage Publications, 1996.

Bennett, Hugh. *Soil Conservation.* New York: McGraw-Hill, 1939.

Benson, Ezra Taft. *Farmers at the Crossroads.* New York: Devin-Adair, 1956.

Benton, Ted. *Natural Relations.* London: Verso, 1993.

Berg, Peter, ed. *Reinhabiting a Separate Country.* San Francisco: Planet Drum Foundation, 1978.

Blakey, George. *Hard Times and New Deal in Kentucky, 1929–1939.* Lexington: University Press of Kentucky, 1986.

Bookchin, Murray. *The Philosophy of Social Ecology.* Montreal: Black Rose Books, 1990.

Borsodi, Ralph. *Flight from the City.* New York: Harper & Bros., 1933.

———. *This Ugly Civilization.* New York: Simon & Schuster, 1929.

Bowers, William. *The Country Life Movement in America, 1900–1920.* Port Washington, N.Y.: Kennikat Press, 1974.

Bramwell, Anna. *Ecology in the Twentieth Century: A History.* New Haven: Yale University Press, 1989.

———. *The Fading of the Greens.* New Haven: Yale University Press, 1994.

Bromfield, Louis. *A Few Brass Tacks.* New York: Harper & Bros., 1946.

Browne, William P. *Cultivating Congress.* Lawrence: University Press of Kansas, 1995.

———. *Private Interests, Public Policy, and American Agriculture.* Lawrence: University Press of Kansas, 1988.

Buranelli, Vincent. "The Case against Thoreau." *Ethics* 67 (1957): 257–68.

Burke, Edmund. *Reflections on the Revolution in France* [1790]. New York: Holt, Rinehart & Winston, 1959.

Cannavò, Peter. "The Familiar Chair and Table: Hannah Arendt and the Politics of Place." Paper presented at the Western Political Science Association Annual Meeting, March 22–24, 2002.

Carlson, Allan. *The New Agrarian Mind.* New Brunswick, N.J.: Transaction Publishing, 2000.

Carruth, Hayden. "Human Authenticity in the Age of Massive, Multiplying Error." *Parnassus* (fall/winter, 1986): 140–43.

Carson, Rachel. *Silent Spring* [1962]. Boston: Houghton Mifflin, 1994.

Caudill, Harry. *Night Comes to the Cumberland.* Boston: Little, Brown, 1962.

Christenson, Reo. *The Brannan Plan.* Ann Arbor: University of Michigan Press, 1959.

Christman, John, ed. *The Inner Citadel*. New York: Oxford University Press, 1989.

Chuse, Steve, ed. *Defending the Earth: A Dialogue between Murray Bookchin and Dave Foreman*. Boston: South End Press, 1991.

Cochrane, Willard. *The Development of American Agriculture*. Minneapolis: University of Minnesota Press, 1979.

Collins, Robert. "A More Mingled Music: Wendell Berry's Ambivalent View of Language." *Modern Poetry Studies* 11 (1/2, 1982): 35–56.

Commins, Saxe, ed. *Basic Writings of George Washington*. New York: Random House, 1948.

Commission on Country Life. *Report*. New York: Sturgis & Walton, 1911.

Commoner, Barry. *The Closing Circle*. New York: Alfred A. Knopf, 1975.

Comstock, Gary, ed. *Is There a Moral Obligation to Save the Family Farm?* Ames: Iowa State University Press, 1987.

Conkin, Paul. *The Southern Agrarians*. Knoxville: University of Tennessee Press, 1988.

Cooke, Morris Llewellyn. "Is the United States a Permanent Country?" *Forum/Century* 99 (April 1938): 236–40.

Coomaraswamy, Ananda. *The Dance of Shiva*. London: Simpkin, Marshall, Hamilton, Kent, 1924.

Cornell, Daniel. "The Country of Marriage: Wendell Berry's Personal Political Vision." *Southern Literary Journal* 16 (fall 1983): 59–70.

Cottingham, John. "Religion, Virtue, and Ethical Culture." *Philosophy* 69 (1994): 291–316.

Council on Environmental Quality and U.S. Department of State. *Global 2000 Report to the President*. 3 vols. Washington, D.C.: U.S. Government Printing Office, 1980.

Cowan, Louise. *The Fugitive Group: A Literary History*. Baton Rouge: Louisiana State University Press, 1959.

Crèvecoeur, J. Hector St. John. *Letters from an American Farmer* [1782]. New York: Penguin Classics, 1963.

Crisp, Roger, and Michael Slote, eds. *Virtue Ethics*. Oxford: Oxford University Press, 1997.

Danbom, David. "Romantic Agrarianism in Twentieth-Century America." *Agricultural History* 65 (fall 1991): 9.

Devall, Bill, and George Sessions. *Deep Ecology*. Salt Lake City: Gibbs M. Smith, 1985.

Devigne, Robert. *Recasting Conservatism*. New Haven: Yale University Press, 1994.

Dewey, John. *Reconstruction in Philosophy*. Rev. ed. Boston: Beacon Press, 1948.

Dobson, Andrew. *Green Political Thought*. 2d ed. London: Routledge, 1995.

———. *Justice and the Environment*. Oxford: Oxford University Press, 1998.

Doherty, Brian, and Marius de Geus. *Democracy and Green Political Thought*. London: Routledge, 1996.

Douglas, William. *A Wilderness Bill of Rights*. Boston: Little, Brown, 1965.

DuBois, W. E. B. *The Souls of Black Folks* [1903]. New York: Penguin Books, 1989.

Duncan, Christopher. *Fugitive Theory*. Lanham: Lexington Books, 2000.

Dworkin, Ronald. *Law's Empire*. Cambridge, Mass.: Belknap Press, 1986.

Eckersley, Robyn. *Environmentalism and Political Theory*. Albany: State University of New York Press, 1992.

Ehrenfeld, David. *The Arrogance of Humanism*. New York: Oxford University Press, 1978.

Ehrlich, Paul. *The Population Bomb*. New York: Ballantine Books, 1968.

Ekirch, Arthur A. *Man and Nature in America*. New York: Columbia University Press, 1963.

Faulkner, Edward. *Plowman's Folly and A Second Look*. Washington, D.C.: Island Press, 1943, 1947.

Fink, Deborah. *Agrarian Women*. Chapel Hill: University of North Carolina Press, 1992.

Foner, Philip, ed. *The Complete Writings of Thomas Paine*. 2 vols. New York: Citadel Press, 1945.

Fox, Warwick. *Toward a Transpersonal Ecology*. Boston: Shambhala, 1990.

Fox-Genovese, Elizabeth. *The Origins of Physiocracy*. Ithaca: Cornell University Press, 1976.

Frasz, Geoffrey B. "Environmental Virtue Ethics: A New Direction for Environmental Ethics." *Environmental Ethics* 15 (fall 1993): 259–74.

Freyfogle, Eric. "The Dilemma of Wendell Berry." *University of Illinois Law Review* 1994 (2): 363–85.

Friedman, Lawrence. *A History of American Law*. 2d ed. New York: Simon & Schuster, 1985.

Fulcher, Clay. "Vertical Integration in the Poultry Industry: The Contractual Relationship." *Agricultural Law Update* (January 1992): 4–6.

Gaard, Greta, ed. *Ecofeminism*. Philadelphia: Temple University Press, 1993.

Garland, Hamlin. *Main-Travelled Roads*. New York: Harper & Bros., 1891.

Gerth, H. H., and C. Wright Mills, eds. *From Max Weber*. New York: Oxford University Press, 1946.

Goldschmidt, Walter. *As You Sow*. Montclair, N.J.: Allanheld, Osmun, 1947.

Goodin, Robert. *Green Political Theory*. Cambridge, U.K.: Polity Press, 1992.

Goodwyn, Lawrence. *The Populist Moment*. Oxford: Oxford University Press, 1978.

Gottlieb, Robert. *Forcing the Spring: The Transformation of the American Environmental Movement*. Washington, D.C.: Island Press, 1993.

Govan, Thomas. "Agrarian and Agrarianism: A Study in the Use and Abuse of Words." *Journal of Southern History* 30 (February–November 1964): 35–47.

Griswold, A. Whitney. *Farming and Democracy*. New York: Harcourt, Brace, 1948.

Habermas, Jürgen. *Structural Transformation of the Public Sphere* [1969]. Cambridge: MIT Press, 1992.

Hagler, Dorse. "The Agrarian Theme in Southern History." Ph.D. diss., University of Missouri, 1968.

Hamilton, Neil. "Agriculture Without Farmers? Is Industrialization Restructuring American Food Production and Threatening the Future of Sustainable Agriculture?" *Northern Illinois University Law Review* 14 (1994): 613–57.

———. "Why Own the Farm if You Can Own the Farmer (and the Crop)?" *Nebraska Law Review* 73 (1994): 48–102.

Hamlin, D. A. "Moral Husbandry: The Nashville Agrarians, Wendell Berry, and the Hidden Wound of Race." *Journal of the American Studies Association of Texas* 28 (1997): 55–78.

Haney, Wava, and Jane Knowles, eds. *Women and Farming*. Boulder: Westview Press, 1988.

Hansen, Mark. *Gaining Access*. Chicago: University of Chicago Press, 1991.

Hanson, Victor Davis. *Fields without Dreams*. New York: Free Press, 1996.

Harbour, William. *The Foundations of Conservative Thought*. Notre Dame: University of Notre Dame Press, 1982.

Hardin, Garret. "The Tragedy of the Commons." *Science* 162 (December 13, 1968): 1,243–48.

Harrison, Lowell, and James Klotter. *A New History of Kentucky*. Lexington: University Press of Kentucky, 1997.

Havard, William, and Walter Sullivan, eds. *A Band of Prophets*. Baton Rouge: Louisiana State University Press, 1982.

Hays, Samuel. *Beauty, Health, and Permanence*. Cambridge: Cambridge University Press, 1987.

———. *Conservation and the Gospel of Efficiency*. Cambridge: Harvard University Press, 1959.

Heilbroner, Robert. *An Inquiry into the Human Prospect* [1974]. New York: W. W. Norton, 1980.

Held, R. Burnell, and Marion Clawson. *Soil Conservation in Perspective*. Baltimore: Johns Hopkins Press, 1965.

Herman, Barbara. *The Practice of Moral Judgment*. Cambridge: Harvard University Press, 1993.

Herzog, Don. *Without Foundations*. Ithaca: Cornell University Press, 1985.

Hicks, Jack. "Wendell Berry's Husband to the World: A Place on Earth." *American Literature* 51 (May 1979): 239–40.

Hightower, Jim. *Hard Tomatoes, Hard Times* [1973]. Cambridge, Mass.: Schenkman Publishing, 1978.

Hill, Thomas. "Ideals of Human Excellence and Preserving Natural Environments." *Environmental Ethics* 5 (fall 1983): 211–24.

Hirschmann, Nancy and Christine Di Stefano. *Revisioning the Political*. Boulder: Westview Press, 1996.

Hobsbawm, Eric, and Terence Ranger, eds. *The Invention of Tradition*. Cambridge: Cambridge University Press, 1983.

Hochfield, George. "Anti-Thoreau." *Sewanee Review* 96 (summer 1988): 433–43.

Hofstadter, Richard. *Age of Reform*. New York: Alfred A. Knopf, 1955.

Honderich, Ted. *Conservatism*. Boulder: Westview Press, 1990.

Horwitz, Morton. *The Transformation of American Law*. Oxford: Oxford University Press, 1992.

Howard, Albert. *An Agricultural Testament*. London: Oxford University Press, 1940.

Hubbard, Harlan. *Shantyboat: A River Way of Life* [1953]. Lexington: University Press of Kentucky, 1977.

Jackson, Wes. "Challenges Facing Kansans: Environmental, Economic and Political." Available on the Land Institute website, http://www.landinstitute.org/texis/scrip...paper/+/ART/2000/07/01.

———. "Ecology Then and Now." *Science, Technology, and Human Values* 17 (winter 1992): 129–31.

———. "The Need of Being Versed in Country Things." *The Land Report* 67 (summer 2000).

———. *New Roots for Agriculture*. Lincoln: University of Nebraska Press, 1980.

Jamieson, Dale, ed. *A Companion to Environmental Philosophy*. Malden, Mass.: Blackwell Publishing, 2001.

Kiffmeyer, Thomas. "From Self-Help to Sedition: The Appalachian Volunteers in Eastern Kentucky, 1964–1970." *Journal of Southern History* 64 (February 1998): 65–94.

Kile, Orville. *The Farm Bureau through Three Decades*. Baltimore: Waverly Press, 1948.

King, F. H. *Farmers of Forty Centuries*. Madison, Wisc: Mrs. F. H. King, 1911.

Kleber, John, ed. *The Kentucky Encyclopedia*. Lexington: University Press of Kentucky, 1992.

Koch, Adrienne, and William Peden, eds. *The Life and Selected Writings of Thomas Jefferson*. New York: Random House, 1993.

Kolodny, Annette. *The Land Before Her*. Chapel Hill: University of North Carolina Press, 1984.

Kymlicka, Will, ed. *The Rights of Minority Cultures*. Oxford: Oxford University Press, 1995.

Lauck, Jon. *American Agriculture and the Problem of Monopoly*. Lincoln: University of Nebraska Press, 2000.

Leopold, Aldo. *A Sand County Almanac*. New York: Ballantine Books, 1966.

Lewis, Martin. *Green Delusions*. Durham: Duke University Press, 1992.

Lewis, R. W. B. *American Adam*. Chicago: University of Chicago Press, 1955.

MacIntyre, Alasdair. *After Virtue*. 2d ed. Notre Dame: University of Notre Dame Press, 1984.

Malvasi, Mark. *The Unregenerate South*. Baton Rouge: Louisiana State University Press, 1997.

Marsh, George Perkins. *Man and Nature* [1864]. Cambridge: Belknap Press, 1965.

Marshall, Suzanne. *Violence in the Black Patch of Kentucky and Tennessee*. Columbia: University of Missouri Press, 1994.

Marx, Leo. *The Machine in the Garden*. Oxford: Oxford University Press, 1964.

Matusow, Allen. *Farm Policies and Politics in the Truman Years*. Cambridge: Harvard University Press, 1967.

McConnell, Grant. *The Decline of Agrarian Democracy*. Berkeley: University of California Press, 1953.

McCoy, Drew. *The Elusive Republic*. Chapel Hill: University of North Carolina Press, 1980.

McGovern, George, ed. *Agricultural Thought in the Twentieth Century*. Indianapolis, New York: Bobbs-Merrill, 1967.

McKibben, Bill. *The End of Nature*. New York: Anchor Books, 1989.

McWilliams, Carey. *Factories in the Field*. Boston: Little, Brown, 1939.

Meadows, Donella, Dennis Meadows, Jorgen Randers, and Williams Behrens III. *The Limits to Growth*. New York: Universe Books, 1972.

Merchant, Paul, ed. *Wendell Berry*. Lewiston, Idaho: Confluence Press, 1991.

Montmarquet, James A. "Agrarianism, Wealth, and Economics." *Agriculture and Human Values* 4 (spring-summer 1987): 47–52.

———. *The Idea of Agrarianism*. Moscow, Idaho: University of Idaho Press, 1989.

Mooney, Patrick, and Theo Majka. *Farmers' and Farm Workers' Movements*. New York: Twayne Publishing, 1995.

Morgan, Speer. "Wendell Berry: A Fatal Singing." *Southern Review* 10 (October 1974): 865–77.

Muir, John. *The Wilderness Journeys*. Edinburgh: Canongate Classic, 1996.

Murphy, Patrick. "Two Different Paths in the Quest for Place: Gary Snyder and Wendell Berry." *American Poetry* 2 (1): 60–68 (1984).

Nabhan, Gary Paul. *Cultures of Habitat*. Washington, D.C.: Counterpoint, 1997.

Naess, Arnold. "A Defence of the Deep Ecology Movement." *Environmental Ethics* 6 (fall 1984): 265–70.

Nash, Roderick, ed. *The American Environment*. 2d ed. Reading, Mass: Addison-Wesley, 1976.

———. *Rights of Nature*. Madison: University of Wisconsin Press, 1989.

———. *Wilderness and the American Mind*. 3d ed. New Haven: Yale University Press, 1982.

Nearing, Helen. *The Good Life* [1954, 1979]. New York: Schocken Books, 1989.

North, Helen. *Sophrosyne: Self-Knowledge and Self-Restraint in Greek Literature*. Ithaca: Cornell University Press, 1966.

Norton, Bryan. *Toward Unity among Environmentalists*. New York: Oxford University Press, 1991.

Oakeshott, Michael. *Rationalism in Politics* [1962]. Indianapolis: Liberty Press, 1991.

Okin, Susan. *Justice, Gender, and the Family.* New York: Basic Books, 1989.

Ophuls, William, and Stephen Boyan Jr. *Ecology and the Politics of Scarcity Revisited.* New York: W. H. Freeman, 1992.

Orden, David, Robert Paarlberg, and Terry Roe. *Policy Reform in American Agriculture.* Chicago: University of Chicago Press, 1999.

O'Toole, Patricia. *Money and Morals in America.* New York: Clarkson Potter, 1988.

Palmer, Bruce. *Man Over Money.* Chapel Hill: University of North Carolina Press, 1980.

Passmore, John. *Man's Responsibility for Nature.* New York: Charles Scribner's Sons, 1974.

Patton, James. *The Case for Farmers.* Washington, D.C.: Public Affairs Press, 1959.

Periam, Jonathan. *The Groundswell.* Cincinnati: E. Hannaford, 1874.

Pevear, Richard. "On the Prose of Wendell Berry." *Hudson Review* 35 (summer 1982): 341–47.

Pinchot, Gifford. *The Fight for Conservation.* New York: Doubleday, Page, 1911.

Pittman, Nancy, ed. *From the Land.* Washington, D.C.: Island Press, 1988.

Pocock, J. G. A. *The Ancient Constitution and The Feudal Law.* Cambridge: Cambridge University Press, 1957.

———. *The Machiavellian Moment.* Princeton: Princeton University Press, 1975.

———. ed. *The Political Works of James Harrington.* Cambridge: Cambridge University Press, 1977.

Pollock, Norman, ed. *The Populist Mind.* Indianapolis: Bobbs-Merrill, 1967.

Polsgrove, Carol, and Scott Sanders. "Wendell Berry." *The Progressive* (May 1970): 34–37.

Ritter, Gretchen. *Goldbugs and Greenbacks.* Cambridge: Cambridge University Press, 1997.

Rodgers, Andrews. *Liberty Hyde Bailey.* Princeton: Princeton University Press, 1949.

Rölvaag, O. E. *Giants in the Earth* [1927]. New York: Harper Perennial, 1991.

Rorty, Richard. *Contingency, Irony, and Solidarity.* Cambridge: Cambridge University Press, 1989.

Rosenblum, Nancy. "Thoreau's Militant Consciousness." *Political Theory* 9 (February 1981): 81–110.

Rosenfeld, Rachel Ann. *Farm Women.* Chapel Hill: University of North Carolina Press, 1985.

Rubin, Louis. *The Wary Fugitives.* Baton Rouge: Louisiana State University Press, 1978.

Ruckelshaus, William. "Risk, Science, and Democracy." *Issues in Science and Technology* 1 (spring 1985): 19–38.

Sachs, Carolyn. *The Invisible Farmers.* Totowa, N.J.: Rowman & Allanheld, 1983.

Salamon, Sonya. *Prairie Patrimony*. Chapel Hill: University of North Carolina Press, 1992.

Sale, Kirkpatrick. *Dwellers in the Land*. Philadelphia: New Society Publishers, 1991.

Sandel, Michael. *Liberalism and Its Critics*. New York: New York University Press, 1984.

Sanders, Elizabeth. *Roots of Reform*. Chicago: University of Chicago Press, 1999.

Scheffer, Victor. *The Shaping of Environmentalism in America*. Seattle: University of Washington Press, 1991.

Schonbach, Morris. *Native American Fascism During the 1930s and 1940s*. New York: Garland Publishing, 1985.

Schumacher, E. F. *Small Is Beautiful* [1973]. New York: Harper Perennial, 1989.

Sears, Paul. *Deserts on the March*. Norman: Oklahoma Press, 1935.

———. "Science and the New Landscape." *Harper's Magazine,* July 1939, pp. 207–16.

Senate Committee on Agriculture and Forestry, *Hearings on the Agricultural Act of 1948,* 80th Cong., 2d sess., 1948.

Sennett, Richard. *The Fall of Public Man*. New York: W. W. Norton, 1974.

Shabecoff, Philip. *A Fierce Green Fire*. New York: Hill & Wang, 1993.

Shi, David. *The Simple Life*. New York: Oxford University Press, 1985.

Shover, John. *First Majority—Last Minority*. DeKalb: Northern Illinois University Press, 1976.

Simon, Julian, and Herman Kahn, eds. *The Resourceful Earth*. Oxford: Basil Blackwell, 1984.

Skinner, Quentin. *Foundations of Modern Political Thought*. 2 vols. Cambridge: Cambridge University Press, 1978, 1: x–xiv.

Slote, Michael. "Virtue Ethics and Democratic Values." *Journal of Social Philosophy* 24 (fall 1993): 5.

Smiley, Jane. *A Thousand Acres*. New York: Ballantine Books, 1991.

Smith, Henry Nash. *Virgin Land*. Cambridge: Harvard University Press, 1950.

Smith, Kimberly. "Wendell Berry's Feminist Agrarianism." *Women's Studies* 30 (2001): 623–46.

Snyder, Gary. *Earth House Hold*. New York: New Directions, 1957.

Statman, Daniel, ed. *Virtue Ethics*. Washington, D.C.: Georgetown University Press, 1997.

Stegner, Wallace. *The Big Rock Candy Mountain*. New York: Hill and Wang, 1938.

———. *Marking the Sparrow's Fall* [1948]. Edited by Page Stegner. New York: Henry Holt, 1998.

Stewart, John L. *The Burden of Time*. Princeton: Princeton University Press, 1965.

Taylor, Bob Pepperman. *America's Bachelor Uncle*. Lawrence: University Press of Kansas, 1996.

———. *Our Limits Transgressed*. Lawrence: University Press of Kansas, 1992.

Taylor, Carl. *The Farmers' Movement, 1620–1920*. New York: American Book Co., 1953.

Taylor, John. *Arator* [1818]. 4th ed. Indianapolis: Liberty Fund, 1977.

Thompson, Paul. "Agrarianism and the American Philosophical Tradition." *Agriculture and Human Values* 7 (winter 1990): 3–8.

Thompson, Paul, and Thomas C. Hilde, ed. *The Agrarian Roots of Pragmatism.* Nashville: Vanderbilt University Press, 2000.

Thoreau, Henry David. *Walden and Civil Disobedience* [1854]. New York: Penguin Books, 1983.

Tindall, George, ed. *A Populist Reader.* Gloucester, Mass.: Peter Smith, 1976.

Triggs, Jeffery Alan. "Moving the Dark to Wholeness: The Elegies of Wendell Berry." *Literary Review* 31 (spring 1988): 279–92.

Tucker, William. "Populism Up-to-Date: The Story of the Farmers' Union." *Agricultural History* 21 (October 1947): 198–208.

Tugwell, Rexford. "Farm Relief and a Permanent Agriculture." *Annals of the American Academy of Political and Social Science* (March 1929): 271–82.

Turner, Frederick Jackson. *The Frontier in American History* [1920]. Malabar, Fla.: Robert E. Krieger Publishing, 1985.

Tweeten, Luther. "Sector as Personality." *Agriculture and Human Values* (winter 1987): 66–74.

Twelve Southerners. *I'll Take My Stand* [1930]. Baton Rouge: Louisiana State University Press, 1977.

Udall, Stewart. *The Quiet Crisis.* New York: Holt, Rinehart & Winston, 1963.

Waldrep, Christopher. *Night Riders.* Durham: Duke University Press, 1993.

Waring, P. Alston, and Walter M. Teller. *Roots in the Earth.* New York: Harper & Bros., 1943.

Warren, Karen, ed. *Ecofeminism.* Bloomington: Indiana University Press, 1997.

Washington, Booker T. *Up from Slavery* [1901]. New York: Airmont Publishing, 1967.

Weaver, James B. *A Call to Action.* Des Moines: Iowa Printing, 1892.

Weiland, Steven. "Wendell Berry: Culture and Fidelity." *Iowa Review* 10 (winter 1979): 99–104.

Wensveen, Louke van. *Dirty Virtues.* Amherst, N.Y.: Humanity Books, 2000.

White, Lynn. "The Historical Roots of Our Ecological Crisis." *Science* 155 (March 10, 1967): 1,203–7.

Whitney, Elspeth. "Lynn White, Ecotheology, and History." *Environmental Ethics* 15 (summer 1993): 151–69.

Wildavsky, Aaron. *But Is It True?* Cambridge: Harvard University Press, 1995.

Wilson, E. O. *Consilience.* New York: Alfred A. Knopf, 1998.

Wish, Harvey, ed. *Antebellum Writings of George Fitzhugh and Hinton Rowan Helper on Slavery.* New York: Capricorn Books, 1960.

Witherell, Elizabeth Hall, comp. *Henry David Thoreau: Collected Essays and Poems.* New York: Library of America, 2001.

World Resources Institute. *World Resources, 2000–2001.* New York: Basic Books, 2000.

Worldwatch Institute. *State of the World 2000*. New York: W. W. Norton, 2000.

Worster, Donald. *Nature's Economy*. 2d ed. Cambridge: Cambridge University Press, 1994.

———. Review of *Ecology in the Twentieth Century,* by Anna Bramwell. *Isis* 81 (4): 799–800 (1990).

Wrigley, E. A., and David Souden, eds. *The Works of T. R. Malthus*. 8 vols. London: William Pickering, 1986.

Yarbrough, Jean. *American Virtues*. Lawrence: University Press of Kansas, 1998.

Zuckert, Catherine. *Natural Right and the American Imagination*. Savage, Md.: Rowan & Littlefield, 1990.

INDEX

direct influence on Berry, 9, 35,
131
critique of politics, 180–82
in Kentucky, 32–34
permanent agriculture and, 49–50,
52
tenets of, 15, 22–27, 49, 57, 138
Port William, 110–11, 115, 123–24,
126, 134, 175–76
Practice, 161, 169, 175
"Pray Without Ceasing" (Berry),
185
Preservationism, 38, 39–45, 57, 67, 93,
140–41, 171
Property rights, 23, 63, 68–69, 70,
93–94, 95
Propriety, 137, 144, 146, 161, 162,
175
Protest, 179, 188–89
Public (defined), 194

Race, 93, 105–07, 193, 196, 197
Ransom, John Crowe, 28, 29
Realism (literary), 125–26
Religion, 172, 174, 176. *See also*
Buddhism; Christianity;
Spirituality
Remembering (Berry), 115
Representation, 180–83, 186, 202
Rights, 68, 70, 71, 199. *See also*
Property rights
A River Runs Through It (MacLean),
159–60
Rodale, J. I., 58, 210
Roots in the Earth, 56
Ruffin, Edward, 67–68
Rugged individualism
agrarian tradition and, 9–10, 38, 57,
137, 205
critique of, 130–36, 139–40, 145,
146, 153
environmental tradition and, 9–10,

38, 42–44, 46, 47, 57, 140–41,
205
grace and, 164–65

Sale, Kirkpatrick, 142
Schumacher, E. F., 209
Science, 82–86, 173
Scientism, 84–85
Sears, Paul, 49, 50, 51
Sense of place, 92, 96, 97, 141–42,
143
*Sex, Economy, Freedom, and
Community* (Berry), 173
Silent Spring (Carson), 56–57
Simple life, 15, 31, 32, 35, 47, 76
Slavery, 18, 25, 29, 30, 105–07, 157
Slote, Michael, 119
Smiley, Jane, 1
Snyder, Gary, 6, 79, 174
Socialism, 30–31, 54, 209
Soil erosion, 22, 50, 56, 65
Soil fertility, 21, 22, 51, 52, 65, 66,
67–68
Solving for patter, 163
Sophrosyne
autonomy and, 151
explained, 136–39
grace and, 160, 161, 162
labor and, 157, 159
politics and, 184
wilderness and, 145, 146, 208
Specialization, 84–85, 168, 173,
186–87
Spirituality, 165, 171–75, 176
States' rights, 6, 196
Steffen, Robert, 58
Stegner, Wallace, 6, 13, 141
Stewardship
agricultural policy and, 211–12
Bible and, 173–74
early agrarianism and, 21–22,
47–48, 55–56, 57, 65–68